Voices of Bereavement

The Series in Death, Dying, and Bereavement
Consulting Editor
Robert A. Neimeyer

Voices of Bereavement

A Casebook for Grief Counselors

Joan Beder, DSW
Yeshiva University
Wurzweiler School of Social Work

Brunner-Routledge
Taylor & Francis Group
NEW YORK AND HOVE

Published in 2004 by
Brunner-Routledge
29 West 35th Street
New York, NY 10001
www.brunner-routledge.com

Published in Great Britain by
Brunner-Routledge
27 Church Road
Hove, East Sussex
BN3 2FA
www.brunner-routledge.co.uk

Cover Design: Elise Weinger
Cover photo: ©Royalty-Free/CORBIS

Copyright © 2004 by Taylor & Francis Books, Inc.
Brunner-Routledge is an imprint of the Taylor & Francis Group.

Printed in the United States of America on acid-free paper.

10 9 8 7 6 5 4 3 2 1

Library of Congress Cataloging-in-Publication Data

Beder, Joan, 1944-
Voices of bereavement: a casebook for grief counselors / Joan Beder.
    p. cm. – (The series in death, dying, and bereavement)
Includes bibliographical references and index.
    ISBN 0-415-94614-X (hardcover) – ISBN 0-415-94615-8 (pbk.)
1. Grief therapy – Case studies. 2. Bereavement–Psychological aspects –
Case studies. 3. Loss (Psychology) – Case studies. 4. Grief – Case studies. I. Title.
II. Series.
RC455.4.L67B43 2004
155.9'37–dc22

                                                                    2003025756

With thanks …

To my family
for their patience and boundless support,
to my friends and colleagues
who helped in this endeavor,
to my beloved Matthew
who taught me joy
beyond anything I have known,
and to my clients who dared to trust me
with their innermost feelings and thoughts.
I dedicate this book to you.
I am grateful to you all.

CONTENTS

FOREWORD

Most practical books on bereavement fall into one of a few predictable genres. Many—perhaps most—are more inspirational than instructional, drawing upon the author's personal experience with a particular loss to offer hope or guidance for those suffering a similar form of bereavement. Others proffer spiritual counsel or religiously oriented advice to those who have lost loved ones, or to those professionals and volunteers who attempt to help them. Still others distill the wisdom of decades of engagement in bereavement work, providing practice-grounded (if occasionally idiosyncratic) principles to fellow professionals. Finally, a few draw on the expanding empirical literature on grief and trauma to portray the symptoms and sequelae of life-altering loss, sometimes featuring the distinctive results of the author's own research program. Each of these genres has its place, and each finds a receptive readership in the diverse and multidisciplinary domain that constitutes the field of grief therapy. Not surprisingly, each also has its limitations, reflecting the selective knowledge and experience base of its author or authors.

It is in this context that Joan Beder's *Voices of Bereavement* makes a distinctive contribution. In a sense, Beder combines the best features of each of the above genres, offering intelligent case-based discussions of a broad spectrum of losses, ranging from the death of a partner or friend to that of a pet, and of bereavement resulting from combat or airline accidents to that stemming from degenerative disability. Importantly, Beder gives special attention to losses that are conventionally disenfranchised, when the dynamics of secrecy and stigma preclude the level of social validation and support that the bereaved require, perhaps especially when they or their specific losses (through miscarriage or murder, or death of a grandchild, divorced spouse, or therapist) are marginalized. Beder structures each case study in consistent fashion, offering a "presenting problem" orientation to the person seeking help, giving a backdrop of his or her relevant history prior to the loss, and then using these to anchor a conceptual discussion of the theoretical and empirical literature most pertinent to the distinctive difficulties the case entails. Beder thoughtfully extracts principles for intervention from this review, and concludes by reflecting on the unique issues the case raised for her as a therapist. The result is a satisfying read, and one that incorporates many of the strongest qualities of the dominant genres of bereavement handbooks, offering a hopeful and sometimes inspirational coverage of a vast range of losses in a volume informed by both scholarly and personal insights.

The astute reader will also detect important strands of continuity against the backdrop of diversity in culture, gender, age, ethnicity, and type of loss that the book features. Chief among these is Beder's clinical style, which focuses prominently on the expression of negative emotion, the normalization of guilt and the gentle insinuation of "reality checks" of the restrictive assumptive worlds that traumatized grievers inhabit, all tempered and timed to accord with the needs of a particular case. For me, Beder's decision not to describe only "star" cases carried an ironic fringe benefit: although all of the clients featured experienced clinically substantial change, few were fully "healed" by her earnest interventions, reassuring me as a fellow grief counselor that therapy can be useful even when it is not fully transformative. I would therefore commend this book for its realism as well as range of coverage, and for its humility as much as for the hope it engenders. I would be surprised if it did not have something of value to offer to nearly every practicing grief counselor.

Robert A. Neimeyer, Ph.D.
The University of Memphis
Series Editor

PREFACE

If we live, we die. It is that simple and that complex. If we love someone or even like him or her a lot, it hurts when he or she dies, and we feel a sense of loss. Sometimes the hurt is manageable and we are able to regroup, rebound, and move on with our lives, holding on to memories or feelings about the dead person. Sometimes we are not able to move forward, getting immersed in the sadness and pain of our loss. Fortunately, there are people who are trained to help those who get stuck on their journey from loss.

Purpose of the Book

I wrote this book to help educate grief counselors who may not have encountered some of the more unusual bereavement situations I discuss in this volume.

Surely, there are other types of loss worthy of exploration but this book deals with death and the aftermath of major loss. The cases presented are all based on actual clients; they are true stories that have been carefully disguised to protect the identity of each person involved.

In this volume, you will meet a variety of individuals; what unites them is their sense of loss and despair when faced with the death of a loved one. Within each chapter I introduce the reader to relevant research on that particular bereavement experience. On the basis of the research and several theoretical orientations, I move the reader toward suggestions for intervention strategies. I must state that there are numerous orientations to bereavement work and none can make the claim that it is the "only" or the "right" way to work with grieving individuals or family members. In addition, many of the theoretical approaches and intervention strategies that I discuss can be used in cases that go beyond the material presented, and can be seen as potentially generic in application.

Bereavement Themes

While immersed in the journey of writing this book, I began to see certain themes that guided the work, a certain level of awareness that informed and expanded my understanding of the task of helping those in grief. There are two themes that I particularly want to highlight: the impact of culture and lifestyle, and the importance of assessing the developmental stage of the bereaved.

Cultural norms and imperatives are a major determinant of individual and family patterns of behavior. As grief counselors, we are bound to encounter those from a different ethnic, lifestyle, or religious group and it is essential that we not act and interact with the bereaved based on our own experiences or expectations. This begs that we as counselors keep an open mind and that we educate ourselves toward understanding that which is different from what we know. Several cases in this book reinforce the need to understand more and seek to acknowledge the dynamics beyond the Caucasian frame of reference: the death of an African American grandmother, the Puerto Rican male experience of miscarriage, the death of a twin, the experience of a lesbian when her partner dies, and the bereavement of an Orthodox Jewish woman when her ex-husband dies.

The impact of the developmental stage of the bereaved is essential in being able to locate the griever within a time frame, with the attendant struggles and challenges imposed at that stage. The stage concept suggests that there are areas of emerging competence or conflict that help to explain the complex range of behaviors of a particular period. The challenges of fitting in and belonging and an evolving sense of self, driven by hormonal changes, are typical struggles for the adolescent. How is that typical struggle affected by the death of someone close to the adolescent?

In several chapters, developmental stage is a major factor informing the understanding between griever and counselor. The death of a pet, for example, is usually a profound experience. For an elderly person, the pet may be the object with whom they have a very close relationship and the level of despair at the death of the animal must be understood in the context of the aloneness of the later years. The death of a grandchild has to be understood within the context of the stage of development of the grandparent who is invested in leaving a legacy for a grandchild. The older adolescent whose disabled sibling dies struggles with issues of finding her way as an adult and her bereavement casts her as a parental figure before she is developmentally ready.

Approaches Toward Helping

The work of many theorists has informed my approach to helping. A key theoretical concept, which applies to almost every case cited, is that of disenfranchised grief. Doka's (1989a, 2002a) conceptualization that because of the nature of the death the griever is denied the right to grieve, that the death is not openly acknowledged or socially validated, is a guiding concept in helping the mourner to accept the loss. The centrality of validating the loss is often the first step in the counseling effort.

Therese Rando's (1993) contributions to the study of bereavement are well-known. Especially useful are her six "R" processes of mourning in which there are three phases of mourning: avoidance, confrontation, and accommodation. This conceptualization has been applied in several of the cases presented. In contrast, William Worden's (2002) task model poses four task areas that the mourner must traverse in healing: accepting the reality of the loss, working through the pain and grief, adjusting to an environment without the deceased, and relocating the deceased and moving on with life.

The work of Rando and Worden has proved useful in much of my bereavement work and my approach to helping.

The concept of the assumptive world and assumptive world violations (Janoff-Bulman, 1992; Kauffman, 2002a) plays an important part in helping the counselor to understand the depth of reaction to certain losses and to be able to relate to some of the struggles of the bereft. The work in the case, which involved a death from the attack on the World Trade Center and the death of a lesbian partner in a plane crash, was informed by this useful conceptualization of traumatic loss.

In writing this book, I have hope that those who use this volume will find it informative and that the knowledge gained will be of value to those we want to help through some of the darkest moments of life.

CHAPTER 1

Bereavement After the Death of a Workplace Friend

The Case—Ernie

At the water department, Dave (46 years old, Caucasian) and Ernie (48 years old, African American) were always seen together. They had joined the department the same year, had been assigned to similar tasks and routes, and for the past decade had been riding in the same truck together as they did their work. Over the years, each found that he enjoyed the company of the other, felt comfortable talking about work events, and felt even more comfortable talking about personal matters. On several occasions, Ernie, who had been divorced for many years, would join Dave's family for an outing or a summer barbecue. Ernie was a frequent dinner guest at Dave's home and was invited to almost all family parties. When Ernie's father died, Dave was one of the first people Ernie called. When a car hit Dave's son, Ernie was at the hospital with Dave and his family.

On a Thursday afternoon, soon after lunch, Dave complained to Ernie that he was not "feeling right, that he must have eaten something bad." They continued their work, checking office-building meters for water use, but as the day progressed, Dave felt worse and worse. Ernie became alarmed when Dave mentioned that he had pains running down his left arm; that was when Dave relinquished the wheel of their truck and Ernie drove to the local hospital's emergency room. By then, Dave was pale, was having difficulty breathing, and had terrible chest pain. The doctors felt quite certain that Dave either was in the process of having a heart attack or had had one. Tests were needed to confirm the diagnosis. Ernie called Dave's wife and they sat in the emergency room together awaiting news.

When they heard the call for a code emergency, they did not realize that it was for Dave. Some minutes later, the doctor came out to tell them that Dave had had a massive coronary episode and it was unlikely that he would make it. Ernie and Dave's wife went into the acute care area. Dave was unconscious, hooked to a variety of monitors, and looked dreadful. He died during the night.

Ernie was devastated. His partner at the water company was gone, but the most profound loss was that of Dave's unlimited friendship and caring. Ernie did not know how he would ever "recover from Dave's death." The funeral was something of a haze to him. He remembered that the funeral home was packed with many familiar faces, people he knew from parties with Dave's family and, of course, the entire water company staff. He said that he felt "funny at the funeral and did not know where to put himself in relation to the family." He stayed toward the back of the church, and he was almost invisible at the funeral home.

After the funeral, Ernie took a few days off. This was not because he was ill but because he could not face going to work without Dave. He dreaded the empty locker next to his, the assignment of a new partner, and the endless hours without his friend. He could feel himself becoming more and more upset, more than a little depressed, and he even had morbid thoughts. His loneliness—he was divorced and had lived alone for many years—weighed on him. Although others at the job mourned Dave's death, none felt it to the degree that Ernie did.

A week after the funeral, Ernie got up in the morning intending to go to work. He got dressed, had breakfast, and returned to bed. He could not get himself to leave the house. He called his supervisor and asked to take a few more days off, but the time did not ameliorate his despair. The supervisor made the suggestion that he speak to the county employee assistance person, and Ernie agreed because he could not bring himself to return to work. A referral for bereavement counseling was made by the social worker at the employee assistance program.

Relevant History

Ernie was the oldest of four brothers; one was deceased and the others lived out of state. He had grown up in a "poor neighborhood, actually the ghetto." He had not known his father but had lived with the father of his three brothers for 10 years. He did not get along very well with his stepfather or his stepbrothers and kept to himself a lot. His mother worked two jobs after his stepfather left, and Ernie remembered lean times. He did not graduate from high school, as it was incumbent on him as the oldest to get a job and help out with the money crunch of the household. Ernie was a "good kid, did drugs for a short time but did not do any really bad stuff." When he quit high school, he got a job at a local market making deliveries. He had one or two friends and a steady girl-friend. He gave most of his money to his mother. He got married when he was 21 years old. Two children were born in quick succession, and Ernie was overwhelmed with commitments and obligations, some of which he was able to manage and some he could not. The marriage lasted 10 years. It dissolved when Ernie's wife decided that he was not responsible enough to have and maintain a wife and family and she left him.

Ernie found his way to the water company when one of his customers at the grocery told him about several openings for meter readers. No civil service test was required and Ernie became a county employee, a job he has held until the present.

Relationally, Ernie was a troubled man. He had difficulty making connections and trusting the intentions of others. Dave had been the first close male friend he had ever had. That he had not known his father, had been estranged from his stepfather, and had had a troubled relationship with his stepbrothers suggests that close male bonding would be difficult for Ernie to maintain. He had lost track of his divorced wife and the two children, who were now adults, and he claimed that he had no interest in trying to find them or connect to them in any way.

Ernie described his life before Dave's death as comfortable: "I had a good job; enough money to keep myself going and I had a good friend in Dave. Sometimes I saw one particular woman but nothing serious." Of course, that all changed with Dave's death.

Conceptual Issues

"Friendships are a core aspect of our lives" (Fehr, 1996, p. 1). *Friendship* refers to voluntary, enduring social relationships that involve choice, sharing, valuing, trust, loyalty, companionship, and sometimes love. Friendships are more significant than acquaintances; they involve self-revelation and disclosure, an exchange of confidences, and acceptance (Doka, 1989a). Although friendships vary in intensity, they can create meaning in lives, lend a focus and support in time of need, and play a significant role in the social structure of our existence. "Although the definition of 'friend' is highly personal and individualized, there are conceptual meanings attached to this term, which involve choice, sharing, valuing, trust, loyalty, and pleasure. From friendship we derive a sense of self-confirmation—a sense of who we are—self-worth and self-esteem" (Albert, 2001, p. 171).

Workplace Friends

The workplace is a natural venue for the development of friendship. Friendships that develop in the workplace have many benefits. They can provide a source of instrumental and emotional support, buffer job-related stress, and reduce job dissatisfaction; they can make work more enjoyable and increase commitment to the job (Yager, 1997).

Friendships that are work based seem to go through a series of three stages as described by Sias and Cahill (1998). The first stage noted was from acquaintance to friend. Proximity, shared tasks, shared projects, and the beginning of socializing out of work—lunches, drinks after work—promote that initial shift. Communication patterns at this level move from discussion of work to nonwork and personal topics with decreased caution, but not at an intimate level. The second stage is friend to close friend. This stage is driven mostly by problems or events in the personal lives of the friends, life events, and perhaps increased work-related problems. At the close friend level, socializing becomes more intimate with vacations or inclusion in family activities. There is decreased caution and increased intimacy of discussion topics. The transition from close friend to almost best friend is associated with extraorganizational socializing, life events, and work-related problems. Because the trust has been developed between the friends, increased comfort and intimacy are felt and opinions and feelings are more easily shared. At this stage, the friends become an important part of each other's personal and work life. It would be accurate to see Dave and Ernie's friendship as being at the third stage in which each saw the other as his "best friend." This is a level of connection that is deeply felt and experienced as a source of comfort and belonging. In the event of a workplace friend's death, the level of friendship outside the job usually dictates the level of reaction to the event.

Work friendships can be intense. Sometimes work friends spend almost half of their waking time together, develop an emotional dependence on one another, see each other daily, and provide a support system for each other. When this tie is broken, the remaining employee is left in a vulnerable state, grappling with the emotions of anger, confusion, sadness, and helplessness (Stein & Winokuer, 1989). What makes this type of loss more complex is that workplace norms ask us to separate our work lives from our personal lives. When these two quadrants overlap, there is no organizational recognition or structure for this to be acknowledged. Grief and mourning are not acceptable at the workplace because grief does not belong at work; work is about productivity, quality, and profit and not about emotional caretaking. In recent years, larger corporations have begun to create employee assistance programs to help manage the emotional life of the company (Lattanzi-Licht, 2002). It is reasonable to expect employers to be more sensitive and aware of the impact of a coworker's death on the other employees and adjust leave time accordingly. Employers need to understand that grief takes time and to be more aware of the impact of death on their staff.

When there is a death in the workplace, it is up to company policy whether and for how long colleagues and coworkers are permitted to observe the rituals of dying. Most companies will allow time off for the funeral and a family visit but any more extended time off is not permitted. In most organizational settings, the amount of time allowed depends on the level of kinship connection to the deceased, with much more liberal absence time granted for death of blood kin. This position is understandable but short sighted.

Eyetsemitan (1998) coined the phrase "stifled grief," which is any recognized grief that has been denied its full course. The workplace is a good example of where such grief is exhibited. Stifled grief has negative implications for workers and workplace productivity (pp. 470–471) and begs a reexamination of corporate policy and personnel practices.

Death of a Close Friend

It is surprising that there are so few studies on the death of a friend even though there are many studies that describe adult friendships, friendship patterns, and the role of friendship in adult lives. The few studies that have been reported used a convenience sample of university students or adolescents as their focus (Archer, 1999). What has emerged from the scant literature is the recognition that the bereavement following the death of a close friend can be as severe and in some cases more severe than that of an immediate family member. In the event of a sudden death of a friend, the opportunity for anticipatory grieving does not exist. The survivors of sudden death may have an intensified need for support as their world has been so abruptly turned upside down (G. Lee, 1994).

Sklar and Hartley (1990) reported on an exploratory study involving a sample of young adults who had a friend die. They used the term "survivor-friend" to denote one who has lost a close friend to death. Their findings indicated parallel bereavement patterns between survivor-friend and family member death. They noted the presence of "...unresolved feelings of despair, guilt (especially for things unsaid), fear for one's own mortality, and a sense of emptiness that had not been resolved since the death" (p. 108). In addition they noted the presence of decreased coping ability, premonitions, anger, feelings of craziness, guilt, anniversary syndrome reactions, and visions. All of these reactions are consistent with emotions and experiences commonly reported by widows, widowers, and other family members.

Weiss (2001) suggested that the grief of the survivor-friend might be severe, especially if there is a deep and long-lasting affiliation but that this loss does not produce the depth of despair and hopelessness that a family-member death can evoke. One reason for this difference (which was not the case for Ernie) is that there is an opportunity for substitut-ability with friends and none for kin. This assumes two things: that the relationship with the kin was positive and that the relationship with the friend was not especially intense.

The death of a friend may place the survivor-friend in an unusual bereavement position in relation to the immediate family. Society does not seem to tolerate or support in substantial ways the grief experiences of the survivor-friend (Rando, 1995). "Grief is a family affair, at least in American society..." and as such "...the ...distraught close friend of someone who dies has virtually no legitimate, public, grief and mourning channels. The close friend is likely to be ignored by the deceased's immediate family and extended family and by others" (Sklar, 1992, p. 109). The survivor-friend may be cast in the difficult position of feeling the need to provide support to the family with limited amount of support going back to him or her. There does not seem to be a place for the survivor-friend in the rituals associated with funerals or the mourning period. As Deck and Folta (1989) observed, "There appears to be a cultural lag between the social definition of rights and responsibilities of family members, and the reality of social relationships" (p. 81). This lack of social definition isolates the survivor-friend from the functions and behaviors the family performs. "The family is expected to behave as mourners, experiencing sadness and crying in amounts deemed appropriate. They are expected to perform a variety of functions such as planning the funeral, greeting guests, dealing with funeral directors or clergy. They are prescribed socially acceptable clothing, places to sit, and things to do. These mourners are released from the usual daily tasks of work and play. Not so the friend" (p. 83).

Besides being marginalized by the mourning rituals of the family, another source of anguish is the loss of the role of a friend. In a sense, when a friend dies, his or her friends lose a part of their identity. Because friendship is such a unique relationship, based on sharing, values, trust, and so on, the sharing that occurred during the friendship is aborted and is not validated easily by another. The loss of that role can negatively affect self-esteem and self-confidence as we strive to replace this type of connection and validation from another.

Suggestions for Intervention

A major underlying belief in this and most bereavement cases is that "...losses not fully mourned shadow our lives, sap our energy and impair our ability to connect. If we are unable to mourn, we stay in the thralls of old issues, out of step with the present, because we are still dancing to tunes from the past" (Albert, 2001, p. 173). Therefore, as a form of disenfranchised grief (Doka, 1989a), one of the first counseling tasks in working with a survivor-friend is to legitimize the loss. The cultural imperatives of being sidelined in this form of death may give the subliminal message to the griever that he or she should not display emotion and thus should not feel any. Sklar and Hartley (1990) spoke of the double burden of grief for the survivor-friend: he or she may experience the social and emotional transformations of bereavement while suffering the lack of institutional outlets that act as support (p. 105). As a marginalized griever, the survivor-friend may even be in denial as to the depth of the loss. This denial points the counseling effort in the direction of having the griever talk openly and freely about the loss and the history of the friendship, being able to describe the depth and breadth of the friendship, the unique aspects of the friend, and what will be most missed about the friend.

"By facilitating respectful recognition of the aspects of the mourner's experience that was originally denied or disallowed, each intervention makes possible the pursuit of various subsidiary goals, such as healing relational fractures, encouraging greater self-acceptance, prompting instrumental changes in one's life to address newly recognized needs, and so on" (Neimeyer & Jordan, 2002, p. 102). The survivor-friend has to feel legitimized in order to move ahead.

Barbant (2002) stated that the tasks for the disenfranchised griever is to cope with, deal with, and grapple with the loss in such a way that the loss is incorporated into one's cognitive life. This is accomplished by keeping the griever focused on the loss to help him or her accept the death and reconstruct his or her day-to-day life in the absence of the friend. This is difficult work for one who is mourning but within the supportive atmosphere of the counseling the counselor may become a transitional figure and facilitate the grief process for the survivor-friend. The counselor's continued interest and presence may be especially needed by the griever, as the sense of abandonment and aloneness can be quite powerful.

For many, the death of a friend is a reminder of one's own death. It is not only that a peer has died but also that the death of the peer destroys the social network in which the individual is a member. As most friendships are dyads, the death of one means the demise of the grouping (Deck & Folta, 1989). Here again, the task is for the counselor to help the griever to look at his or her resources while attempting to empower the griever toward linking with others.

Major Issues in This Case

Ernie was suffering when he first came for counseling. His appearance was careless: he was unshaved, was wearing wrinkled clothes, and was generally not well groomed. He had not been to work for more than a week and did not know when he would be able to return.

Early in the counseling relationship, he was encouraged to speak of Dave and his friendship, how it had started, grown and become such a substantial part of his life. Initially, Ernie was slow to respond to this form of guided questioning, as he seemed uncomfortable talking about Dave and what had happened. In moments such as this, when a mourner seems uncomfortable with early content, it is helpful to acknowledge this resistance and say something along the lines of "Beginning is always hard" or "Everyone seems to struggle when they start talking about feelings." This puts the griever at ease for two reasons: his or her anxiety is acknowledged as "normal" and the counselor is seen as someone who understands the client.

Ernie said that he had had very few male friends over the years and that he had not been "brought up to think that men would come through for you. You can usually depend on women to be there, but not so with guys." So when he first met Dave, he was wary and "there was the color thing." But he really felt that Dave was a "good guy and we started to hang out together a lot. Then they put us on the same route and finally on the same truck so if I didn't like this dude I would have had way too much of him." Slowly, he said, they began to have some social contacts and the friendship expanded. He related the details of Dave's last day and the experiences in the truck and hospital. He said that he felt guilty that he had not acted sooner when Dave began complaining; he wondered whether acting faster might have saved Dave's life.

In the counseling, it was important to reassure Ernie that his feelings of guilt were normal and that the pain that he was expressing was part of sustaining a loss; we all question what we could have done after someone is gone. It was especially important with Ernie to keep in mind his aloneness and to be careful that the depression did not take a more serious turn into suicidal thinking. This had to be assessed—by direct questioning as to whether he had thoughts of ending his life, whether he had the means and a plan to kill himself—and Ernie reassured the counselor that he was not contemplating suicide.

The option to make a referral for Ernie to a group was not realistic. Most bereavement groups are for direct kin and this would not have helped Ernie, although the additional support would have been helpful to him. Unfortunately, Ernie would have to shoulder his grief alone.

For Ernie, the resumption of work was directly related to the pain of his loss. This was unfortunate, as the structure of working, being around other work friends, and getting back to a routine probably would have helped him along. The return to work became the initial goal of the counseling. Ernie was asked to consider what would be the most difficult moments upon entering the locker room, for example, and to think how this could be managed. Role play was suggested to help prepare Ernie for comments that other employees might make regarding Dave and his death. Ernie played the role of an employee and the counselor modeled responses that Ernie could use to deflect some of the emotion that might be provoked by the questions from other employees. Ernie was further reassured that the first few days back would be difficult and that it was normal to feel the stress of returning. At many junctures in the counseling, the counselor felt that Ernie needed to be reassured that his reactions were within normal bounds; this was especially important for Ernie, who seemed to have few social contacts and internal measures of "normal" and "crazy."

He had been told that one of the other water department employees, Bob, was to be his new partner on the truck. Ernie knew Bob and felt "he was OK but he surely was not Dave." The counselor suggested that Ernie might speak with Bob before going back to the job to get a feel for whether they would be able to work together. Ernie did not want to do this as he felt that it was "disloyal to Dave to be driving with someone else." This notion had to be addressed and corrected. The counselor suggested that although Bob could never replace Dave, Ernie had to adjust to a new partner and that it would take some time for that relationship to feel comfortable. Ernie was told, "Dave could never be replaced in your memories and heart." Bereavement counselors sometimes need to reiterate to the mourner(s) that bereavement does not mean forgetting the person who died but that the mourner can remember him or her without a terrible amount of pain. If this is reiterated for the mourner, it becomes a bit easier to move on, as there is no fear of losing the memories and feelings for the deceased.

Ernie was urged to consider what the reaction of the other men might be on his return to the department. This was designed to help Ernie feel that he was part of a larger community and in this case, a community of those who knew of his relationship with Dave and were sympathetic to his loss.

Ernie had taken a month off, using sick time and vacation time, and if he was not able to return, he was advised that he would be put on disability. Although Ernie did not really feel ready to go back, he did not want to be put on disability. On the day of his return, Ernie tried to "put up a strong front. When I got there the other guys were very happy to see me and were very nice to me. They even put up a 'welcome back Ernie' sign for me." It seemed to go more smoothly than Ernie had anticipated. The evening of his return, there was a scheduled session with the counselor and Ernie cried during most of that session. Although he had begun to accept the loss, the finality of the relationship was now fully realized. The crying was a necessary release for him. He was able to resume his work responsibilities by the end of the first week. He and Bob are "not great together but as long as he doesn't ask too many questions and does his work, we will be all right."

The employee assistance program limited Ernie's counseling to eight sessions. Although Ernie could have probably benefited from several more sessions to examine his basic difficulty in trusting and connecting, there was no option to extend the service. The insurance limitations have become a reality of certain counseling situations in which managed care dictates the duration of any counseling effort. It is helpful to know this in advance, as it will define the degree and depth of the counseling. Occasionally, an insurance company can be prevailed upon to extend benefits, sometimes at reduced cost. This was not the case for Ernie; the water department had rather strict limitations on benefits.

At the funeral, the relationship with Dave's family began to shift for Ernie. As he thought back to it, he had felt uncomfortable there, not sure what his place was, and although Dave's wife had been warm and cried with him, she was occupied by others and with the funeral arrangements. Dave, in Ernie's eyes, was the glue and without him Ernie felt that there was no spot for him. In counseling, this was challenged and seen as another way for Ernie to isolate himself. Ernie did mention that Dave's wife had called him a few times and invited him for dinner but he had declined. He was encouraged to stay connected but, as the counseling relationship was ended after eight sessions, it is not clear how Ernie finally made out. He did return to work but whether or not he returned to a life of isolation is not clear.

Issues for the Counselor

This case did not present any major issues or particularly difficult areas. The only frustration was dealing with the managed care situation and trying to stay within the eight-session limit and do an effective job. Ernie would have benefited from a more intense counseling relationship. It would have served him well to affix to a counselor and go through a positive, planned termination to undo some of the ruptured terminations of his life: father abandonment, divorce, Dave, and so forth. At best, this counseling effort helped Ernie to deal with the present situation in a more positive way and allowed him the space to grieve for Dave.

One of the ongoing struggles in counseling those who grieve is for the counselor to not assume the grievers' pain and overidentify with their situation. This can cloud the responses of the counselor especially in a short-term model when focus and clarity are essential. In addition, Ernie's isolation was a cause for concern and provoked a strongly empathetic and sympathetic reaction. The urge to take care of Ernie was very much present and had to be monitored. Although it is important to monitor these urges, the counselor's humanness comes through and should be capitalized upon. The necessity of empathy in this work is high and the maxim "Step into the shoes of the client and see how it feels" should be adhered to and used to help the counselor phrase and structure interventions for the griever.

2

Bereavement After a Grandmother Dies

The Case—Delores

As far back as Delores (14 years old, African American) was able to remember, her grandmother was an integral part of her life. There were periods of time, after Delores's father left, that Grandmom, as she was called, practically lived with Delores, her brother Isaac, and her mother Marti. And when Delores's mother had to go back to work full-time, when Delores was 5, Grandmom moved in and took care of Delores and 2-year-old Isaac. In fact, Delores would say that Grandmom was often more available than Mom. Yes, Mom had to earn a living as there was no other source of family income, but even when she was home, she was often too tired to help with some of the routine chores in the house or "be there" for the kids. One thing about Grandmom, she was always there. By the time Delores was 6, Grandmom had given up her apartment and moved all her belongings into the small, somewhat rundown, one-family house that Delores's family owned.

Grandmom was 55 years old when she moved in with her daughter and grandchildren. She was widowed at a young age when her husband was killed in a construction accident. He died when Delores was 3; Delores has no memory of her grandfather except through the eyes of her mother and Grandmom. There were always money problems in the household but Delores was somewhat immune to the problems except when she needed new clothes or something special. When Delores was 9 she had a very serious case of pneumonia and she remembers Grandmom staying with her in her room and taking care of her throughout the illness. When Isaac, at 5 years of age, broke his arm when he fell off the stoop, Grandmom took him to the hospital. In Delores's memory Grandmom was the steady parent figure and Mom was more the "shadow person" in the household. Although Delores loves her mother and they actually have a caring relationship, Grandmom was the one who took them to the clinic, went to the school functions, and took them shoe and clothes shopping.

At the age of 63, when Delores was 14 and Isaac was 11, Grandmom had symptoms that were diagnosed as advanced colon cancer. At first, there was no remarkable change in the tempo of the household; the kids went off to school, Grandmom stayed in the house, and Mom went to work. But as the weeks went by, Grandmom began to lose weight and it was an effort for her to get out of her favorite chair and do her regular things. She was still able to keep up with most of the household chores but it was becoming difficult. On her 65th birthday, Grandmom collapsed in the house—the family was home as it was a Sunday—and they called the doctor. The doctor came to the house, examined Grandmom, and told the family that there was some internal bleeding, that it did not look very good, and that it was a matter of days for Grandmom. The decision to keep Grandmom at home was made by her daughter, as was the custom. Grandmom fell into a coma and died at the age of 65 years, 5 days. Her daughter, Delores, and Isaac were "there when she passed."

Delores missed a few days of school for the church service, funeral, and wake. Some relatives came from out of town for the funeral, and there were many people who came, especially from church, to pay their respects over the rest of the week. Delores told everyone that she was "fine" and she almost believed that but she started to not feel so fine about 3 weeks after the death and ritual observances. She woke up crying in the middle of the night, cried for a long time, and went to find comfort from her mother. She got a bad cold and stayed home alone for a week, for the first time in her life. She began missing classes at the junior high school and the guidance counselor called her mother to discuss the situation with her. When questioned, Delores said, "I just feel bad." Delores's mother was immersed in her own grief and wondered how she was going to be able to manage her life and the lives of her children without her mother. Two months after the death, for the first time, Delores received two failing grades on her report card. The guidance counselor called again and suggested that Delores might benefit from some counseling and made a referral for bereavement counseling.

Relevant History

Delores was a fairly well-adjusted young woman. She had a few girlfriends and was a solid B and B+ student in school. The family went to church every Sunday and Delores could be termed a very decent girl. She had a regular babysitting job in the neighborhood and was considered responsible and "on a good track." There was minimal history of "acting out" or inappropriate behavior.

Delores had no memory of her father and what went into his eventual departure from the home. She had seen pictures of him and when she questioned her mother regarding his whereabouts, she was told that he lived somewhere out west. This satisfied her and there was infrequent mention of him. She was attached to her grandmother and all of her family memories included her.

Conceptual Issues

There are three parallel conceptual threads involved in this bereavement experience: adolescent patterns of grief, the death of a grandparent, and the cultural significance that death signifies in the Black community. The experience of kinship care serves as a backdrop to understanding the relationship between Delores and her grandmom.

Kinship Care

"In response to changes in family structure and changing social conditions, the role of grandparents in U.S. society is being redefined. Increasingly, grandparents, rather than playing secondary roles in the lives of their grandchildren, are assuming complete responsibility for raising them" (Cox, 2002, p. 45). In 1997, 3.7 million grandparents were raising their grandchildren; the majority, 2.3 million, were grandmothers. Census data indicate variations by race and ethnicity, with 4.1% of White children, 6.5% of Hispanic children, and 13.5% of Black children living with grandparents or other relatives (Casper & Bryson, 1998). Kinship care is defined as the caring of children by nonparent relatives when parents are absent, unwilling, or unable to parent effectively. Kinship care has been identified as a major strength of Black families and is consistent with the Black community's commitment to assisting family members by providing a safety net for grandchildren (Gibson, 2002). The Black woman in her role as grandmother is the relative most frequently accepting the role of primary caregiver (Dubowitz, 1994).

Several factors explain the dramatic growth in kinship care, especially in the Black community: parental substance abuse, AIDS, incarceration, homicide, and other illnesses (Cox, 2002). In addition, beginning in 1979, federal and state laws changed, which had the effect of encouraging or requiring that precedence be given to next of kin in the placement of foster children (Fuller-Thomson & Minkler, 2000). For many of these new-parent grandparents, the assumption of this role requires a long-term commitment to provide care and support for their grandchildren. For most grandparents, this new role proves very challenging, is laden with responsibility, may mean putting their own needs and commitments on hold, and takes a toll on their lives. At the same time, the rewards are many: the opportunity to parent again, to nurture a legacy, and to be the recipient of the love and companionship of the grandchildren (Burton & Devries, 1992).

Adolescent Patterns of Grief

Writing in 1996, Fleming and Balmer observed, "...Until recently, theories of adolescent bereavement have been virtually nonexistent. One exception to this is the model formulated by Fleming and Adolph (1996) which integrates theories of adjustment to loss with theories of adolescent ego development" (p. 140). The explanation for this lack of inquiry may relate to the fact that death and grief are not normative transitions of adolescent life; adolescents are more engaged in physical and developmental transitions and this seems to be the focus of much of the writings about this age group (Balk, 1996, 2000).

But, what of the adolescent who is involved in a major loss to death? The work of Fleming and Adolph (1996) helps delineate what can be expected for the griever at the nexus between the emotional experience of death and a maturational phase of ego development. Taking a developmental view, the authors proposed five core issues that vary according to the maturational phase of the adolescent: predictability of events, mastery and control, belonging, fairness and justice, and self-image. Within these core areas there are behavioral, cognitive, and affective responses that are consistent with the current maturational phase of the adolescent. For early adolescents, 11- to 14-year-olds (the subject of this case), the maturational and developmental issues revolve around emotionally separating from the parents, developing and sustaining a positive self-image, and shifting of loyalties toward peers and away from family. A death at this time can unseat the adolescent as he or she learns that predictability marks some events and not others; that mastery and control are elusive; that belonging means that peers, not family, are better able to understand his or her struggle; and that realizing that fairness and justice mark some outcomes but not all. Self-image, which is so fragile for most teens, is also seriously shaken with a death. Often a teen will feel marked by the grief and feels "different" from others. In other words, it is reasonable to observe that for the early adolescent, a death is disruptive to the extent that the core issues identified by Fleming and Adolph have been resolved. Although it is one of the tasks of adolescence to begin to grapple with the meaning of life and death and to come to a philosophical and religious stance, clearly it is not easily accomplished (Gordon, 1986).

One variable that affects the degree of reaction for the adolescent is the closeness of the deceased to the youngster and how embedded in his or her life was the person who died. In recent literature on adolescent bereavement, researchers assessed the degree of depressive symptoms. Typically, adolescents became depressed when the death involved a first-degree relative (a close family member) or a second-degree relative (close friend, more distant relative, or pet). The greater the number of losses, the more depressive symptoms the adolescent has to struggle with (Harrison & Harrington, 2001). Another variable in reactivity is gender. Balmer (1992) studied sibling-bereaved adolescents, finding that female respondents exhibited lower self-esteem and higher anxiety and insomnia levels than their male counterparts. Another aspect of her study showed that for the first year, the bereaved adolescents, regardless of gender, were less well adjusted than were nongrievers but by the second and third year after the death, the adjustment scores of the bereaved and nonbereaved were indistinguishable. This speaks to a level of resiliency associated with adolescent bereavement.

Worden (1996) studied adolescents in his Child Bereavement Study. Findings showed that bereaved adolescents were more anxious and fearful over time compared with nonbereaved peers; bereaved adolescents considered their conduct and academic performance inferior to nonbereaved peers but considered themselves more mature; and bereaved adolescents had greater difficulty getting along with peers and struggled with a sense of belonging more than nonbereaved peers.

In summary, the impact of death on an adolescent can be manifested behaviorally, cognitively, and affectively. Variables of gender, age within the adolescent span, and maturational levels are factors in the depth of the bereavement experience; closeness to the deceased is also a major factor. Coping with bereavement involves the interplay between the tasks and conflicts of each maturational phase of adolescence and the grief experience.

Death of a Grandparent

An adolescent's first experience of death may be the death of a grandparent or of a pet. The reaction to these deaths varies depending on the quality and level of relationship attachment and the warmth and frequency of their interaction. In addition, for many adolescents, this will be the first time they have seen their parent(s) deeply upset and it may be their first funeral and period of mourning. The adolescent will have a dual experience: he or she will experience a sense of personal loss if he or she was close to the grandparent and has the larger experience of the family system being shaken by the loss (Webb, 2002).

The death of a grandparent may bring a whole set of confusing thoughts and feelings to an adolescent. The existential questions that we all grapple with—what is death, where do you go when you die—will plague the adolescent. These questions may lead to feelings of anxiety and confusion and a loss of a sense of mastery and control. Concerns may surface about the safety of other family members as well as fears for his or her safety (Hatter, 1996).

The centrality of the relationship with the grandparent is perhaps the most powerful predictor of adolescent grief. Grandparents potentially occupy a unique place in the life of the grandchild, often offering a level of unconditional love and acceptance that can be found only in the grandparent-grandchild relationship.

When there is a death of a grandparent who has served as a surrogate parent in a kinship care capacity, the response for the adolescent is as powerful as the death of a parent would be. The grandparent, one of the adolescent's life anchors, has been ripped from his or her life and although there is the constant struggle for the young adolescent to assert adulthood, there is still the child who wants and needs care and parenting. What may serve to buffer the death of the grandparent is the relationship that the adolescent has with his or her parent(s). But the loss is still significant.

For the adolescent who has lived with the grandparent, who does not have a parent(s) because of a variety of experiences, there is the possibility that the youngster will be placed in a foster care situation or group home. This upheaval on top of the grief may be very difficult for an adolescent to manage. Particular care has to be initiated to protect this youngster from serious emotional harm.

Death in the Black Community

Different cultural traditions approach the social and personal issues of death and bereavement in their own unique ways. These approaches are consistent with long-standing traditions and beliefs, ritual, and custom regarding life, death, and an afterlife, emphasizing certain aspects of the broad range of human experience while diminishing the importance of others (Shapiro, 1994). Each cultural perspective assigns roles, beliefs, values, ceremonies, and rituals to integrate death and the process of dying into the culture as a whole and to help individuals cope with the mysteries and fears of death (Kalish, 1977).

Death viewed from an Afrocentric perspective is a rite of passage wherein the soul passes into another phase of continuous existence. The soul leaves the material world and crosses over into a spiritual world. The underlying belief is in the continuity of the soul and life of the spirit after death. The implication of this belief is that death is not final as the soul survives and the spirit has everlasting life (Bolling, 2000). The belief that there is a life after death makes death less threatening (Gordon, 1986).

Within the Black community, dying family members are kept at home more frequently than in the White community. This may be a reflection of socioeconomic variables as well as an expression of family and religious networking. There is a strong tradition in the Black community of turning to religious persons and symbols for comfort, while relying less on relatives for support. Support is typically garnered from the church and church members. Funerals are seen as a vehicle for confirming self-worth and positive self-identity on the deceased and are strongly religious in content. Because the Black family sees death as a significant life transition, family members will make every effort to attend the funeral and wake of a relative or friend. Funerals might be delayed for days to make sure that all family members can attend. Black families tend to express their grief directly with verbal expression through song and prayer (McGoldrick, 1989).

The three themes of the specific death of a grandparent, the nuances of adolescent grief, and the cultural rituals of death in the Black community help in understanding the particular struggle for Delores when her grandmother died.

Suggestions for Intervention

Two areas of awareness guide intervention strategies with the grieving adolescent: what it means to be an adolescent when a death occurs and the impact of culture or race on the bereavement process.

An overriding sensitivity of any intervention with adolescents must take into account that adolescents, especially early adolescents, are struggling with issues of identity, self-esteem, and pressures of school and of "fitting in." A death in the life of an adolescent can topple the fragile sense of self that holds the adolescent together. After a death, many adolescents, with the aid and support of family and others, will recover a sense of equilibrium within months of the death. Others may require professional evaluation and intervention.

The profile of the adolescent who needs professional intervention is one who, several months after the death, has persistent difficulty talking about the dead person, is exhibiting aggressive behavior that persists or takes the form of property destruction, is experiencing anxiety that is turning into phobic reactions, is experiencing disturbed eating and sleeping, is withdrawn socially, is having newly identified school problems, and is self-destructive. All these areas must be assessed when referral is considered (Worden, 1982). In addition, it is important to look at historical antecedents such as the number of previous losses experienced by the adolescent survivor and how they were handled. If previous losses were not fully grieved, the present loss may be more difficult to manage. The counselor should assess mental history, history of depression, and history of levels of anxiety (Valentine, 1996). Grieving adolescents, like adults, will experience the conflicted emotions of guilt, anger, powerlessness, withdrawal, and isolation. The question becomes how does the adolescent express these confused feelings (Lattanzi-Licht, 1996).

Within the counseling context, the adolescent is encouraged to address his or her feelings and concerns in a safe, nonjudgmental environment. Adolescents often comment that they need and want opportunities to express their feelings, especially around death. Sometimes they are afraid to share these feeling with family members, as family members are going through their own experience of grief. The teen is afraid that he or she will be further burdening grieving parent(s) or others.

In general, the strategy for working with adolescents is cognitively based, consisting of confrontation of feelings and helping them to restructure their world without the deceased. This involves going over the events before and at the time of the death, focusing on memories, and working toward restructuring the former relationship with the deceased (M. S. Stroebe, Stroebe, & Hansson, 1993). This approach helps facilitate the reality of the loss in the thinking and awareness of the adolescent. Complicated grief and mourning usually result when there is a denial of the pain of the loss, avoidance of discussion of memories or feelings regarding the deceased, and a hurried reentry back to one's life (Valentine, 1996).

Intervention with the family and the adolescent can be especially important as the family grieves collectively. Frequently, adolescents feel marginalized when decision making occurs; urging the family to include the adolescent in planning the funeral and what occurs after helps bring the adolescent into the circle of mourning where support can be more forthcoming. The family can be pivotal in quelling anxious feelings that may arise within the adolescent because of the death. If the family is available, it may be the role of the counselor to bring the family together to facilitate the discussion of feelings related to the loss. If the family is unavailable, either mentally or physically, the counselor may have to be more available to the adolescent griever and offer greater levels of support through phone calls and additional appointments. While making an initial assessment of an adolescent mourner, the counselor should consider the availability and receptivity of the family, as they suggest a level of emotional support that may or may not be available to the adolescent.

It is imperative for the counselor to be aware of cultural differences in the experiences and rituals of death because there can be no solid definition of "normality" in assessing responses to death. Every culture expresses grief in unique ways: the dominant American pattern is often to deny death with a minimization of all rituals. Traditional Greek and Italian women bear the outward signs of mourning for their spouse by wearing black for the rest of their lives. Jewish people have a prescribed pattern of ritual that mandates burial within 24 hours of death and a week of family mourning. Irish families consider death a significant life cycle transition and family members will make every effort to attend the funeral and wake, sparing no expense for drink and funeral arrangements. In Puerto Rican culture, women often express their sorrow dramatically by having seizurelike attacks (*ataques*) with uncontrollable emotions (McGoldrick, 1989). In the death culture of Korea, there are four stages or days of handling of the deceased in preparation for the burial: the first day is preparation, on the second day the deceased is cleaned with honey and is clothed and covered with cloth, on the third day the body is wrapped in a blanket and wrapped with ropes, and the fourth day is the burial. No conversation is allowed during this period as a show of respect. The mourning period goes from 3 months to 3 years, depending on the degree of the relationship (D. Lee, 2000). What becomes clear is that practices and attitudes vary, mandating an awareness of difference and a broader base of understanding and acceptance by the counselor.

Major Issues in This Case

By the time the guidance counselor from school contacted Delores's mother, more than 2 months after Grandmom's death, Delores was beginning to sink into a period of depression and withdrawal. Her grades had dropped, and she was cutting classes, was absent from school more than her mother realized, and had stopped seeing several of her friends. She had kept up with the babysitting job but the woman who hired her had begun using some of the other girls in the neighborhood because she did not show up on a few occasions. Delores's world, as it had been defined before Grandmom's death, was now quite unfamiliar. She and her mom were getting along, sort of, as they redefined the household responsibilities, but their relationship had been secondary to Grandmom, and although Isaac was there, he had his own friends and they "just lived in the same house." Her developmental struggles were toward self-esteem and independence, and it appeared that the death had set her back in each of these areas.

She initially presented in a detached way and had difficulty establishing and maintaining eye contact. She was not forthcoming and did not volunteer much information. She answered questions with one-word answers and gave the impression that she was angry. She had some 'right' to this anger, as she had not wanted to go to a counselor but her mother had given her no choice.

Delores was tall for her age, was well developed, moved with a certain amount of grace, and was quite attractive. Her clothes were of the most recent style but she was not well groomed. There was almost a sloppiness about her that would have been consistent with a low-level depression.

This was Delores's first direct experience with death. Her mother had attended a funeral of an aunt a few years ago but Delores had not really known her. As a first experience, especially of someone as central to Delores as her grandmother, this was a devastating and profound hurdle for Delores to overcome.

It took several sessions for Delores to begin to open up. Efforts to engage her included talking about school, questioning her about her interests, commenting on her clothes; anything that might promote a verbal interchange was tried. What finally worked was when the counselor told Delores that her dog (the counselor's) had died over the week and that the counselor was struggling with feelings about the death. Delores was visibly shaken when told about the dog that often came in and out of the treatment room. Sometimes, self-disclosure can facilitate discussion; it may give a patient hope that he or she too will be able to survive a significant loss. In addition, especially for a teen, the reassurance that the counselor will not judge him or her is inherent in the counselor's disclosure. In this case, the dog's death seemed to open up some need in Delores to talk and she began with the time of the funeral. Although Grandmom had been mentioned numerous times, this was the first discussion, initiated by Delores, about her. She began tentatively to tell the counselor about the funeral, perhaps a safer spot to begin talking about her loss. She described the funeral as best she could, with prompting, but she said that she was not able to remember a lot about it. She was able to talk about who was there, who conducted the service, the food at her house, her mother crying, and so forth. She talked from a distant place, almost as a reporter rather than as a participant.

In the following session she was a bit more relaxed and open and responded to questions about the time when her grandmother first became ill. The tradition of taking care of family members while they were terminally ill (Gordon, 1986) meant that their very small home had been transformed. Delores was reluctant to discuss some of her feelings and memories of this time—was she feeling especially guilty about some aspects of it?—and kept moving away from the topic.

Delores became very verbal when exploring some of her favorite memories of her relationship with Grandmom. There was the time "when we went to the beauty shop together and we both had our hair curled in the exact same way." There was the time when "Isaac broke his arm and we had to go to the hospital. Grandmom had to hold his arm a certain way so the bone would not stick out"; "Grandmom took us kids to the movies on Saturday afternoons and laughed at the same cartoons that we did"; "We all, my mom and brother and Grandmom, went on a vacation together one year to visit relatives and Grandmom rode a horse with me on the front part of the saddle with her." There were endless stories and as Delores told them, she became more and more animated. Prompting Delores to remember and tell the stories was part of the counseling strategy to help her begin to confront her feelings about the loss.

Delores's resistance to confront her feelings fell apart during the fifth session when, in the middle of recalling her sixth grade graduation party that Grandmom had made for her, she realized that Grandmom would not be there for her high school graduation. It was a dramatic moment in that Delores, it seemed, realized for the first time that Grandmom was no longer a part of her world. And that was when the tears began to flow. Delores had been holding all this grief inside and it seemed to burst forth at this pivotal trigger moment. She cried for quite some time and then talked more about what Grandmom would miss—her graduation, her college years, her possible marriage and children; she was all over her future map. It seemed necessary to shift the focus away from what Grandmom would miss and move it more toward what Delores was going to miss by Grandmom's not being there. The counselor made that reframing and Delores began to talk more about herself, albeit slowly and tentatively.

During the next several sessions—there were 20 in all, over a 6-month period—Delores began to address her anger and sadness, emotions that are so easily intertwined in loss. She began to be more animated, began to look less depressed, and her grooming improved. She was more engaged at school and had resumed most of the babysitting jobs. She was "hanging out with her friends" more.

A critical juncture with Delores was forged when she began to speak of her guilt feelings and her anger. Feelings of guilt and anger are part of every bereavement experience and Delores was no exception. The counselor asked Delores to talk about the time when Grandmom had got so sick that she needed a lot of care; did Delores have any angry or bad feelings about that time? This issue was very hard for Delores to discuss but the trust was there between Delores and the counselor; Delores was reassured that everyone has those feelings as times and that they are part of what goes on for most people. Delores said that she was very upset during that time, she hated seeing Grandmom in pain, and there were times that she left the house rather than witness it. She also had "wished that Grandmom would die so that she would stop hurting." She felt especially guilty over that admission. In helping the mourner cope with this guilt, the counselor normalized this reaction by recognizing that there are often circumstances that we would want to have ended but despite this wish, we cannot make things happen. Also, she was reassured how difficult it is for most people to see someone whom they love in pain or in compromised circumstances.

Another area that needed attention was the evolving relationship that was developing with Delores's mother Marti. In fact, her mother had been more of a shadow figure in the household for the years that Grandmom had been there. She worked in a shift job and often worked nights, so she was sleeping during the day and was gone when the kids were home. She now had rearranged her schedule so she worked during the day and she and Delores were sorting out the details of their relationship. When suggested by the counselor, Delores agreed to a double session with her mother. The goal was to facilitate discussion between them about the loss and to establish some new ground rules between them.

The session between Delores and her mother began with some tension, as Marti was unaccustomed to sharing emotions with a counselor. Also, Marti might have suspected that she would be walking into a situation in which she would have to defend herself. To allay some of these anticipated concerns, the counselor tried to explain that this was an exploratory session to see how Delores and Marti might work on their newly revised relationship now that Grandmom was gone. Delores quickly jumped in with some concerns about household responsibilities—laundry, cleaning, food shopping—which she felt would now be her responsibility as Marti returned to work. Some of the nuts and bolts of running the household had to be addressed but underlying the relationship between Delores and Marti was the sadness that they both felt and were having some difficulty expressing to each other, often picking at each other rather than supporting each other.

After the household responsibilities were sorted out, the counselor asked how they were each handling their grief; Delores admitted that she was still very sad and that she thought about Grandmom every day. Marti appeared surprised to hear the extent of Delores's pain. Perhaps that allowed her to open up to her own pain; perhaps it was coincidental, but Marti began to cry (the first time that Delores had seen her mother in tears except at the funeral) and in a particularly poignant moment, Delores went over to her mother and they cried together. When they were able to talk, the counselor suggested an exploration of how they could emotionally support each other, perhaps spending time together outside the house, perhaps talking together and sharing their memories of Grandmom, even coming to additional sessions if they felt that it would help. It was decided that they would try talking together. Marti did not return for any additional sessions and Delores reported that although there were still house things that were not fully operational, she and her mom were getting along well.

By the end of the 6 months, Delores was well on her way to incorporating her loss. She had resumed most of her activities and her outlook and demeanor were very positive. Her relationship with her mother was still somewhat strained but not much more than the relationship of most adolescent girls and their mothers. Delores commented, "Grandmom is with me; her spirit and what she wanted for me will guide me. I sure do miss her."

Issues for the Counselor

Working with adolescents has its share of frustration, especially with younger adolescents. They are not adults and they are not children and as such some of the sophistication is lacking and some of the needy child is still there. Does the counselor deal with the child part or strengthen the adult? In this case, realizing the level of maturity of Delores—she was much more little girl than young woman—and that she was scared, angry, and guilty, trying to access her emotions and helping her put words to her feelings were especially important. Thus, the counselor structured the helping as being catered much more to a girl than a young woman.

An additional struggle for the counselor revolved around trying not to apply White, middle-class values or timetables to the work, being sensitive to other customs and ways of handling situations. This included not only the illness and death of Delores's grandmother but also the living and life arrangements of this family. It was necessary to see Marti in a nonjudgmental way in relation to her necessary abdication of some aspects of the maternal role. By having the joint session, Marti became a person to the counselor rather than a figure only known through the eyes of Delores. It facilitated the work greatly to have the session with her and added a dimension missing until then between Delores and Marti.

Another struggle for the counselor was wanting to protect Delores and care for her, as a mother might. She was so raw and angry when she first came for help and there was the inclination to try to make it all OK for her, sparing her the pain of having to look at her emotions. These feelings had to be pushed aside so the work could be done.

A follow-up appointment was scheduled for the year anniversary of Grandmom's death. Delores was now 15, looked more mature, and carried herself well. She was busy at school, had a part-time job, and had picked up her grades somewhat. She thought of Grandmom every day but she had stopped crying about her on a daily basis. She spoke to her in her thoughts and her goal was to make her grandmother proud.

3 CHAPTER

Bereavement After Multiple Losses

The Case—Laura

After the death, Laura (48 years old) continuously questioned why she had been singled out to be so tortured. Her life had been going along fairly well: she had had a serious, committed, loving relationship with a man, Sid (53 years old), for the past 7 years; her three children were grown, one living nearby, the other living upstate, and her oldest son, David (24 years old), living at home and working. She was healthy and had a steady job, and although she was not rich, she lived comfortably. She had limited contact with the husband from whom she had been divorced when the children were very young; she spent weekends with Sid and during the week she would see friends and "do her thing."

Sid was a magazine editor and had never married; when he had met Laura 7 years prior they just seemed right for each other and a deep and abiding love developed between them. They were each other's best friend; the separate living arrangement seemed to suit both of them, allowing each some freedom while being deeply committed to time together. Sid had not been feeling just right for a short time before consulting his doctor. Tests showed some type of malignant mass in his pancreas, and he was to begin chemotherapy as soon as it could be scheduled. This weighed heavily on Laura and Sid, despite the optimistic prognosis offered by Sid's doctors.

In Laura's life, the routine of the household was that she woke David up in the morning, as he was notorious for sleeping through his alarm clock and arriving late for work. One morning, she went down the steps to his room and bent over to shake David awake, but this morning he could not be awakened; he had died during the night. Laura ran through the house screaming, called 911, and within minutes the medics and police were there but he had been dead for several hours. The final determination was that he had died from an embolism that probably began in his leg and traveled to his heart. No explanation was forthcoming from the doctors about why a clot had formed. David had been treated for recurring allergic reactions over the years and the doctors speculated that perhaps an explanation resided there. An autopsy was ordered; to this day, Laura has not looked at it.

The next days were a total blank as Laura went through the motions of all that had to be done. The family gathered, the funeral took place, and Laura blocked most of it out.

Essentially, she was unable to function. Her grief and depression were crippling and overwhelmed everything. For the first few weeks, she could not eat or sleep; she was unable even to consider returning to work, as she was immersed in her grief. Sid and others suggested that she should get some help, so Laura went for group counseling at a local mental health agency. The group proved somewhat helpful; it enabled Laura to return to work about 5 weeks after David's death. At work, she found herself short tempered, snapping at those who worked with and for her; she was preoccupied and could not focus; and she was frequently late. Somehow she was able to get through most days, only to come home and cry.

David died in April, and Sid died in November. Sid began to spiral downhill about 3 months after David's death. He was losing weight and strength and was forced to leave his job. The doctor began to use words such as "hospice" and "care facility," which was the signal that Sid was not going to improve. During the last months of Sid's life, Laura was very involved in his care, and to the end she believed that he would get better. Even on the last day in the hospital when Sid died, she remained hopeful. Again, the family gathered, hers and Sid's, the funeral took place, and Laura blocked out most of it.

It was her anger that finally propelled her into individual counseling; she was unable to be civil to those at work "who were idiots." The few friends that she still had, her mother, and even the people in the grocery store "who push ahead as though I am not standing there" were objects of her wrath. She found herself irrationally lashing out at anyone who even slightly annoyed her, and she began to feel isolated and frightened by her own actions. She began bereavement counseling in December, 8 months after David had died.

Three months after Laura had entered counseling, in March, she got word that her former husband had died suddenly from unknown causes. Within 11 months, there had been three deaths: her son, her partner and life mate, and her ex-husband. "How much can a person take?" Laura lamented.

Relevant History

Laura would never define herself as upbeat but she would say that she was "steady." As a deeply religious woman, she had been brought up to "do the right thing" and to be respectful of others. She had an older brother with whom she kept in touch and was in frequent contact with her mother who lived in another state. She had married young and quickly had three children, but the marriage proved unsatisfying and she and her husband parted. According to Laura, her ex-husband maintained contact with the children and "was a better distant father than when he was present."

Her emotional history was not particularly complex. She did not suffer with moodiness, had never had a serious depression, and was an even-keeled person. Many years before David's death, her father had died after a prolonged illness. Although Laura felt close to him, she had lived apart from her parents since college, and although she had grieved his death, she was able to move ahead in her life.

The decision to divorce her husband had been facilitated by his indiscretions, and once divorced she decided that she would never marry again. She had been a single parent, minimally subsidized by her ex-husband, and had managed well with the income from her job. When she met Sid, she cautiously allowed him to enter her life and slowly found a safety and comfort with him that was enduring. And then everything came apart with the death of her son. Then it came apart again with Sid's death and then again, but not with great pain, with the death of her ex-husband. Laura would accurately be described as someone who had sustained multiple losses occurring over a short time. With each new loss, her ability and willingness to cope with these losses was seriously compromised. Instead, she became depressed, barely functional, angry, and despondent.

Conceptual Issues

The majority of research material that describes the impact of multiple losses comes from two areas: multiple losses in relation to the elderly and deaths from HIV/AIDS. Although it surely occurs in other populations, it is especially pronounced in these two groups and because of its prevalence, it has been studied. I explore these areas of bereavement knowledge in relation to this case, and I provide a discussion of those struggling with morbid grief. Both concepts—multiple losses and morbid grief—define Laura's bereavement experience.

Multiple Losses

Multiple losses, also known as multiple deaths, refers either to the loss of two or more loved ones in the same event or to the experience of a number of losses occurring sequentially within a short period of time (Rando, 1993). In this case, I am using the second definition, the experience of a number of losses within a short time frame. Bereavement from multiple losses is different from standard bereavement in several ways. Individuals who face loss after loss cannot be expected to bounce back, as one death occurs that has not been grieved and then the next occurs that compounds the grieving process. In multiple losses, there may not be time between traumas to work through the many feelings associated with each grief experience. Also, because of the repeated emotional assaults, survivors tend to turn inward, which frequently creates a more protracted grieving period (Biller & Rice, 1990). For those who have sustained multiple losses, the coping mechanism of building a protective wall is an emotional barrier to loss and pain and becomes an adaptive, protective response that keeps others at bay while it prevents much needed closeness.

Discussion about multiple losses occurs in the bereavement literature regarding the AIDS epidemic. The gay community in the United States has been devastated by the AIDS epidemic, with most homosexual men having experienced multiple losses of friends and lovers (Neugebauer et al., 1992). The compounding effect of multiple losses is a constant theme in the homosexual community and is a source of concern and anguish; the impact on survivors of multiple losses complicates the resolution of their grief, in part, because there is insufficient time between deaths to work through the grief process before another death occurs (Nord, 1996b).

The range of emotions in multiple losses is wide. Researchers have observed and documented that the survivors experience periods of emotional shutdown (Carmack, 1992); psychic numbing to screen emotions that are overwhelming, which is a frequent defense used against the pain of the losses (Boykin, 1991); and depression and anhedonia (the inability to enjoy pleasurable events). Drinking and drug use may increase (Carmack, 1992; Cherney & Verhey, 1996) as do feelings of hopelessness, demoralization, and helplessness (J. L. Martin, 1988). Moodiness and tendencies to react in rage, even to minor or small irritation, are observed and can be directed against those closest to the survivor or at the deceased (Nord, 1996b). Symptoms such as preoccupation and searching behavior also have been noted in those struggling with multiple AIDS losses (Neugebauer et al., 1992). As shown in this literature, multiple losses have an impact on the grief experience in terms of prolonging and compounding it, and the losses have the potential to evoke a wide array of emotional responses.

Multiple losses in the elderly are a frequent occurrence. With age, the number of deaths of friends and family members increases, which can cause a person to feel so overwhelmed by the pain of loss that he or she is not able to grieve. Worden (2002) pointed out that the elderly are also struggling with losses of occupation, environment, family constellations, physical vigor, and, for some, loss of cerebral functioning. All of these changes need to be addressed, but with the compounding of so many losses in an abbreviated time, grieving responses may not be fully realized, creating the possibility of protracted depression. The concept of bereavement overload (Kastenbaum, 1969) speaks to the condition of loss upon loss in later life that taxes the individual's ability to cope. The reality is that the longer we live, the greater the potential is for multiple losses to assail us; by just staying alive over an extended period of time, we will accumulate losses, of mates, friends, loved ones, physical viability, jobs, financial security, and mental acuity (Kastenbaum, 2001).

Multiple losses to death, whether in the AIDS community or for those who are aging, create special bereavement challenges including how to cope with the assault of the losses to fend off depression and hopelessness, how to adjust to a shifting personal landscape, and how to grieve each loss. For the elderly and those with AIDS, the impact of multiple losses has posed a serious emotional health challenge for the survivors and for those from whom they seek help.

Morbid Grief

Morbid grief has been referred to in the literature as complicated grief, unresolved or exaggerated grief, or pathological grief. Morbid grief reactions can be defined in different ways: by depth of despair or reaction and time.

Morbid grief reactions that are defined by time include those situations in which the survivor has not been able to adapt to the loss, has had an exaggerated or prolonged grief response, has not been able to modify his or her self-image around the loss, and has remained rooted in the death experience with depression and anger (Kastenbaum, 2001; Worden, 2002). The level of despair that signals morbid grief may be unrelated to time; this aspect of morbid grief is defined as a constellation of symptoms (Lindemann, 1944).

The classic work on morbid grief was written by Erich Lindemann (1944), a psychiatrist who observed the bereavement behaviors of 101 patients during a series of psychiatric interviews in a clinic that he had set up following a fire in the Coconut Grove nightclub in Boston. He concluded that there were five characteristics of those suffering with normal grief: somatic distress, preoccupations with the image of the deceased, guilt, hostile reactions, and loss of patterns of conduct. A sixth reaction, seen in those bordering on morbid or pathological grief, is the appearance of traits of the deceased in the behavior of the bereaved. He stressed that successful completion of bereavement involved grief work aimed at helping the bereaved adjust to the environment without the deceased and give expression to the pain of the loss.

Morbid grief is a distortion of normal grief with symptoms that include overactivity without a sense of loss which may include expansiveness and replication of the behaviors of the deceased; the acquisition of behaviors related to the illness of the deceased; a recognized medical disease with a psychosomatic origin; a major alteration in relationships to friends and relatives with avoidance of social interactions; lack of interest and critical attitudes; furious hostility against specific persons; wooden and formal appearance which often covers the hostility; loss of patterns of social interaction; actions detrimental to one's own social and economic existence; and agitated depression with tension, insomnia, feelings of worthlessness, bitter self-accusation, and punishment (Lindemann, 1944).

Lindemann's conceptualization has created the basis for established views on morbid grief reactions (Parkes, 2001). Lindemann's work and that of others (Rando, 1993; Raphael, 1983) rest on the assumption that the overwhelming crush of several losses causes the individual to inhibit his or her grief, which can lead to psychiatric symptoms and physical morbidity. Unresolved grief tends to be tenacious, chronic, and persistent unless treated (DeVaul, Zisook, & Faschingbauer, 1979) and may have a corrosive impact on the survivor.

Suggestions for Intervention

Two approaches to bereavement work for those with multiple losses will be suggested: Worden's model of grief therapy and guided mourning.

Grief Therapy—Worden

Worden (2002) outlined nine procedures to follow for those struggling with complicated mourning, for those suffering multiple losses, or both. I list these procedures numerically, but it should not be assumed that they must be followed in a lockstep manner. When dealing with multiple losses, Worden suggested that generally it is best to explore the loss believed to have the fewest complicating factors first and then apply the same schema to the subsequent losses.

1. *Rule out physical disease.* If the mourner presents with physical complaints, it is important to assess the mourner for any physical problems to be certain that the complaints are not emotionally based.
2. *Set up a contract for the focus of the work and establish an alliance.* Setting up a contract may be difficult for the mourner but it is wise to adhere to Worden's procedures. Within this step, the multiply bereaved agrees to reexplore his or her relationship with one of the deceased persons (as noted, the client should decide which is the least complicated loss, which would be the first addressed). The counselor reinforces the beneficial aspect of this part of the work despite the pain that it might provoke in the survivor. The focus is specifically on the loss and what is directly related to it. Within this procedure, the counselor temporarily becomes a substitute for the lost person, offering hope and comfort. Establishing an alliance may be difficult, as those who have been faced with multiple loss do not easily connect for fear of losing yet another person.
3. *Revive memories of the deceased person.* Talk about the person who died, his or her respective qualities, what he or she was like, what is best remembered about him or her, what he or she enjoyed doing, and how he or she related to the bereaved. Once some of these positive memories have been discussed, a slight turn is needed to help the mourner look at some aspects of the deceased person that have a negative quality such as anger, hurt, and disappointment. By looking at the deceased in a more balanced way—as possessing good qualities and bad—the griever is helped to see the deceased as less idealized. This balance can help in integrating the

loss by seeing that much will be missed and some aspects of the deceased will not.

4. *Assess which of the four mourning tasks are not complete and make an effort to address the gaps.* The four tasks of mourning as detailed by Worden are to accept the reality of the loss, experience the pain of grief, adjust to the environment in which the deceased is missing, and withdraw emotional energy and reinvest it in another relationship. If the mourner has not accepted the reality of the loss, the survivor has to begin the letting go of the deceased; if the difficulty is in experiencing the pain, the counselor has to help the mourner feel safe enough to feel both the positive and negative aspects of his or her grief. The safety is built up through the accepting relationship established between counselor and griever. If adjusting to the environment seems to be the hurdle, then problem solving becomes the focus to help the bereaved to make the needed accommodations to get back to living. If the bereaved is unable to engage in a new relationship and withdraw his or her emotional energy from the deceased, the counselor has to work with the mourner to help release him or her from a binding attachment to the deceased and to be free to develop a new relationship. Often mourners are afraid to let go of the deceased for fear that the deceased will be forgotten. It may be constructive to counsel the griever to build new connections to the deceased, new ways to think about him or her in a more spiritual or ethereal manner. The counselor who urges social connectedness with others and by encouraging and supporting efforts in that direction can facilitate this. Often membership in a bereavement group can be the first step in that part of the healing process.

5. *Deal with effect or lack of effect stimulated by memories.* There is a tendency for the bereaved to speak of the deceased in overly glowing terms. Early on in the counseling this is encouraged but it is suspect later on in the work as this hyperbole often covers angry, unexpressed feelings. The counselor must urge the survivor to feel the anger and hurt, which facilitates the verbal expression of these emotions. Guilt, as well as anger, is often not directly expressed. The feelings of guilt are to be reality tested by the counselor, as often these feelings are irrational.

6. *Explore and diffuse linking objects.* Linking objects are symbolic yet concrete objects—such as a watch, camera, or clothing—that the survivor retains that keep the deceased's memory alive. Counselors are urged to discuss these objects with the survivor and encourage the survivor to bring them into the counseling session. The problem with linked objects is that the survivor often becomes compulsively attached to the object and may experience anguish if the item

is misplaced. In addition, the retention of the object(s) can restrict the grieving process. The letting go of the linked object is seen as a step toward letting go of the deceased.

7. *Acknowledge the finality of the loss.* Some survivors harbor the belief that the deceased will return, holding on to a chronic hope for reunion. The counseling effort is to help the bereaved accept the loss and understand why he or she is holding on to this belief.

8. *Deal with the fantasy of ending grieving.* Help the bereaved to explore the fantasy of what it would be like to complete grieving, what would be lost and what would be gained. Does he or she want to relinquish the role of mourner?

9. *Help the mourner say a final good-bye.* Survivors need to be reassured that saying good-bye to the deceased does not mean that the deceased will be forgotten. In addition, the process of saying good-bye to the grief counselor has to be handled well, with the counselor initiating and discussing the ending of the relationship with the bereaved, giving the bereaved a lot of notice and time to adjust to the loss of their relationship. For those who suffer multiple losses, leaving the bereavement counselor might activate some of the previous losses (Worden, 2002). Worden suggested that a scheduled recheck with the counselor be agreed upon, especially if new issues arise.

Guided Mourning

As described by Mawson, Marks, Ramm, and Stern (1981, p. 185), guided mourning "...likens unresolved grief, to other forms of phobic avoidance which have been treated successfully by exposure to the avoided situation." Multiple losses usually create unresolved grief, and patients are amenable to this approach. Guided mourning involves intensive exposure to reliving of avoided painful memories and feelings associated with bereavement. It entails repeated description of difficult situations pertaining to the loss, encouragement to visit places that have been avoided since the loss, encouragement to verbally and behaviorally say good-bye to the deceased, assignments consisting of forced writing and thinking about the deceased, facing the grief, and daily viewing of the deceased's photograph (Rando, 1993).

In their investigation on the effectiveness of guided mourning, Mawson and colleagues compared two groups of 6 patients each. The patients in the control group were encouraged to avoid thinking of the deceased, to not give much attention to painful memories, and to employ distraction whenever possible. The guided mourning group was directed to immerse themselves, in imagination and real life, in their loss. All patients were assessed as having morbid grief reactions and had been on a clinic waiting list for bereavement counseling. Each group had six sessions with a grief counselor over a 2-week period. After 2 weeks, the guided mourning group showed significantly greater improvement on three measures and a trend toward improvement on four measures on a grief measurement inventory. In contrast, the control group showed no significant improvement or trend on any measure. These findings have led the researchers to state, "Results suggest that guided mourning is a useful ingredient in the management of morbid grief" (Mawson et al., 1981, p. 191) despite the limited sample.

As an approach, guided mourning appears most useful in survivors where mourning has been avoided, repressed, or delayed. For the mourner with multiple losses, because of the potential for numbing based on repeated losses, it would be advisable to look at each loss separately and experience the loss as an entity unto itself.

In summary, the individual who sustains multiple losses can be helped using various intervention approaches. Guided mourning and Worden's procedures for helping those with complicated mourning are suggested because they address the aspects of multiple losses that keep the mourner from experiencing grief and moving through it.

Major Issues in This Case

The compounding of loss for Laura was overwhelming, as it might have been for anyone. The first of the losses was her child, and the enormity and assault of a mother's grief experience is enough to cause major emotional disruption. Within months, and actually as Laura was grieving the death of David, Sid's condition had been diagnosed and he was spiraling into a terminal situation; the major support in her life who could have made a substantial contribution to Laura's healing, was fading from view. Fortunately, Sid's condition at the time of David's death, while diagnosed, had not affected Sid's functioning and he was able to be there for and with Laura, initially and for several weeks thereafter. But that support and person was taken from her as well. It was soon after that Laura entered individual grief counseling.

Laura's demeanor, appearance, and affect were those of a seriously depressed person. She had minimal eye contact, looked down most of the time, was not well groomed, and spoke in a monotone. She could be described as "flat" yet when she was asked why she had come for counseling, she mentioned her anger. This was not consistent with how she carried herself. She spoke of her work situation that was becoming more troublesome because of her absences, attitude, and lateness. She mentioned that she had no interest in anything or anyone and that she felt like "a windup toy that is put on the floor and does what it is supposed to and falls down." She had difficulty staying awake and "felt nothing but cried a lot." When asked if she had considered suicide, she said no but felt that there was no purpose in her life. "I am alone, my son has died, my boyfriend is gone and there just doesn't seem to be a purpose to any of this," she said. In viewing Laura's condition, she had several of the symptoms consistent with morbid grief described by Lindemann (1944): she expressed furious hostility, she was wooden in her self-presentation, she had a loss of patterns of social interaction, she was jeopardizing her economic existence by her lateness and absences, and she was sleeping all the time.

The approach to working with Laura combined Worden's procedures with some of the techniques of working with those struggling with morbid grief. The procedures were not all addressed and the sequencing was shifted; some of the suggestions in the morbid grief material were implemented. This blending of approaches is often how the work proceeds, as the counselor's level of skill and comfort in applying the approaches broadens. People and their emotions are not always linear and strict adherence to an approach is not feasible as the emotional swings of grief pull on an individual in unpredictable ways. Also, in some circumstances, individuals will follow the template suggested in the literature and the work with them is effective as well as linear.

It was clear from Laura's brief description that Sid's death was the less complicated of the two. She was able to describe some of the details of Sid's illness and their relationship but had not even been able to say her son's name during the first few meetings. Following Worden's suggestion to address the less complex loss, the counselor focused on Sid's death for the initial work. For Laura, David's death so close to Sid's diagnosis meant that she was less available to Sid and was not able to give to him as fully as she would have wished. The counselor assumed that there was a lot of guilt about this that lay under the surface of her grief and that might be the source of some of her depression. The contract to reexplore the two lost relationships starting with Sid was agreed to with no resistance.

The counselor and Laura slowly began to discuss Laura and Sid's relationship: how they had met, what was the first attraction, what were the circumstances of the first date, and so on. The questions are designed to get the patient talking about the deceased. This part of the work combined the two approaches as guided mourning asks the survivor to relive some of the avoided memories, the good and the bad. In the telling of the early history, Laura was more animated than she had been up until that point. She was able to smile and reminisced freely. The chronology of their relationship was followed from first meeting to greater and greater degrees of involvement. She described some fond memories of the early years and slowly segued to the present and how Sid had been so helpful during the funeral for David. In sum she felt that Sid "was a tender and gentle man who was very special." What made Sid unique, according to Laura, was "his perspective on the world, he never thought within the box, he was creative and had an unusual kind of intelligence which I appreciated."

To shift away from only seeing Sid without flaws, the counselor suggested, "Perhaps there were some qualities about Sid that you didn't fully appreciate. Can you tell me what they were?" This was to try to put Sid in a realistic framework noting some aspects of their relationship that were less than perfect. Mostly, Laura resisted this path but was able to acknowledge that Sid was "not the most perfect of men but he was close to ideal and he took a lot of crap from me."

During the session devoted to the relationship with Sid, it became apparent that Laura was only just beginning to accept the reality of this loss and the associated pain, Worden's second task. In this part of the work, the counselor hoped that Laura might be able to express some of her guilt about not being fully engaged in Sid's dying and death. The emotional pain is not only about the loss for the survivor but may be for the pain of his or her own behavior as well. Laura was not immediately forthcoming with this emotion but did say, "I did not give as much to Sid as I wanted." To push Laura, who was so vulnerable, would have been a mistake in timing, so early in the counseling relationship.

Throughout the many weeks of the counseling that focused on Sid, Laura's feelings about David started to merge within the content of the sessions. With the best of intentions, the counselor found it difficult to confine all of the discussion on Sid. Laura's anger began to emerge, albeit slowly, as more of David entered the explorations. The merging was not totally discouraged as it was thought that encouraging Laura to vent these feelings would be helpful, if done in a safe environment—one where feelings were encouraged and intellectualization discouraged. Along with the anger came the guilt: about Sid, about not knowing that David was not well, about not going downstairs earlier to wake David, about not making Sid see a doctor sooner. There were so many "shoulds" and "oughts." After Laura's expression of guilt, the counselor made every effort to introduce the factor of reality—how it was impossible for any one person to do all things perfectly, that as humans we are bound to make many mistakes by virtue of our humanness—and to challenge the guilt to have Laura reevaluate her role with both Sid and David. One impossible question for Laura to avoid was why Sid had not gone to a doctor on his own when he first began to have symptoms. In other words, why was it Laura's responsibility to tell a grown adult that he had to see a doctor?

By the beginning of the fourth month of weekly sessions, the counselor began to feel that Laura was making some progress. She trusted the counselor and was more open with her feelings. She had been asked to bring in pictures of both David and Sid (linking objects) and she complied. She was still deeply depressed, and the counselor initiated a discussion regarding antidepressant medication. Laura agreed to a psychiatric consultation and she agreed to try some antidepressant medication. As it takes a few weeks for the medication to take effect, no immediate relief was felt. She was struggling with "trying to hold everything together" and there was only a slight elevation of mood even when the medication was at its most effective.

When the counselor feels that the mourner is not functioning in several key areas of life such as not being able to work, not relating to others, crying much of the time, and having depression so overwhelming that he or she is not able to benefit from any of the supportive efforts from the counseling, consultation for medication with a psychiatrist is suggested. Psychiatrists are able to prescribe from a broad range of antidepressant medications and are entrusted to monitor the side effects of medication. It is suggested that the bereavement counselor establish a relationship with a psychiatrist for just such situations. Periodic check-in with the psychiatrist to discuss the client's progress is warranted. Many clients are reluctant to take medication; the counselor may be able to educate the griever to some of the benefits of medication and its utility in helping people function better.

And then came the call from her ex-husband's wife telling her that he had died. Laura gathered her strength and went to the funeral, out of state, with her two children. It was anticipated that Laura would have a reaction but when she returned from the funeral, she said that she had "felt almost nothing about his death. It was too bad for the kids, but I was more annoyed than sad." Her son, who lived upstate, was detached from Laura and had not been an active part of the family for many years. Her daughter had been in individual counseling for several years and was addressing her difficulties with these several losses on her own.

Laura had built up that wall against feeling that is referred to in the literature. She was almost unable to incorporate another loss into her being. Thus, at the news of the sudden death of her ex-husband, Laura went into shutdown mode and had almost no response to this additional loss. When she resumed counseling after the funeral for her ex-husband, the focus of the work was on David's death.

Of the three losses, it seems that there was no dealing with David's death. This is understandable as all of the literature supports that the death of a child is the most difficult to overcome. Laura will forever be in mourning about losing her son, the favorite child. Over time, Laura will be better able to think of him and talk in very general terms about him but, after more than a year of counseling, she is not ready or willing to examine that loss. The first year was the hardest, but within that first year, she sustained two other deaths, thus complicating her bereavement experience.

Bereavement can be seen as a time of transition (P. Silverman, 2002) from one part of life to another. For Laura, her transition has been from a good life with love and connection to one bereft of any of those feelings. She will surely heal and have many good days, but it is accurate to imagine that much of what remains of her life will be tinged with periods of sadness. It seems quite possible that Laura will be able to enter a relationship with another man and find contentment and solace within it. But as a child is not replicable or replaceable, Laura will struggle to release the bonds that keep her connected to David.

The counseling will support Laura's efforts to rebuild her life by allowing her free emotional expression and understanding. She will be encouraged to speak of David, to remember him, and to still love him. It is hoped that she will be able to forgive herself for his death as she was in no way responsible for what happened. Hopefully, this relief of guilt, frequently explored in the counseling, will allow her to release the energy she needs to deal with each day. It will be a very long time before Laura will be able to enjoy life again.

Issues for the Counselor

Laura's sadness was overwhelming for the counselor. When confronted with a survivor with so much pain and anguish the counselor found it very difficult to maintain boundaries, be restrained, and not become overwhelmed as well. With so much sadness in the room, it is sometimes difficult to focus and even breathe. To lose a son and lover within months seemed almost too cruel for one person to bear and the feelings evoked in the counselor were those of horror at what Laura had to overcome. A case of such intensity can push the counselor into a parallel depression with the client and the counselor can become almost as weighed down with feelings as the client is. If this happens, the counselor compromises his or her effectiveness, and this must be guarded against.

What was helpful in this case was having the counselor set reachable goals such as helping Laura to express some of her despair and helping her to touch her guilt and anger. If the counselor believed that it was possible to fully relieve Laura's depression and have her fully engaged in life, there could have been only disappointment. Too much had damaged Laura and the repair was aimed at keeping her as functional as possible. The frustration of the work with Laura was in knowing that she would never be whole again, that she would show some signs of reconnecting with life but that she would always be weighed down by her losses. Stating this in a more positive way, the counseling, which continues, will help relieve her, will offer her a venue for expression, and will serve as a transitional relationship until she is able to establish herself on more solid footing. It will be a long road.

CHAPTER

4

Bereavement After the Death of a Pet

The Case—Herb

Every day for the 15 years that Herb had the television repair store, he took Emma to work. They would leave the house before 9 a.m. and walk the four blocks to the store. Emma would go to her accustomed corner while Herb repaired the sets and helped customers. Herb and Emma were known all over town; everyone spoke of Herb the TV guy and Emma his black dog. Emma was a mixed breed, calm, and used to people, and she seemed to know her place in the world. She ate, did her business outside, and was a silent companion for Herb as he did his work. After Herb had the repair store for 5 years, his wife died of cancer. Herb was 55 years old then, and his wife was 54. The cancer was incurable and she died soon after diagnosis. Their married daughter, who lived in a nearby city, stayed with Herb for a few weeks after the death and then returned to her life; Herb and Emma returned to an altered existence without Herb's wife.

When his wife was alive, they frequently went to the movies, had some friends with whom they socialized, and enjoyed the quiet of their home and life. After her death, Herb's life followed a routine that hardly varied. He kept the shop open 6 days a week and when the workload was too demanding for him to manage alone, he hired a part-time worker who was there 2 days a week. Herb had a few friends, and he usually went out one night a week to play cards. Every other week he visited with his daughter and family. Most evenings, Herb was content to be home, reading or puttering around the house. As he said, "I see enough television during the day. I am glad for the quiet." Herb's only sibling, David, lived far away but they spoke on the phone at least once a week. It was a quiet life. Emma was his constant companion.

Herb was a conscientious caregiver for Emma. She had the requisite inoculations and when she seemed ill he took her to the vet. She ate well and although not a very frisky animal, she walked back and forth to the store with Herb and got a minimum of eight blocks of exercise from the walking each day. As a mixed breed, it was not possible to guess her life expectancy. She seemed fit well into her 14th year. On one Thursday morning, Herb and Emma left the house to walk to work. For reasons that Herb will never understand, as they were about to cross an intersection, Emma tugged at the leash and ran into the street. Herb ran after her but he was too late and a car making a left turn struck her. She was bleeding from her mouth and her body was limp. The car driver took Herb and Emma directly to the vet, who felt that there was nothing she could do to address the multiple problems caused by the accident. Herb agreed to have her euthanized. Emma died within a few moments of the injection and at that instant, Herb's world collapsed. Herb called his daughter, who came immediately.

After a week, Herb's daughter insisted that he go for bereavement counseling. He was not going to the store and seemed "frozen." She said, "All of a sudden my father became an old man." In the first counseling session, Herb was able to answer only "yes" or "no" to the many questions asked and did not volunteer any information or personal history. He was truly a sad man.

Relevant History

The only other period of depression that Herb could remember was after his wife's death. Theirs was a solid marriage and they did most things together. After her death, he remembered going though a difficult period in which he had lost weight and had not been motivated to return to work. After a few weeks, he basically "became bored with himself" and reopened the store. He had no interest in remarrying, stating, "She was the only woman I ever loved and I knew it the first time we spoke to each other."

As a young adult, Herb had attended a technical high school where he learned his trade. His parents died young and his only sibling had moved across the country soon after Herb was married. Herb and his

wife had wanted a large family but she was unable and they felt fortu-
nate that they had their daughter. He was healthy and did not have any
major financial concerns. Some might say he lived a quiet life; Herb
would describe himself as content. "I have my store, my daughter and
grandchild, and that's enough for me. Oh! Yes, I also have Emma."

Conceptual Issues

To understand the bereavement experienced through the loss of a companion animal, we must acknowledge that "the depth of a human–animal bond
often exceeds that between a person and close kin" (Weisman, 1991, p. 247).
"The relationship is normal, deep, loving and authentic. Many people consider their pets to be members of their family" (Margolies, 1999, p. 290). Pets
have some outstanding qualities as partners in a relationship—they are
loyal, uncritical, nonjudgmental, and relatively undemanding. They often
are intuitive and engaging and have a presence that for most pet owners, is
soothing (Rando, 1988). Pets often become active members of a household,
participating in a variety of activities with their owners (Lagoni, Butler, &
Hetts, 1994).

In North America, pets most often are owned for the purpose of companionship. As a source of companionship, a pet (generally a dog or cat)
may be the ideal mate or partner, ever faithful, patient, and welcoming,
loving unconditionally, and offering a constant level of friendship. "Pets
provide structure, organization, steadiness and a sense of purpose for
many people, particularly those living alone who do not have a regular
schedule or source of other relationships" (Weisman, 1991, p. 246). Pets
are dependent on people, and the caretaking and nurturing of a companion animal can lend a sense of purpose and connection to the owner
(Ross & Baron-Sorensen, 1998).

Rynearson (1978) asserted that the bond between pets and their owners pivots on their commonality as animals. As such, the pet and owner
are not only psychologically but also biologically bonded and are significant attachment figures for one another. When this bond is broken, "It
can create complicated and enduring psychiatric reactions" (p. 551).
When the counselor acknowledges the depth of the bond, then the ensuing bereavement becomes more understandable and the potential for
emotional and physical disruption can be envisioned and understood.
The severity of the bereavement period can be especially intense if the
significance of the pet loss is unacknowledged (Sharkin & Bahrick, 1990).
Increasingly, more veterinarians and humane societies are offering grief

counseling after pet loss; grief counselors are advised to acquaint themselves with the resources in their community.

Empirical research on bereavement after the loss of a pet is informing of the depth, texture, and duration of the grief experience. Keddie (1977) studied three cases of pathological bereavement (a prolonged, deeper, and more depressed form of bereavement) after the death of pets. In each case—all were women—the pets had been owned for more than 13 years and severe psychiatric symptoms had surfaced immediately after the death. In each case, on an unconscious level, the pet represented a surrogate relative. Pathological bereavement, according to Harris (1984), occurs in fewer than 15% of cases. In his study of 76 patients, half had resolved their grief within a month and 29% had reached partial resolution and were still working through the loss by themselves.

Quackenbush and Glickman (1984) examined the reactions of 138 pet owners to the death of their pets. Their veterinarian, family member, or friend had referred all of the owners for social work services at a university veterinary hospital for psychological stress related to the death of their pets. Although many more participants were women (79%) than men (21%), all shared the reality that the death of their pets had influenced unusual behavior patterns of eating and sleeping and having nightmares. Overall social activities decreased for 70% of participants, with participants tending to remain home more, talk less, and spend a great deal of time thinking about and longing for the deceased pet. Forty-five percent of the study participants missed from 1 to 3 days of work. Many complained about the insensitivity of response from family, friends, and colleagues. Most participants cried easily and uncontrollably and talked mournfully to the dead animal; guilt and anger reactions were common. Quackenbush and Glickman concluded, "In general, the behavior of the pet owners at the time of their animals' death appears to mimic in many ways the stages or phases that have been described as characteristic of bereavement after human death" (p. 44).

Archer and Winchester (1994) observed that of the 88 participants recruited within a year after the death of their pets, 25% showed signs of depression, anger, and anxiety, with grief being most pronounced among those living alone, for those who experienced a sudden death, and for those who were strongly attached to their pets. Jarolmen's (1998) study of 270 adults, 106 children, and 57 adolescents who had lost their pets within 12 months showed that the greatest period of distress over the loss was within the first 4 months; anguish began to wane from 5 to 8 months. An interesting aspect of this research was the finding that children and adolescents grieved more than the adults in this study, as measured by the Grief Experience Inventory (Sanders, Mauger, & Strong, 1985) and Pet Attachment Survey (Gosse, 1988).

Pet Loss and the Elderly

There is particular concern for elderly pet owners and their bereavement. Loss and sequential bereavement is a prevailing theme in the lives of the elderly. By old age, most have lost parents, spouses, siblings, friends, and children to death. Their physical strength, stamina, and mobility may have been compromised. If they are retired, a piece of their identity has been lost along with the routines associated with work. Many elderly live alone. In view of these losses, commonly associated with advancing age, it is not surprising that many older people develop profoundly deep relationships with their pets.

Loving and caring for a pet allows the older person to feel connected to and companionable with another, to feel unconditional and consistent love, and to feel touched by another both physically and emotionally. The constant proximity offered by a pet, with the pet staying by the owner's side day and night, is a source of great comfort (Sable, 1995). Levinson (1972) noted that especially in old age, the presence of a companion animal could make the difference between tolerable life and intolerable misery.

Ross and Baron-Sorensen (1998) pointed out that an elderly person's ability to work successfully through the grief over the death of a pet might be inhibited by a diminishing support system. Not only may there be fewer people in an elderly person's day-to-day life but, also, many people may not respond supportively to the death of a pet. In addition, elderly people may not be aware of existing support services or may not be able to afford or be able to travel to obtain such services to help them adjust to their bereavement situation.

The greatest concern for profound bereavement reactions is for the elderly pet owner who lives alone. The social isolation of the elderly person's life and the dependency on his or her pet as a companion puts him or her at highest risk for complicated and pathological bereavement reactions.

Disenfranchised Grief

In Weisman's (1991) work with bereaved pet owners, he noted a strong reluctance on their part to tell others about their grief. In group counseling sessions with other pet owners, he observed that members spoke freely about their loss and cried frequently. He also noted the expression of shame by bereaved pet owners at the intensity of their feelings for a nonhuman attachment. Others who describe pet owner bereavement (Lagoni et al.,

1994; Ross & Baron-Sorensen, 1998; Rynearson, 1978; Sharkin & Bahrick, 1990) have echoed Weisman's observations.

In many respects, pet death is an example of disenfranchised grief. This is grief that is not socially acknowledged, as it does not involve a blood or kin bond. "Contemporary customs do not approve of mourning a pet; at best, it is indulged" (Weisman, 1991, p. 248). This lack of recognition leaves the bereaved in a situation in which they may not receive the support of family, friends, and others who potentially could help ease the pain and help to buffer their loss. There are few socially sanctioned mourning rituals to help grieving pet owners; although there are many pet cemeteries, formal funeral services by clergy or others are limited. There is no option to place an obituary notice in a newspaper. Verbal discussions of the loss often are met with insensitivity and the suggestion to replace the deceased animal as soon as possible. The attachment to the animal is downplayed (Doka, 1989a; Margolies, 1999) to the point of creating discomfort and even shame. This situation seriously hampers the healing from the pain of the loss.

Suggestions for Intervention

The depth of the bereavement experience is affected by a number of variables including the age of the owner, the level of cognitive and emotional development, the length of time the owner had and cared for the pet, the quality of the bond between the owner and pet, the circumstances surrounding the death, and the quality of family support available during the grieving process (Marrone, 1997). Awareness of these variables may help the counselor in assessing the course of the bereavement. Studies suggest that grief over pet loss lasts between 6 months and 1 year, averaging 10 months. The acute phase may last 1 to 2 months (Stallones, 1994). For many, the loss is profound and counseling is needed for those who experience greater and more prolonged depressive symptoms.

Because of the frequent lack of social sanction for bereavement over a pet's death, the first step in helping people cope is to acknowledge their loss. The unwillingness to legitimate the responses of those who openly grieve often complicates the course of bereavement (Quackenbush & Glickman, 1984). Acknowledging the loss is done in an atmosphere that respects the consequences of the death for the client and provides an acceptance for the expression of the psychological, physiological, and social responses to the loss (Margolies, 1999; Sharkin & Bahrick, 1990). If the bereaved feels that he or she is in a safe and respectful atmosphere, it becomes easier to give voice to the many feelings of loss that have accumulated. The strategy of acknowledgment is to encourage the griever to talk about his or her pet and the nature or circumstances of the loss: illness, accident, or runaway (Sharkin & Bahrick, 1990). The griever is urged to speak about the endearing qualities of the pet; favorite pet stories as well as shared activities are to be described. Grievers are encouraged to bring pictures for the counselor to see. To legitimize their loss, the counselor should help clients create mourning rituals that honor and memorialize their pets. There are more than 600 pet cemeteries in the United States. These facilities offer burial plots and grave settings for animals, urns for remains, as well as caskets and tombstones. The ritualization of the loss may help to begin the process of the bereavement experience.

Counselors are to be especially sensitive to the griever who has euthanized his or her pet. Despite the reality that the animal may have had a terminal condition, the owner will still tend to question the timing of the decision. Ending the suffering of a pet is the positive side of euthanasia, but there is usually lingering doubt and feelings of guilt. Sometimes an owner is faced with having to decide whether to euthanize the animal or authorize extensive and expensive medical procedures. In some cases, the costs are prohibitive and there remains only the decision to end the animal's life. Under these circumstances, the guilt may be intense for the griever.

Anger is another frequent aspect of bereavement. In the case of pet loss, anger may be directed toward the family, friends, and others but especially at the veterinarian. Counselors should recognize this as a phase in the bereavement process and encourage its verbalization.

Frequently, adults who lose a pet experience a reactivation of earlier unresolved losses. This can be used as an opportunity to explore other losses and to comment on the nature of deep attachment. For an elderly person, who may have experienced sequential losses, this is especially prominent in the bereavement experience.

In terms of attachment to an animal companion, Rynearson (1978) suggested that it might be helpful to point out to the bereaved that deep attachments form over time and that upset and depression are natural responses when bonds are broken between humans and their pets. We choose pets because of our need for attachment, and what develops is a dynamic aggregate of behaviors that flows between the pet and his or her owner; it is the aliveness of the relationship that appears crucial—a vital, reciprocating balance of attachment.

Although individual counseling can be effective with those bereaved from pet loss, group sessions with others who have sustained such a loss also should be encouraged. Within the confines of the group, grief can be more openly expressed and emotions more easily accessed. In view of the acknowledged lack of social and family support for pet grievers, the group offers a haven of acceptance where grievers can give voice to the loss and despair they are feeling. Groups that begin for emotional support may continue for a period of time and become more social in their purpose, even though emotional support is offered (Worden, 2002). Friendships based on mutual loss can be formed, and these friendships are especially valuable for the elderly person.

In a recent feature story about the Paw to Heart group, which was founded in 1992, members spoke about their bereavement group experience. At their meetings, members took turns speaking about their losses. Some pet deaths had occurred a few years before, but what kept members engaged was that "You come, maybe you can give a wise word, maybe you can help." The overwhelming sentiment was that in the group, it was acceptable to cry, mourn, and actively evoke the deceased pet. One member commented, "It's great to have support because you feel so unique, like such an oddball. Just to be with people, it helps so much—to know that I am not alone" (Flaim, 2002, p. G11). The freedom to express emotion and feel supported in an understanding atmosphere makes the group experience a valued addition to individual counseling.

Major Issues in This Case

Herb was a great risk for a protracted and serious bereavement experience. He fit the profile described by Archer and Winchester (1994) for a complicated bereavement experience: he lived alone, he had a long-term relationship with his dog (14 years), and the animal had died suddenly. Indeed, his grief was intense. He presented initially—1 week after the accident—in an apparent state of shock. He answered questions but volunteered very little information or emotion. He was almost devoid of emotion. When asked to fill in the details of what had happened, he answered in three word sentences with information offered haltingly. He did not cry. He was hardly engaged with the counselor, there was virtually no eye contact, and he would easily be described, in both content and emotional affect, as depressed.

By the second session, held a few days after the first, Herb was somewhat more animated. He had begun eating, at his daughter's insistence, and was able to speak about the details of the Thursday when Emma was struck down. He blamed himself for the death. Although Herb had Emma on a leash for their accustomed walk to work, he held it loosely because she always stayed beside him. She had never run into the street before; he felt responsible because he had not held the leash tightly enough to prevent her running into the street. The counselor gently challenged this admission, asking Herb, "Did you usually anticipate when Emma would pull strongly at her leash? How could you have known that she would run into the street?" It gave Herb pause but not a strong response.

The counselor encouraged Herb to share the history of his "getting Emma," how he had trained her, and some of his favorite "Emma stories." This was an effort to get Herb talking, to bring him out of the dark place of his sadness, and to bring a bit of life into his being. He told of going to dog obedience training classes with Emma when she was a puppy where they were both taught certain commands and behaviors that helped Emma to become socialized. He recounted the story of how Emma hid the first time his baby granddaughter came to visit and the baby started to cry. He spoke of how Emma would curl up on the bed when his wife was ill and dying and stay there for hours with her. When he mentioned his wife, he began to cry and spoke of her illness and final days. The ricochet effect of reactivating past losses based on the loss of his pet was certainly present for Herb. The counselor reassured Herb that sometimes present losses can stir up a lot of memories of other losses and that it was entirely normal to feel these memories and feelings.

Herb was spared the experience of disenfranchised grief cited in the literature. Perhaps because he and Emma were known in their community and because family and friends had acknowledged their closeness, there was a substantial level of social support and understanding. Strangers came up to him on the street asking where his dog was. This reduced Herb to tears each time it happened.

By the third and fourth counseling sessions, Herb spoke of his aloneness and the weight of time. Herb showed no interest in going back to work or resuming any of his usual activities. He could not imagine going to the store without his dog and was inclined to close the store and never return to his work. Every time he thought of going back to the store he said, "I don't know how I will be able to open the door and go into the store without her." Two suggestions, tentatively accepted, were made to him at this time. The counselor offered to go with Herb to the store to help ease the transition and strongly urged Herb to consider joining a bereavement group for pet owners. This would not preclude the individual meetings scheduled with him but was to be seen as an adjunct to the counseling. Herb agreed to go to a group session, "Just one as I am not much of a talker." The store suggestion was put on hold.

The counselor made the suggestion to attend a bereavement group for pet owners on the basis of the positive outcome literature on support groups for pet owners. Weisman (1991), a noted bereavement expert who actually ran a pet bereavement group program, noted, "Clients spoke freely and with relief; the discovery of acceptance and respect for their bereavement was in itself appreciated. Clients felt their grief was both exceptionally strong and abnormally tenacious, and they wept accordingly, as if confessing something unmentionable" (p. 245). If Herb could be motivated to join such a group, the counselor thought that it could legitimize his loss in a way that no other experience could and would allow him a venue to avail himself of support and even offer support to others.

By the fifth week, Herb had attended his first group session and was beginning to show signs of a lifting of his depression. He was more verbal, was groomed, and was more responsive in the sessions. He reported that the other members of the group were interested in his situation and most members had been as attached to their dogs or cats as he had been to Emma. He even admitted to having shed a few tears during this first session. Weisman (1991), in his groups, observed that many people apologized for crying; Herb was no exception.

Herb did not, however, return to his store. He discussed his decision to close the store with his daughter, who supported the idea. He felt that he might want to sell his house and move closer to where his daughter lived and spend more time with his grandchild. He could not bear to be in the store without his dog, feeling the terrible weight of his loss as intolerable. His retirement was not out of the question: he was 65 years old, had a fair amount of savings as he had lived very frugally, and would realize some money from the sale of his house. The counselor, who felt that Herb's life would be more emotionally comfortable and much less isolated by such a move, supported this plan.

After the sixth session, Herb decided to end individual counseling; he wanted to continue with the support group that went on for many more weeks. He felt that although the individual sessions had been very helpful, he was choosing to attend more group meetings based on the shared experience of losing a pet and being understood in a better way. Herb said that the group members accepted his grief and that he felt comfortable with most of them.

When Herb was asked what he spoke about in the group, he commented on his anger. This was a new area for Herb, who presented in a very passive way. He said, "I am angry at God for having taken my wife and my dog. It is not fair." As this was the final session with Herb, it would not have been prudent to explore his anger in a major way and end the counseling on such a note. To pretend it was not there would have been equally unwise. His angry feelings were acknowledged as expected reactions to loss.

A follow-up individual session was planned for when the group ended. This occurred a few months later. Herb was more animated than he was in the sessions a few months before. He had put his house up for sale, sold his business, and was looking forward to living close to his daughter. The plan was not for Herb to move in with her, but for him to find a small house within walking distance of his daughter's home. He wanted his independence. He also said that he wanted some yard space for a dog to play in. He was not ready for another pet, but he felt that the day would come soon. In commenting about the group, he said that it had been very helpful to talk with others going through what he went through. He admitted that he had made friends with some of the members and that they frequently went "out for coffee" after the meetings. He was appreciative of the individual sessions and especially the suggestion that he join a group. In fact, he hoped there might be a similar type of group in his daughter's community.

Herb moved about 8 weeks later. It would not be a surprise to find a puppy in his backyard.

Issues for the Counselor

When working with pet owners, counselors can find it sometimes challenging to relate fully to the depth of their loss. For the counselor who has never experienced the death of a pet, the patience and pacing of helping those saddened in this way may be challenging. For those who have had such an experience, the reawakening of those memories can be problematic.

In this case, the timing of a referral to a group was difficult to assess. There was little doubt that a group experience would be beneficial, especially for someone like Herb, who, although working with the public, was essentially a very private, reserved person. The group referral was based on two of Herb's needs: the need to talk with others about his experience and the need to break into his shell of isolation. But was Herb ready to confide in others, was he strong enough to be supportive to someone else and relate to his or her situation? The counselor discussed the group option with Herb and he was tentative in his interest. Despite these reservations, the group seemed to work well for Herb.

The counseling effort of combining both individual and group support sessions was considered successful. Herb's personality and reserve suggested that he was not a joiner and that he had to be pushed to go to the group. Dealing with a griever's resistance to support has its share of frustration, especially when the suggestion comes out the counselor's practice wisdom and conviction. This was the case with Herb.

The depth and complexity of loss must never be underestimated. Herb's situation points to the aloneness of some lives but not the sterility:

Herb was not the object of pity. He had developed a comfortable life, which revolved around his relationship with his dog, and when this bond was broken, Herb was broken. This relationship was central to Herb, and it kept a lonely man quite content. In the wake of his loss, Herb slowly regrouped and his resiliency was impressive. The follow-up session a few months after Emma's death was especially gratifying, as Herb seemed, for the first time, to be more forward thinking and acting than rooted in the past.

CHAPTER

5

Bereavement After Catastrophe: Deceased Unfound

The Case—Helen

Helen (29 years old) and Michael (30 years old) had been married for 3 years when the disaster at the World Trade Center occurred on September 11, 2001. Helen, a nurse, had worked the Monday evening shift and was actually settling in for a day of sleeping when the first call came telling her to put on the television, that something hideous had happened. Michael, a stock analyst with a major brokerage firm housed on the 97th floor of the World Trade Center, Tower 1, had been at work for more than an hour in the first of the two buildings to be struck. He and 20 other employees with whom he worked were among the hundreds reported missing on that ill-fated day. Michael's remains had not been found and he became a statistic with no confirmation of his death.

Like hundreds of others, Helen was faced with the situation in which she had news that someone she loved was missing but had no definite details or absolute information to confirm the death. In a tragedy as profound and far reaching as the attack on the World Trade Center, the range of possible situations was vast and ambiguity surrounded thousands of lives on the day of the attacks and for weeks afterward. The emotional fallout from the attacks unsettled the world and upended the personal world of countless numbers of people. The lives of those who lost loved ones were changed forever. As did thousands of others, Helen became a secondary victim of the attack.

Helen did not know where to turn for information about Michael. She tried calling the police, the office, the branch office in another part of the city, members of the staff, anyone she could think of who might, just might, have some news. She was thwarted at every turn. No one seemed to know anything for sure, only that the floor and adjacent floors near Michael's offices were destroyed and that the Towers had collapsed. As the days passed and the extent and depth of the attack was revealed, as the death toll mounted, as the country mourned, Helen's hopes that she would ever see Michael again sank lower and lower.

She decided to seek counseling because she thought she was losing her mind: "I don't know what to do, where to put myself, how to think. I cannot turn on the television and see those planes hitting the buildings and I cannot turn off the television because I might miss something, and my friends told me I had to get help or else." Work was out of the question, as were an appetite and sleep. Friends suggested that she seek help and she accepted the suggestion with minimal resistance. Her major reluctance was that she did not want to leave the house lest she miss the call she so eagerly wanted to receive.

Helen came for bereavement counseling in early October, approximately 3 weeks after the disaster. She was convinced that Michael was gone but a small kernel of hope still existed that somehow he had been spared. Helen had many of the symptoms of depression: she was unable to sleep, eat, or feel much of anything. The only emotion she did feel was intense anger. She was unable to work or concentrate on any one task for more than a few minutes. She stated that she could not accept Michael's death and still held out the belief that he would "turn up" because his body had not been recovered. Her equation, which was beginning to crumble, was no body, no death. She had lost 10 pounds and her sleep was seriously disrupted.

Relevant History

Helen is the oldest of three sisters, all residing in the New York area. Her parents are deceased, her father died when Helen was 9 years old, leaving the children and her mother in desperate financial straits. Somehow, they managed and Helen had gone away to a state school and met Michael while at college. They graduated within a year of each other and moved to New York. Helen had no history of depression or major anxiety symptoms. In 1998 her mother's illness was diagnosed as breast cancer and she had been

treated, but during the course of the treatment she developed heart problems and had a fatal heart attack.

A year before Michael's death, her best friend from college died in a
tragic accident on Helen's 28th birthday. After both of these significant
deaths, Helen went through a period of mourning that was not unreason-
ably protracted or pathological in nature or duration.

Helen described her marriage as good. Neither Helen nor Michael
were temperamental types, both were easygoing, and what had drawn
them to each other was that they both liked the same type of music, movies, and books. Helen marveled at how compatible she and Michael were
and she noted, "We almost never fought as it would have been like fighting with myself as we were so alike." Michael and Helen had discussed
having children and decided they wanted to wait for 1 more year to be
comfortable with Helen's decision to stay home with the baby for the first
few years and have no financial worries. Essentially, before the World
Trade Center attack, Helen would define herself as happily married,
looking forward to a long life with Michael with the prospect of having
children with him in the next few years. And then the Towers fell.

She defined the loss of Michael as no other loss she had ever
experienced.

Conceptual Issues

For those affected by disaster, the reality of the loss of loved ones becomes
complicated by the lack of physical confirmation of death. These losses, in
which there are no remains to bury and no definite confirmation of death,
extend the grieving period and can produce complicated or pathological
mourning. For many, the ability to move past the pain of the loss is seriously
compromised. Indeed, based on the levels of anger, rage, and anguish that
continue after a disaster, short-term recovery may be unrealistic. Long-term
grieving may ultimately lead to peaceful acceptance of the death.

Role of Rituals

Of the many activities we engage in as human beings, few are as prescriptive
and repetitive as the rituals surrounding death. Many of these rituals are culturally mediated with all cultures having certain prescribed ceremonies and
practices for dealing with those who die (Romanoff & Terenzio, 1998). We
are a culture with rituals embedded in our lives. To be classified as a ritual,
behaviors have to be codified and repetitive. The rituals around death dictate

certain ceremonies and practices; these rituals lend structure to our experi-ences and offer socially sanctioned expression for our feelings and emotions (Kollar, 1989). The funeral is one of the essential elements of the rituals asso-ciated with death. For most, the funeral marks the beginning of the period of mourning; it is believed that participation in funeral and burial rituals is instrumental in the healing after a death (Bolton & Camp, 1987). The funeral serves both a social and a psychological need. The social aspect provides group support for the mourners and an opportunity to experience the rela-tional changes brought about by the death. The psychological aspect of the funeral reinforces the reality of the death (Kollar, 1989).

When bodies have not been recovered, the trajectory of the postdeath experience is altered for the bereaved. For these families and individuals, the loss has to be handled differently and the situation can prove to be highly stressful. For them, the loss is incomprehensible, as there are no remains to bury and to focus the grief on; many people need the concrete experience of seeing a body to make the death real (Beder, 2002). Boss (1999) coined the term "ambiguous loss" to describe the situation that occurs when there is no verification of a missing person's status. The loss is ambiguous because the mourner is not and may never be certain that the loved one has died; the mourner is in an ambiguous state between actively mourning and not knowing whether the loved one is alive.

In ambiguous loss situations, people are more prone to feeling help-lessness, depression, anxiety, and relationship strain. These reactions are understandable for several reasons. First, because the loss is confusing, people tend to become immobilized and baffled as they strive to make sense of their situation. Individuals are reluctant to leave their homes as the call they are eagerly awaiting might come when they are absent. Rumors abound during these critical times, while hopes escalate and are shattered within an instant. Second, the uncertainty prevents people from adjusting to new roles required of them in relation to their loss; the ambiguity of the situation makes it difficult to act. In many respects, peo-ple are frozen in time until they know for sure what has happened to their loved one(s). Third, the individual and family are deprived the ritu-als that attend death in their culture and the needed closure is absent (Boss, 1999).

Additional reactions associated with loss when no body has been found include denial, confused boundaries, continuous information seek-ing, and emotional swings. Denial allows the person to remain hopeful and optimistic. If denial is strong, it is possible to keep the relationship with the presumed deceased as though they are on an extended vacation, with the certainty of reunion as a possibility. Confused boundary issues occur, as a new configuration of roles cannot be assumed until death is confirmed. Is a wife still a wife if her husband's body has not been recovered? The continuous search for information is exhausting for those awaiting definitive news, and the emotional swings that this provokes can be debilitating. This does not mean that the individual is resisting reality, but there are no facts available to confirm or deny his or her worst fears (Boss, 1999). Other possible reactions include a posttraumatic stress response, with the obsessive need to relive and replay parts of the disaster.

Challenges to the Assumptive Worldview

Another aspect of this type of dramatic, unanticipated, unconfirmed loss is the shattering of what researchers have called the assumptive worldview (Janoff-Bulman, 1992; Kauffman, 2002a; Rando, 1993). When the worldview is shattered by a sudden, unexpected, and violent death, the individual suffers a shift in conceptualization about the safety of the world. This affects the bereavement experience, making it more complex and longer lasting.

As human beings, we have constructed a view of the world based on certain assumptions. These assumptions lend shape and stability in our environment and allow us to function optimally. The three core assumptions are that the world is benevolent, that the world is meaningful, and that the self is worthy. The benevolence of the world refers to the belief that the world is a safe place; the world as meaningful suggests that things make sense and happen for a reason, that there is a cause-and-effect relationship between events and outcomes. The worthiness of the self allows us to perceive ourselves as good, capable, and moral, functioning with others in a benevolent world. In the event of catastrophic trauma, these assumptions are shattered and a violent disruption to one's worldview can occur (Kauffman, 2002a). This disruption creates a situation that complicates the bereavement experience because, in essence, the griever not only is dealing with the loss of a beloved individual but also is dealing with the shattering of a belief structure that has lent a structure to his or her life. Healing from this type of grief may be protracted and painful as new assumptions are created.

This type of loss does not make sense in how most people construct and negotiate their lives. As such, emotional reactions are heightened and confusion and disorganization are frequently experienced. In national disasters, the violence, trauma, and horror of wide-scale death exaggerate all bereavement situations. The more random and wide scale the event, the greater the anger, fear violation, and sense of powerlessness experienced by the griever (Rando, 1993).

Traumatic Grief

Prigerson and Jacobs (2001, p. 615) defined the concept of traumatic grief. They explained this form of grief as "falling into two categories:

1. Symptoms of separation distress, such as preoccupation with thoughts of the deceased to the point of functional impairment, upsetting memories of the deceased, longing and searching for the deceased, loneliness following the loss.
2. Symptoms of traumatic distress, such as feeling disbelief about the death, mistrust, anger, and detachment from others as a result of the death, feeling shocked by the death, and the experience of somatic symptoms of the deceased."

It is the presence of the dual categories that defines the reaction.

This conceptualization fully captures the experience of Helen and many of the survivors of the World Trade Center and similar disasters. The ability to distinguish normal grief from traumatic grief is important in that it alerts the counselor to the possibility that the duration and challenges of the bereavement are altered. The traumatic griever will grieve longer and will not be able to reinvest in life or activities as smoothly or quickly as one who suffers from normal grief. The gradual return to life of the normal griever is complicated for the traumatic griever by the symptoms of separation and traumatic distress. These symptoms have to be addressed so healing can proceed.

Suggestions for Intervention

As with other bereavement situations, the goal is to help the individual or family accept the reality of the loss, to experience the pain of the grief, to adjust to the environment in which the deceased is missing, and to help redirect emotional energy to other relationships (Worden, 1982). This is accomplished over time; some people are able to mourn, feel their feelings and express them in a productive way, and move ahead. In some instances, the time to make these adjustments is quite long and torturous and relief from the pain of the loss does not abate. "Complicated mourning" is the term used to describe this situation.

Several factors come together in a loss situation to promote complicated mourning: the suddenness of the loss, the compounding and reactivation of several losses, the level of disruption to our assumptive world, and the depth and centrality of the connection between the survivor and the deceased. In Helen's case, all factors were present. When addressing situations of complicated mourning, the counselor has to assume that the bereavement period will be long and will provoke levels of internal struggle and rearrangement for the survivor; relief from the pain will not occur quickly and the ability to move on may not be tapped for many months or years. In general, each aspect of the complicated mourning will have to be addressed.

Initial strategies for those who are grieving a sudden loss is to support their anguish and to reassure them that loss that occurs with no warning is very hard to incorporate into reality. To help the survivor to acknowledge the death, the counselor must use words diligently. Terms such as *widow, widower, death,* and *deceased* are to be used frequently. In situations in which there is ambiguity surrounding the death, the counselor must be reality based, while allowing the griever some measure of hope, and continue with the counseling effort toward acceptance. Acceptance of death means that the survivor has to experience the pain of the experience; this may prolong hope longer than is reasonable to forestall the pain.

Rando (1993) commented on the importance of realizing that with this type of loss—one that is so unexpected—the bereavement tends to be longer and that the intensity of reactions is more volatile. If the deceased has not been found, an additional layer of anguish exists. She suggested that normalizing of some of the reactions to violent loss is helpful. These reactions include numbing, denial, intrusive thoughts and reactions, a heightened startle response, and sleep and eating disruptions.

When dealing with the kickback effect of past losses exacerbating the current one, the counselor is advised to help the griever recall what strategies helped during previous grief experiences and to make a effort to help the mourner see that he or she was able to reinvest in life after other losses. If the history of grief has been particularly traumatic, the counselor needs to be aware of potential areas of sensitivity and help the mourner through them.

The struggle to gain meaning from the loss, the lack of control that is experienced, and the anguish of not knowing are all to be acknowledged and discussed. Whenever possible, group support for those with unconfirmed loss is to be encouraged. Many feel that those having a similar experience are the only ones who can understand their anguish. The recognition of the power of the group experience in legitimizing the loss and in lending needed social support is an additional component in the healing process.

For those whose assumptive worldview has been shattered, a group experience may be especially helpful. As members attempt to rebuild and repair their assumptive worlds, the connective resources offered by the group can provide a vital step toward healing (Liechty, 2002, p. 91).

In general, bereavement support groups have many valuable functions: group members find validation by connecting with others who share similar losses, suggestions for coping are freely offered, hope is provided by members who are at varied levels in their grief journeys, and members can enhance their self-esteem as they help other members. Although not a panacea for every grieving individual, groups can offer much needed or additional support (Pesek, 2002).

Individual intervention that attempts to address the violation of the assumptive world includes cognitive techniques that keep the focus very much on the here and now and involve relearning and realigning assumptions about life. Continued discussion about the basis for worldview assumptions is encouraged, with new ways to experience and assess being in the world as a goal.

Another tool is to ask the griever to imagine what the deceased experienced. Although initially a very difficult task, by retelling and reexperiencing the event, the potency of the actual event is diminished. The translation from thoughts about the event into language helps the griever calm some of his or her intrusive and disruptive thoughts (Janoff-Bulman, 1992).

Within a certain time frame, dictated by the circumstances and considering the powerful role of ritual, a funeral or memorial service should be initiated for the unfound deceased that serves to facilitate acknowledgment of the death. This service allows the mourning to have a specific or identified beginning and will facilitate communal support. Although the burial is symbolic, it is suggested that it take place at a cemetery and that usual religious rituals and observances are adhered to. This ceremony can bring the closure needed to move the griever forward after the loss.

Major Issues in This Case

Helen's depression was deep. She was unable to move ahead as she was still hoping for Michael's return, even though it was 6 weeks after the disaster. Understandably, Helen was caught in a void in which she was trapped and this was philosophically problematic in the counseling. Should the counselor help Helen begin her bereavement for her deceased husband or should she be supported in her denial and hope? Logically, she needed to begin mourning Michael's death and that was ultimately the direction the counseling took as a few more weeks went by with no new discoveries. Reluctantly, Helen had to begin facing life as a widow of the World Trade Center attack. "Widow, how could someone 29 years old be a widow?" Helen lamented tearfully.

The initial task in the counseling was to help Helen accept Michael's death as she still vacillated from day to day, but eventually she admitted that she had lost hope and was beginning to feel the overwhelming sense of depression and fear that accompanied her recognition. The counselor agreed that it felt hopeless and suggested that Helen had to begin looking at her life and what lay ahead. As Helen was suffering from ambiguous loss, there was equal effort at legitimizing Helen's confusion at her inability to move forward. Helen was encouraged to talk about her feelings of loss, to express her emotions about the injustice of Michael's untimely death, and to repeat and repeat the details of her imaginings of the circumstances of his last day and hours. Encouraging this aspect of her thinking, as painful as it was, helped her to accept the reality of his death.

In the counseling sessions, she questioned and replayed the days before his death and admitted to feelings of guilt as they had argued about money 2 days before the attack. She found herself thinking about her mother and wishing that she were still alive. This is consistent with the ricochet effect of loss, that new loss triggers past losses and often increases the bereavement burden for the griever. Helen was encouraged to talk with other women who had lost their husbands in the blast, to reach out to her sisters for support and to other friends who were eager to help carry her pain. As this was so soon after the tragedy and many people were suffering collectively, Helen could have been helped by joining with others. She did lean on her sisters more than usual; one came to stay with her in her apartment for a few weeks.

An additional area of pain for Helen was the recognition of secondary losses. Secondary losses are those physical or psychosocial losses that accompany or are a consequence of an initial loss (Rando, 1995). Secondary losses are the empty spaces we find in our lives as we adjust to the world without our loved one. These are the changes in our lives and environments that begin to emerge slowly after a death. They include intellectual, emotional, and financial shifts, the mundane changes and the major changes. For some, it may mean having to leave their homes, return to work, seek other employment, be financially compromised, and so on (Marrone, 1997). For Helen, Michael's death meant that she had to accommodate to almost a complete social and emotional realignment. Michael's income was larger than Helen's and it had dictated their current lifestyle. Helen's earning had gone into a fund earmarked for the purchase of a house. Helen was faced with having to decide whether to use that money to pay bills and rent or to move. Although there was some insurance money due her, it would take a long time to sort that out and she had to make some decisions fairly quickly. There were many such decisions that weighed on Helen. To the mourner, these secondary losses can sometimes be as disruptive and disabling as the primary loss.

In the counseling Helen was encouraged to bring these more practical concerns in for discussion and the stance of the counselor was more exploring and directive to help jump-start Helen into acting on her own behalf. Each area of loss was examined one by one with the goal not necessarily for the counselor to come up with solutions but to have the counselor frame each situation so that Helen could decide solutions to her own practical problems.

But, according to Helen, the most painful times were the small things that set her off—finding a note that Michael had written for her to pick up stamps at the post office, opening the medicine chest and finding his shaving brush, going to his closet and smelling his scent on his clothes, and looking at the calendar, marked when they were to have taken a vacation in November. It was the constant, sometimes subtle, reminders of him and her sudden aloneness "…that grabbed her heart and twisted it."

As the counseling extended past 3 months after the attack, and the impossibility of Michael's return was solidified, a funeral or memorial service was discussed. The counselor felt that Helen needed the finality of a ritual to truly begin her mourning and initiated this discussion. Helen was initially reluctant as deep down inside she still had a spark of hope, but she said, "Intellectually I am fully aware that Michael is gone but I am not emotionally ready for any of this. But, perhaps it is best that we do this." Her trust in the counseling relationship was enough that she was able to accept this direction for action despite her reluctance.

Her sisters joined Helen and the counselor for a joint planning session for a funeral. Michael was to be symbolically buried in a site adjacent to Helen's mother. It was hoped that this would serve as both an ending and beginning point for Helen. The service was held on the 4-month anniversary of Michael's death. Family and friends gathered and a rabbi conducted the service. Helen sat *shiva* (the Jewish period of mourning) for 1 week after the funeral. The counselor attended the funeral as a show of support that Helen appreciated.

The funeral service moved Helen into the beginning stages of acceptance and, in some respects, a deeper level of sadness emerged as she finally gave up hope of Michael's return. At that point, more familiar bereavement issues began to surface and Helen's recovery had begun.

Issues for the Counselor

One of the areas of struggles for a bereavement counselor with a situation that is so outside the normal range of losses is the maintenance of boundaries. When disaster occurs, many people are affected and it becomes very difficult for the counselor to manage one's own grief while helping others. Personal feelings of loss and existential questions concerning security and worldview are challenged and the anger experienced by the client over the senselessness of the act can exacerbate the same feelings for the counselor. The counselor may mirror the feelings of helplessness and powerlessness that are experienced by the griever. Recognizing this is the first step, and then marshalling the capacity to keep the boundaries clear are the harder parts.

With Helen, there were additional struggles for the counselor. She was a young, vital woman who was planning a future with her husband and, as yet, unborn children. Her youth and sense of life being cut short made it difficult to not be overcome with sadness for her. As in many bereavement experiences one of the tasks for the mourner is to reiterate and repeat the supposed details of the dying. With so much death on the news and television, it became very difficult to carry the additional pain of Helen's loss. If a counselor feels overburdened by personal loss, it is unrealistic to imagine that they can be receptive to more anguish and pain. Researchers suggest that caseloads be varied so that a level of burnout is not reached when the counselor might become ineffective in his or her work.

As Michael's death was sudden and was the result of terrorist activity, there was a level of vengeance felt toward those who perpetrated the action. In addition, Helen confessed to anger at those who had escaped from the World Trade Center and even felt anger at those who had not escaped but whose remains were found. It was a tangle of emotions that Helen brought to each counseling session and each one had to be ventilated over time. Keeping the needed objectivity was a challenge, as Helen's anger was intense.

The decision to suggest to Helen that there be a funeral or memorial service was well received and then came the dilemma of whether the counselor should attend. In favor of nonattendance was that the counselor was not a family member and did not have any knowledge of the family or others who would be in attendance. Therapeutic distance would suggest not being there. The counselor made the decision to attend the service. It was based on reinforcing the need and importance of the rituals attending death and the desire to support Helen's acceptance of her loss. It was not seen as the ending moment of her counseling; instead, it was quite the contrary. It was the beginning of her ability to mourn her loss in its own right.

Helen ended counseling a few months later. She felt that her anger had subsided enough to allow her to "just be sad" and that it might be time to "...try to put my life in order." Just before the 1-year anniversary, the counselor checked in with Helen. She had returned to work, had become involved in a widow's support group, and had been to the World Trade Center site on several occasions. She planned to be there for the ceremonies on the 1-year anniversary of the attack.

CHAPTER

Bereavement After a Plane Crash:
A Lesbian Couple

The Case—Barbara

Barbara (57 years old) and Ruth (48 years old) began living together after knowing each other for 2 years. They had met at a lesbian bar in their city, hit it off, and began dating. The dating turned into a more committed, monogamous relationship and the decision was easily reached to move in together. Barbara was an executive secretary in a law firm and Ruth worked for a local cable station doing home repairs. Barbara was not "out" at work nor with her family, who lived far away; they believed she led the life of a spinster. Barbara had had a number of failed relationships with men and always wondered about her sexual orientation. She had begun going to bars to meet women. Ruth was open about her sexual identity with family (they were not very supportive but had accepted her choice), who lived nearby, and had confided in several work companions of her life choice. Ruth had a long-term relationship with a woman that had broken up about a year before she met Barbara. Because of Barbara's need for secrecy, she and Ruth had a very small circle of friends and were rarely out in public together. This was a source of frustration for Ruth but she treasured their privacy and the relationship thrived. They were a deeply committed couple, married in all but the legal sense of the word.

To celebrate their 4-year anniversary, Barbara and Ruth planned a vacation that would take them to a resort area in the Caribbean that was "gay friendly." They had tired of being on vacation and having to hide their relationship in a heterosexual environment. The night before they were to leave, Barbara's boss called with an emergency and asked her to postpone her trip by 1 day as some important contracts had to be prepared. He was not aware of Barbara's private life but knew of her vacation plans and told her that he would compensate her for the additional plane fare and hotel costs incurred by this change. Ruth and Barbara talked it over and decided that Ruth would go as planned and Barbara would join her the next day, especially because her boss was going to cover the expense of the change in plans. The next morning, Ruth left for the airport and Barbara went to work. This was the last time Ruth and Barbara saw each other.

For Ruth, the plane trip to the Caribbean area was effortless, but the small prop plane that had to be taken to the resort area encountered a sudden thunderstorm, lost altitude, and disappeared into the ocean. All 12 passengers and 3 crewmembers were killed. Barbara heard the news of the crash on her car radio as she was driving home from work; she felt a darkness descend over her and she was barely able to get home. Once at home, she began calling the airline to get information to see if there were survivors. When she finally reached an airline representative, she was informed that all had perished in the crash. Barbara shouted in horror as her world crumbled and she fell in on herself in a bleakness from which she would not emerge.

By the next day, several of the bodies of the passengers had been recovered, including Ruth's, and her body was being flown back to their home city. Ruth's family had been notified and they were beginning to make funeral arrangements. In the past, Barbara and Ruth had spent time with Ruth's family and they had welcomed Barbara, but it was clear that they wanted to handle all of the funeral arrangements. The few friends who knew of their relationship rallied around Barbara but she was essentially closed off to their concern. She was not going to contact her family or any work friends because of her need for secrecy. Barbara, who was supposed to be on vacation, was not expected to return to work for 2 weeks, so she was able to keep the tragedy and funeral away from her work life. That was the least of her concerns at the moment. She was unable to sleep, eat, think, or do anything that was familiar. She wandered around the apartment, wailed, felt guilty, and was in a state of complete despair. The funeral was a dreadful experience for Barbara; there was no mention of their 4-year relationship or of their life together. Although some family members were invited to speak at the service, Barbara was constrained by suggestions from Ruth's family that it would be better if she "kept a low profile." It seemed to Barbara that the family wanted to deny Ruth's present life. Barbara felt pained, marginalized, angry, and essentially alone.

Barbara's depression was crippling to her. She told her boss that she needed an extended leave; she fabricated a reason for this time off. She was listless, unfocused, did not leave the house, and cried constantly. Finally, after 4 weeks, a friend who knew of the relationship with Ruth forced Barbara to call a therapist for some help. She had lost 25 pounds in the 4 weeks since the crash and was barely functioning. Barbara became a client for the first time in her life.

Relevant History

Barbara had grown up in a conservative household where the values of home and church were uppermost. She was the youngest of three sisters, and both parents had worked. Her childhood was unremarkable as were her high school and community college years. In high school, she became aware of her interest in girls both as close friends and as intimates but had not acted on any of those feelings. She had dated several boys in high school and college but none held her attention for more than a few months. Over the years, she had wondered whether she might be attracted to women but felt constrained from acting on her curiosity. She had an active cultural life, sang in her church choir, and played cello in a semiprofessional string quartet. She "had made peace" with her life, did not expect to marry or have children, and was satisfied to live a quiet life alone. She had occasional visits with her sisters and their families. Periodically, if she felt lonely and wanted female companionship, she would go to a lesbian bar, many blocks away from her home, for fear of being seen and "outed." She enjoyed the company of women and had a few flirtations but had not formed an emotionally connected or sexually committed relationship with a woman.

When she first met Ruth, she was startled by her own reactions. She felt energized in a way that she had not known and was eager to learn as much as she could about this young, very energetic, and attractive woman who made her feel alive and beautiful. Ruth and Barbara fell in love; for Barbara, this was her first true romance and love relationship.

Conceptual Issues

There are three intertwined crosscurrents when considering the bereavement experience of this case: the sexual identity of the deceased and her partner, the impact of death caused by a plane crash, and the violation of the assumptive world caused by sudden, unpredictable death.

Lesbian Death and Dying

To discuss this as a separate form of death is, in itself, a statement about our culture and its readiness to accept all persons as equals. Unfortunately, the experience of death and dying for the homosexual person is still more complicated than for the heterosexual. As Dworkin and Kaufer (1995) noted, "...The larger social environment in which the gay and lesbian community exists, adds a dimension that must be taken into account" (p. 41) in a bereavement situation. There are several issues unique to the homosexual lifestyle and environment that affect the death and dying experience: the role of stigma, sociocultural factors, and the alienation experienced by the hidden griever.

It has been more than 25 years since the American Psychiatric Association removed homosexuality from its list of mental disorders. Although it has been accepted that homosexuality is not a mental illness, lesbian and gay people still are exposed to high levels of external and internal stress over their lifestyle choices (Hughes, Haas, Razzano, Cassidy, & Matthews, 2000). Many in contemporary culture still see homosexuality as a "deviant lifestyle" in conflict with mainstream moral and religious values. For this reason, the risk of stigma promotes many homosexuals to conceal their lifestyle as a way of avoiding possible interactional problems within their families and at work, thus compartmentalizing many aspects of their lives (Cain, 1991; Ryan, Bradford, & Honnold, 1999). For an individual such as Barbara, the necessity of personal concealment was deemed essential. Along with this level of concealment from family, some friends, and coworkers comes a sense of stigma that can lead to shame and the fear of being found out. In the event of a death, not "being out" potentially aborts much needed social support from family, friends, and coworkers, and the mourner is deprived of participation in certain rituals of death.

Concealing homosexual identity when there is a death creates a situation defined by Doka (1989a) as disenfranchised grief. This is grief that a person experiences that is not or cannot be openly acknowledged, publicly mourned, or socially supported. When the death and grief are disenfranchised, it complicates and prolongs the bereavement process of healing.

Sociocultural factors that can affect a bereavement experience include the survivor's having a lack of institutionalized rituals. A surviving partner with no legal status may face a conflict with family members over final disposition of the deceased partner; there may be disagreement over plans, rituals, and ceremonies (Evans & Carter, 2000). If the deceased was "not out," the identity of the partner is surely obscured to the public. The social expressions of grief have to be hidden by the partner who was not out, and social support may be withheld.

The hidden griever is one who, because of the clandestine nature of their relationship, is not connected to whatever bereavement rituals are available in the larger homosexual community. For many, the need to protect another aspect of their lives keeps them apart from available support within the homosexual community, making the period of bereavement much more pained and stressful (Dworkin & Kaufer, 1995). These three factors—stigma, sociocultural friction, and the alienation of hidden grievers—can profoundly affect the bereavement trajectory in disruptive and powerful ways.

Sudden and Violent Death

In Rando's (1993) conceptualization, the experience of a sudden, unexpected death raises the potential for complicated mourning for the griever. Although it might be argued that all deaths are sudden and traumatic, death through disaster "...so severely disrupts the mourner's life that uncomplicated recovery or accommodations to the loss can no longer be expected and functioning is seriously impaired" (p. 554). It seems that the loss and shock are so profound that the survivor is not able to incorporate it or even begin to process it.

A facet of sudden and violent loss is survivor guilt. This form of guilt poses endless questions to survivors as to why they were spared, what could they have done to prevent the death, and why did the event happen. In 1982, for example, an Air Florida jet plunged into the Potomac River. A stewardess was one of the five survivors. In an interview she commented that she felt guilty about so many things: that she was alive, that she was not more patient with the passengers, and that she could not control what happened. Another survivor of the crash commented, "There was something unexpectedly painful about the experience of being spared when so many died" (Yoffe, 2002, p. 39).

Loss of the Assumptive World

"The assumptive world concept refers to the assumptions or beliefs that ground, secure, or orient people, that give a sense of reality, meaning or purpose to life" (Kauffman, 2002a, p. 1). These assumptions include those actions, behaviors, and responses that can be counted on. The assumptions form a conceptual system, developed over time, that provides us with expectations about the world and ourselves. They guide our interactions in the world and generally enable us to function optimally (Janoff-Bulman, 1992). Three fundamental assumptions identified by Janoff-Bulman (1992) are that the world is benevolent, the world is meaningful, and the self is worthy. Benevolence of the world refers to the belief that the world is a good place, that the people in it are kind and well intentioned, and that events usually have positive outcomes. The world's being meaningful means that things make sense, that there is a cause-and-effect relationship between events and outcomes. The notion of the self as worthy means that we perceive ourselves as good, capable, and moral individuals. In essence, we believe we are good people who live in a benevolent world where things make sense, more or less (Janoff-Bulman, 1992, pp. 4-12). In the event of trauma—violent tragedy and death—each of these assumptions is challenged and a loss of the assumptive world can occur (Kauffman, 2002a). These assumptions, which have kept us steady and have given coherence to our lives, are soon discovered to be illusions and an abrupt, terrifying disillusionment occurs (Fleming & Robinson, as cited in Strobe et al., 2001).

When the assumptive world is shattered through traumatic loss, the guidelines with which the self navigates the world are shattered. The world is no longer a safe, benevolent place, peopled with good, caring individuals who have a modicum of control and impact over what happens to them. "Traumatic loss overwhelms and floods the self with negative assumptions deviant from the protective norm of the good... The terror that shatters the assumptive world is a violent deprivation of safety. ... What is lost in the traumatic loss of the assumptive world? All is lost. Hope is lost..." (Kauffman, 2002b, p. 206). For the griever, there are no answers, safety, clarity, power, or control. There is a low-level panic; the self is in danger. Healing from this type of grief may be especially painful and, of greater concern, more protracted as new assumptions have to be created in the worldview of the griever.

Suggestions for Intervention

Especially in these circumstances, the level of bereavement intervention is guided by the degree of reaction to the loss. Assessment of grievers should include the degree of violation to their worldview and whether they have shifted in their fundamental belief structures regarding the benevolence and safety of their lives. If the assumptive world of the griever appears to be more or less intact, bereavement interventions can proceed in the direction of dealing with disenfranchised or stigmatized grief, or both, and management of sudden and violent loss.

Disenfranchised and Stigmatized Grief

Because of the nature of the relationship prior to the death, the disenfranchised griever may not be able to reveal publicly the impact the death has had on him or her. The griever may have had to camouflage his or her feelings and thoughts lest others make assumptions about the relationship (Meagher, 1989) that the griever has attempted to hide. This hidden aspect of the grief guides the counselor's intervention approach, which is geared toward helping the griever accept the reality of the loss, experience the pain of the grief, adjust to an environment without the deceased, withdraw emotional energy, and reinvest in new relationships (H. Stroebe & Stroebe, 1987; Worden, 1982). To accomplish these tasks, the counselor must be available and encouraging of the venting and validating of the lost relationship. Guilt must be examined and discussed, as unresolved guilt may lead to self-punishment (Meagher, 1989). All acts of commission and omission, thoughts, and feelings that seem to be related to the guilt must be examined, including the feelings of disenfranchisement, in order that a process of self-forgiveness can ensue (Rando, 1984). Ritual may help facilitate some of the healing.

Bereavement rituals are a part of all cultures. These rituals are used to facilitate relinquishing of relationships and transitions to a new social role (Rando, 1993). Funeral rituals mediate the transition of the deceased from life to death and help grievers accept the finality and reality of their loss; it moves them from a reality-based relationship to one of memory and meaning (Romanoff & Terenzio, 1998). The homosexual griever may be deprived of the benefits of the funeral rituals, thus complicating his or her grief experience. A function of the grief counselor could be to assist the griever in creating a meaningful ritual (Dworkin & Kaufer, 1995) that would affirm the social networks of the survivor and facilitate integration and recovery (Katz & Bartone, 1998). The counselor could suggest a private funeral ceremony or memorial service, more in keeping with the social relationships that were meaningful to the mourner and deceased. The energy and genesis for this may fall within the realm of the counseling relationship.

Sudden and Violent Loss and the Assumptive World

Sudden death occurs without warning and requires dedicated interventions to address the needs of the griever who might be is such a state of shock or denial that the death has not registered. Worden (2002) set out several intervention strategies to help the survivor begin to accept the death. He suggested that the counselor can help the griever actualize the loss by urging him or her to view the body of the deceased: There is no greater reality than seeing the dead person. In the counseling relationship a step toward acceptance is to keep the griever focused on the death, not on the circumstances of the death. Frequent use of the word dead helps bring home the reality of the loss (pp. 119–121).

Normalizing reactions to sudden death is a facet of intervention strategy suggested by Rando (1993). She urges the counselor to offer normalizing information about posttraumatic responses that can cause the griever anxiety or fear of losing his or her mind. Typical posttraumatic responses include numbing, denial, intrusive thoughts and reactions, sleep and eating disruption, depressed mood, and irritability (pp. 593–608). By having the counselor reassure the griever that his or her responses are normal, the mourner is free to begin exploring other aspects of the loss.

Sudden and violent loss also triggers challenges to the assumptive world. There are a variety of approaches to addressing assumptive world violations: using a cognitive–behavioral approach, relearning and rechallenging, and reliving the trauma. It is assumed that a griever who has experienced a loss of assumptive world would necessitate longer term counseling—more a matter of many months than not—to rebuild their inner world.

Stated simply, using a cognitive approach, the counselor examines with the client a certain affect-laden belief related to his or her worldview. The counselor then "…patiently explores with the client the evidence both for and against such an interpretation, then encourages consideration of an alternative or balanced construct that simultaneously acknowledges and contains these conflicting elements. This would be done repeatedly around specific incidents…" (Fleming & Robinson, 2001, p. 656). Part of the healing is done through "the generation of imagined alternatives to actual events, or counterfactual thinking" (p. 664).

Relearning new assumptions about the world and coming to terms with the loss of violated assumptions is a matter of learning new ways of acting and being in the world. "It is a matter of coming to know how to go on in the world where so much of what we have taken for granted in the emotional, psychological, behavioral, social, soulful, and spiritual dimensions of our lives is no longer supportable or practicable... It is a matter of taking in the truth (of the loss) in the depths of our being, allowing ourselves to feel the impact of the absence in all dimensions of our lives, experiencing the difference that absence makes in the world around us and in our daily lives... reorienting ourselves to those differences" (Attig, 2002, p. 64). As such, cognitive therapy can be very useful with the helping being viewed as teaching; part of the teaching supports revised adaptations to a world that has been so dramatically undermined and changed.

Reliving the trauma is based on the belief that intrusive thoughts and images are ultimately adaptive because they result in a weakening of distressing emotions. In counseling, the griever is urged to reexperience the event of the death. Each time the event is reexperienced, the new data can be worked on so that it assumes less potency and can be assimilated more easily. There is a necessity to talk about the trauma as it is by using language with which the survivor can calm intrusive thoughts and memories. As well, in speaking about an event, survivors can revise it in ways that make it more tolerable; they can impose some order on the experience (Janoff-Bulman, 1992, pp. 107–109) as they struggle to understand their grief.

Major Issues in This Case

Barbara was experiencing a full gamut of emotional and psychological reactions to Ruth's sudden and tragic death. She, as a closeted lesbian, was deprived of customary social support and ritual observance surrounding a death; she was a disenfranchised griever and had suffered a violent rupture within her assumptive world. When she first began counseling, the most immediate concern was the depth of her depression. She had lost a considerable amount of weight, was crying much of the time, and was unable to go to work. She had folded in on herself and could not seem to find any reserve from which she could draw to begin the recovery process. In the first session, she was only able to relate the sequence of events leading to Ruth's death. Intertwined in this description was a substantial component of guilt—guilt that Barbara had not been with Ruth, guilt because it was Barbara's idea to go to a distant place, and guilt that she had not died and Ruth had. The guilt was anticipated and was not to be challenged at this juncture because the counselor was just beginning to establish a relationship with Barbara.

The positioning of the counselor in the early stages, especially with a disenfranchised situation, can be critical. The counselor is urged to remain as accepting and neutral as possible, urging the venting of feelings, even feelings of guilt. Reassurance of the universality of guilt in loss (Meagher, 1989) can be reassuring in the early discussions. The acceptance of guilt as a widely held emotional reaction seemed to ease Barbara. At one point in the third session, she said, "I guess I am not such a terrible person, I just feel like I am."

Along with protestations of guilt, there was continuous questioning of why this had happened and at the same time there were expressions suggesting the unreality of the death. Barbara lamented, "What have I done wrong to have had Ruth snatched from me? Perhaps if we had remained friends and not led a life in secret, she would have been spared. This is truly God's way of punishing me for loving her!" and in the next sentence, "I can't believe that she is gone, that I will never see her again." This dreamlike quality of initial grief is particularly poignant. Initially the best posture for the counselor is to encourage these laments and show support by asking more questions and validating the emotional impact for the griever.

In the beginning it was difficult for Barbara to focus on issues related to the relationship with Ruth. She was too immersed in the immediacy of her pain. But by the fifth weekly counseling session the counselor began to slowly focus Barbara more on the relationship she had with Ruth: How long did it last? How did it begin? What were the dynamics between the two? By asking questions such as these, the counselor was helping to validate the relationship that had been lost and was demonstrating an acceptance of choices made by the griever. Barbara, in her reminiscing about the relationship, was calmed and seemed to relish talking about Ruth. And, then in the midst of a memory, she would begin to cry and question why this had happened.

To further help Barbara resolve the loss of Ruth, the counselor suggested a ritual that celebrated the relationship between Barbara and Ruth. Barbara had felt so marginalized by the whole funeral situation and she was angry and very hurt. As noted, rituals help the griever accept the reality of the death; some form of remembrance would allow Barbara the opportunity to say good-bye. Barbara seemed open to having a memorial service and accepted the suggestion to write a eulogy for Ruth. The counselor also suggested that the few friends who did know of their life be invited to the service, which would be held at Barbara's home. This was scheduled to take place at the 3-month anniversary of Ruth's death.

As Barbara began to demonstrate an easing of her pain—she was able to mention Ruth's name and not cry and generally seemed in tighter control of some of her emotional pain and anguish—the sessional content began to shift more toward a review of the entire relationship, back to its beginning. This was to help Barbara create what Meagher (1989, p. 326) called a "mental scrapbook," which contains memories, mental pictures of where each person was during an event, tender moments seen in the mind's eye. Grievers also can be encouraged to create their own personal memory album of treasured photos. Either way, it is a bittersweet memory album.

Addressing the broader issue of Barbara's assumptive worldview was more complex and necessitated getting past some of the more pressing issues of a new loss. This aspect of the work was ongoing but began much more in earnest after plans were set for the memorial service. Barbara indicated that she believed herself "...to be fundamentally altered. I felt my insides shift when I heard about the plane crash and I don't think I will ever see the world in the same way. It is a dark place, empty and cold." To address these more existential concerns, the counselor encouraged Barbara to talk about the trauma of her loss from a different perspective and to try to imagine a life without Ruth.

Simultaneously, the counselor asked Barbara to retell some of her perceptions of the events of the loss (4 months prior) and to consider different interpretations of those events. One of the interactions that Barbara felt the most guilty about, for example, was the decision to go to a "gay only" vacation spot. Barbara felt that she had imposed this on Ruth. This was challenged, and the counselor, armed with a sense of Ruth from previous discussion, was able to state, "Ruth was a strong woman and would have not agreed to something that she did not want to do." This approach, of challenging assumptions, is influenced by Janoff-Bulman's (1992) view that the retelling with revision is helpful to ameliorate assumptive worldview violations.

On another level, through the accepting relationship with the counselor, Barbara was able to make some indentation into her torn assumptions. On a regular basis, the counselor held up a "mirror" to her that was accepting and nurturing and was supportive of her behavior and decisions. The negative worldview interpretations about self-worth were constantly challenged and reworked. Barbara stayed in counseling for more than 12 months. She was able to return to work, part-time, 6 months after Ruth's death, but she did not feel fully engaged in the effort, leading to the part-time hours.

By the 10th month, Barbara was beginning to feel "almost human." She wanted some of the "peace in her life" to return. She spoke of picking up some of the interests she had when Ruth had been killed. She actually said that she "had looked at her cello for the first time in months and bought some new strings for it." These steps were supported fully. She did not mention wanting to start a new relationship or to connect with people or friends at all. She seemed to want to be almost reclusive in her life.

The question of terminating the sessions was discussed and it was the strong feeling of the counselor that Barbara should stay in counseling through the 1-year anniversary of the plane crash. Anniversary dates are usually a difficult time for most who grieve, and the counselor imagined that Barbara, who felt that she was grieving mostly alone, would struggle during that time. Indeed, the anniversary was a sad and difficult day, and Barbara spent some time at the cemetery, trying to avoid Ruth's parents and find quiet solace in her time there. In the counselor's view, Barbara could have benefited from additional supportive counseling to help her find her way in her essentially solo lifestyle. This was discussed, but Barbara decided that she would take a few months off and then reevaluate whether she wanted to continue counseling. The termination experience in counseling is important and the counselor insisted that there be a verbalization of the feelings associated with the termination of the counseling relationship, which had served as a bridge relationship between the griever and her new life without the loved one. For Barbara, the counseling terminated on a note of sad acceptance of her life and of her loss but with some self-forgiveness and calm. She did not return for additional counseling.

Issues for the Counselor

There are a number of difficult areas in a case such as Barbara's in which there are so many layers of anguish and pain that had to be addressed in the counseling relationship. One of the more challenging areas is asking the counselor to examine his or her own beliefs and reactions to a disenfranchised lifestyle, in this case, the life of a homosexual. It is only through this self-scrutiny that the counselor will be able to be fully accepting of the client's choice(s). In an interesting study of "secret survivors," participants commented that the helping person had to be assessed to determine whether they ascribed only to traditional family values or were open to alternative situations. Participants felt that they had to feel respected and safe to be honest with the counselor (Weinbach, 1989). If the counselor has difficulty accepting this life choice, researchers suggest that a referral be made to another counselor. Although all counseling professionals are pledged to be nonjudgmental, this may an unrealistic expectation and if a counselor has any hesitancy, he or she should refer the client to another counselor.

In working to address issues of violation of the assumptive world, the need for patience on the part of the counselor is often tested. Revised assumptions take a long time to emerge and need extensive reworking and support. This may be very difficult for some counselors to accept. This is surely a case in which the process—the patience to let things unfold in a nonlinear progression—can be taxing. Recovery from assumptive loss is slow and can be overwhelmed by the undertow of grief and sadness experienced by the griever. This pace can be frustrating for the counselor.

Working with Barbara was challenging and often emotionally taxing, as her sadness was so profound. She healed, or rather continues to heal, in measured steps. This was part of the challenge, to accept her for the somewhat changed person she had become: from an outgoing, happy woman with Ruth back to the person she described pre-Ruth. Barbara had become so much more actualized through her life with Ruth, and it was difficult and sad to see her retreat to the "old Barbara," who felt emotionally and experientially restricted. This was one of the areas of frustration, and Barbara left counseling somewhat healed from Ruth's death but emotionally bereft.

7

Bereavement After Death by Murder: A Mother's Grief

The Case—Donna

After months of anguished worry, the definitive call came from the police in March, telling Donna, Jack's mother, about his death. Jack's body was found buried in concrete, 50 miles away from his home. He was 26 years old, a drug dealer by profession. He had been missing since November. Donna went into a state of shock.

When she had not heard from Jack for a few days, Donna became worried and had a sinking feeling that something terrible had happened. She knew of some of Jack's dealings but had been spared a lot of detail and had been lied to in order to protect her. Nonetheless, she was afraid for him. She began calling some of Jack's friends, she questioned his sister and girlfriend, and she called his apartment and neighbors. And then she called the police, who began an investigation. "To speed things up," Donna hired a private investigator, but between the police and the investigator, details were scant and it seemed that Jack had truly vanished. The months went by ever so slowly. The details began to emerge painstakingly, culminating in the visit to Donna's home by the police to fill in the missing pieces of a fragmented and confused story of how Jack's body had been discovered and the details surrounding his murder. The devastation that this brought to Donna was immeasurable. At the same time, she was relieved that the search was over and the truth was finally known.

Up until the time of his disappearance Jack had been working at a gym. He was never late for work and was very well liked at the gym by staff and patrons. He had just moved out of his mother's home, had a steady girlfriend, and seemed to be doing well. The dark side of Jack, the side that dealt in illegal transactions, had been hidden from most people and many were shocked when the details of Jack's business arrangements and subsequent murder were revealed.

Donna came for counseling a month after Jack's body was discovered. Throughout an extremely tearful first session, she explained that her son had been involved with drug dealing for many years and that he had been in prison on two occasions. She described him as engaging, bright, a "good and dutiful son, a loving young man," and a wonderful person who had one fairly substantial problem: "He wanted to have lots of money and only knew one way to get it."

Donna had been married to Jack's father for 12 years when he died of alcohol abuse. When Jack was 10, Donna left the marriage to live with another man and she moved away with Jack's 8-year-old sister. Jack stayed with his father. Two years later, when Jack's father died suddenly, Donna left the man she was living with and returned with Jack's sister to start a renewed life together as a family. Jack's acting-out behavior began when he reached adolescence and he was caught and prosecuted several times for selling drugs. Over the years, his drug dealings grew and he was seen as a major distributor, despite the jail time and higher risk. During the deal that was "to be his last and biggest," a mix-up occurred and the drugs that he had been promised did not meet the agreed-upon standards. The recipient of the drugs kidnapped Jack and subsequently killed him, burying his body in concrete. The murderer was apprehended and put in jail. At the time of the murder, Donna was living with her daughter and Donna's boyfriend; Jack had his own apartment.

Donna was an administrator in a textile company, 48 years old, well dressed, and outgoing. She was subdued, outwardly calm and reserved, and just seemed to be able to hold in her emotions. She explained that since Jack's disappearance, her relationship with her boyfriend had deteriorated and their distance was growing, as she had no interest in anything other than finding Jack. At her work she was barely able to concentrate to perform her responsibilities. She had faced many months of anguish as the criminal justice system brought the murderer to trial. She did not know how she would be able to live with the pain and sorrow she felt. In addition, she was struggling with managing Jack's 24-year-old sister who was going through her own bereavement and anguish. Donna vacillated between being deeply depressed, being barely able to function, and being in a state of denial that allowed her to pretend that Jack was still alive. This enabled her to just get by at work and be minimally functional.

She cried almost constantly during the first few sessions and expressed a gamut of emotions, including guilt, shame, rage at the murderer and anger at Jack for being such a risk taker. The loudest lament was her overwhelming grief over her son's death. She stated, "There will be no more warm embraces, no more giggles at silly jokes, no more fireworks. There is nothing but memories." The competing lament was her guilt. She strongly believed that she had been responsible for Jack's illegal behavior because she had been married to an alcoholic—Jack's father—and because she had left Jack with him when she went to live with another man. She felt that all of the bad things that she had done over the years had created a situation for Jack that left him no option but to pursue something illegal.

Relevant History

Donna was an only child. Her father had died several years before Jack's murder and she was the caretaker for her aging and ailing mother. She briefly described a growing-up period that was not dramatic. She met her future husband in high school and married him knowing that he had an alcohol problem. She used a lot of denial in trying to handle her feelings about his drinking and the problems that it brought into their life and the life of the children. Her current live-in boyfriend had been with her for 7 years; the relationship between them had been faltering for some time. Donna described herself as having lived a rebellious life, having had alternative relationships of several types over the years. She had never had a profound depression of the type she currently described.

Conceptual Issues

The literature that informs the conceptual underpinnings of this case is drawn from two parallel streams: the management of maternal grief and grief after homicide.

Maternal Grief

The death of an adult child is a particularly traumatic event as compared with other deaths; it is unlike any other loss known (Rando, 1986).

According to Fish (1986), "The loss of a child ...requires adaptation to an irretrievable loss" (p. 417). The reality is that something essential to the life of the mother has disappeared. She may appear to be functioning well, but inwardly she may be crying for help to understand why this tragedy occurred (Sprang, McNeil, & Wright, 1989). The grief process for a bereaved mother is lengthy and intense.

The factors that contribute to the intensity and duration of the grief of a mother are age of child at death, circumstances of the death, and role of the child in the family system. Despite the reality that at any age the death of a child is deeply upsetting, when an adult child dies, a mother has worked through the developmental years, many of which are difficult, and often a mature relationship of adults has evolved with shared interests. The mother is grieving for what might have been, for the loss of a future in which there would be events to celebrate including marriage, birth of grandchildren, and the development of a career, all of the celebratory milestones that mark an adult life as well as the companionship and caretaking that might eventually define the relationship. If the relationship with the deceased child has been a positive one, there is the loss of a friend as well as someone with whom a life has been shared (Schatz, 1986).

An additional aspect of the mourning that relates to age is the norm that children outlive their parents. The death of the child alters the "normal course" of things and is seen as "unnatural." The bereaved mother is constantly searching for a reason that explains why her child died, some explanation that clarifies and substantiates this untimely death (Brice, 1991). Guilt is inevitably a consideration that permeates the bereavement circumstances. Often, the surviving parents have particularly strong feelings of guilt because of their perceived failure to provide and protect (Rynearson, 1995). These feelings, once worked through in the counseling, become less prominent and are replaced with a more profound sense of loss.

Maternal mourning is marked by a series of paradoxical situations, according to Brice (1991). He noted that to a bereaved mother, her child's death signifies the death of her world, the world she inhabited with the child. Although she wants to have the child back, she has to die to obtain him; thus, the wish to both live and die is present in the grieving mother. The *emptiness* of the bereaved mother's life is lived by someone who is *filled* with grief and sorrow. The additional paradox of the acknowledged goal of mourning—to somehow accept the death of her child—which will never be realized leaves the mother in an impossible emotional bind. In a twist of logic, as long as the mother continues to grieve and cannot get over the death, there is the illusion of a relationship with the child.

Research on the intensity of grief reactions by Fish (1986) illuminates additional aspects of the bereavement experience. In his study of 77 women and 35 men, he found that the grief of mothers was more intense after 2 years than was fathers' grief, that bereaved parents felt socially isolated and had difficulty maintaining relationships even with people close to them, that fathers experienced greater grief as the death age went up but that age was not a factor for the mothers, and that mode of death (sudden and traumatic versus illness or slower dying) was more significant in the grieving experience for fathers than for mothers.

The unique factors for parents of children who are murdered explain another dimension of this form of bereavement.

Grief After Homicide

Parkes (1993) commented, "Bereavement following murder or manslaughter must surely be one of the most traumatic types of loss experienced" (p. 49). Because of the degree of trauma, the potential for dysfunctional bereavement response is high. Loss through murder surely leaves a great deal of pain and anguish in its wake. The mourning is more profound, more lingering, and more complex than normal grief (Sprang et al., 1989). The suddenness, preventability, and violent nature of the death account for the propensity for complicated mourning and extended psychological problems (Asaro, 2001).

Drawing from participant observation in a group of Parents of Murdered Children, Peach and Klass (1987) discussed the special issues for parents. They noted the unique aspects of this form of grief: the presence of overwhelming anger and a drive for revenge, the fears for self and other family members, and the sudden loss of the social role of the parent. Parents described the sense of rage at the perpetrator as overwhelming and nearly impossible to overcome. Often the anger takes the form of fantasies of revenge that provide an outlet for the frustration and impotence experienced. In addition, the slow movement of the criminal justice system, which protects the rights of the accused, exacerbates the anguish of the bereavement period.

Family members of murder victims are doubly victimized, first by the criminal and second by the criminal justice system. Often, even when the murderer has been identified and apprehended, the time between crime, trial, and prosecution is a matter of many months or years of agonized waiting on the part of the parents or survivors. If apprehension does not take place immediately, and the murderer is not identified, the parents suffer the anguish of not having closure to the death of their child. The media attention and the tendency for the media to sensationalize this type of crime are high. Reporters and photographers are often intrusive visitors in the lives of survivors. The potential for the survivors to feel victimized by the police is another level of intrusion. Often, through innuendo, survivors are made to feel responsible for the murder by the police and those investigating the murder (Sprang et al., 1989). All of these factors negatively affect the bereavement experience.

Empirical research on the bereavement trajectory following homicide is limited. Rynearson (1984) did a retrospective study of 15 individuals who lost a relative through homicide and noted that all participants experienced cognitive, affective, and behavioral reactions that differed from their previous bereavement experiences. All participants, who were 3 or more years from the homicide, noted the continued presence of intrusive and repetitive images of the homicide with accompanying fear and anger. The anger was directed at the murderer. In hindsight, most participants noted that it took 12 to 18 months for the anger to subside but it never fully disappeared. Parkes (1993) studied the bereavement reactions of 17 participants, half seen within a year of the homicide. The immediate reaction to the homicide for most of the participants was numbness, blunting, or disbelief that made it difficult for the participants to express their grief. Strong feelings of rage were common as were haunting nightmares and feelings of guilt and self-reproach. Parkes concluded, "The overall feeling [of the parents] was of sadness, bitterness and disillusionment as if the powers that be had failed to provide the protection from danger we all expect, and the very basis of a just society was in question" (p. 51). Rynearson and McCreery (1993) gathered data from 18 participants, up to 2.5 years from the homicide, using self-report measures. They observed that most participants commented on an idealized attachment to the deceased, disorganizing flashbacks, dreams of death, and high levels of trauma and grief.

Dannemiller (2002) reported a study involving reactions by 11 parents of murdered children. She noted that parents spoke of a sense of emptiness. Although this is a universal reaction when a child dies, whether by murder or illness, the unique aspect of a murder death is the context of violence that surrounds the dying. This brings a level of horror that affects the bereavement experience and infuses an additional level of pain to the survivor's grief. Dannemiller suggested that parents go through a process of informational synthesis that ultimately leads to an understanding of the details of the death and a more complete scenario. "Because they have such a strong desire to understand their child's death, parents strive to recreate the scenario of the murder. To accomplish this goal, they need information about various areas of the death: the cause, the sequence of events, the contextual factors, and responsibility for the death. The process of synthesis leads them to recreate a scenario that is more complete and detailed…" (p. 16) and facilitates their ability to integrate the death and cease their quest for additional information.

Suggestions for Intervention

To be truly effective, the counselor must be willing to enter the often conflicted and torturous emotional world of the bereaved mother. The counselor, who can gain entry into this space, will become acquainted with the mother's overwhelming pain. It is the slow releasing of the pain that moves the mother toward some degree of acceptance of her loss. Each bereaved mother goes through her own unique process toward healing, but it must be understood that maternal bereavement never fully subsides (Brice, 1991).

The approach to interventions is guided by the emotional state of the bereaved. If the bereaved is assessed as having many of the symptoms of post-traumatic stress disorder, various cognitive and relaxation approaches must be used to help stabilize the individual. At the same time, reenactment imagery in which the "story" of the death is told is suggested (Rynearson & McCreery, 1993). The bereaved should be encouraged to review the events leading up to and following the death and to express any feelings that emerge (Parkes, 1993). Reenactment should be encouraged and done repeatedly in an atmosphere that is accepting, nonintrusive, and nonjudgmental (Brice, 1991). The aim of the reenactment imagery is decathexis from the deceased that is accomplished by the repetition.

Schatz (1986) offered some suggestions from the vantage point of her participation in a bereavement group when her son died. She urged counselors to understand that a bereaved mother needs to tell her story, time after time, and that the healing is dependent on the willingness of the caregiver and others to listen. A bereaved mother will never forget her child who died, and the goal of the bereavement counseling is to help the mother remember her deceased child as a special part of her life; the counselor must accept the anger and rage that facilitate that goal.

"In order to be most helpful to bereaved parents, caregivers [counselors] must be realistic about the extent to which they can relieve the parents' suffering" (Rando, 1986, p. 380). We cannot take away all of the pain, but as Rando pointed out, the counselor can offer the "gift of presence" which must not be undervalued. There is something very logical in seeing the counselor in this role. The family and friends of the bereaved parents are suffering in their own ways, and, if they are like most people, are uncomfortable with death and especially the sorrow of a bereaved parent. For the bereaved parents, the counselor is someone who does not need to be taken care of or protected. The counselor is also not judging them. This gives the bereaved people license to express all the rage, anger, and guilt that they feel and not have to worry about any consequences. In many communities, groups under the auspices of Compassionate Friends, an organization that addresses the bereavement needs of grieving parents, are a useful referral in addition to individual counseling.

Expressions of guilt are to be anticipated. Treatment requires that bereaved parents discuss their guilty feelings and evaluate their legitimacy. In the death of adult children, there may be guilt over events from long ago. These are to be explored and put in perspective. In-session questioning can focus on the time before the murder, what the nature of the relationship(s) had been, and how the family functioned. Sometimes the counselor has to address the question of guilt more forthrightly, asking whether the bereaved is feeling guilty over some aspect of the interaction(s) with the bereaved. This is not an initial intervention but one that can be attempted when some level of trust and empathy has been established between the survivor and the counselor.

Helping the bereaved parent accommodate to the loss of the role of parent is a particularly difficult area of intervention. If there are surviving siblings, the parent is still an "active" parent able to maintain the role; if not, finding a reason to live by investing in other relationships is essential and, in time, can be supported by the counselor. This must be done with care as the mother still wants to see herself as the mother and is struggling to keep the deceased alive in some manner.

It is especially important for the counselor to recognize that grief after a child dies lasts a very long time and may actually intensify over the first 1 to 2 years following the child's death. This observation affects the pacing and expectations of the counseling efforts (Videka-Sherman, 1987); parents are not expected to heal in 6 months or a year and may reexperience their loss in a more exaggerated way after the first or second year after the death.

Major Issues in This Case

Consumed with pain and guilt, Donna began counseling 6 weeks after the death of her son had been confirmed (he had been missing for 6 months when police found his body in concrete many miles away from his home). She described the period before he was found as initially filled with anguish and hope, and as time went on, she felt a sense of dread as she suspected something dire had happened. In this initial stage of meeting with a griever, the counselor is faced with the dual task of emotionally connecting to the client while exploring relevant history and assessing the emotional stability of the griever. To facilitate the connection, the counselor should ask a lot of questions, listen attentively, and be as supportive as possible. Donna was easy to connect to, as she was personable despite the depression that gripped her. She was able to relate a good deal of her personal and family history but, quite naturally, kept coming back to her anguish about Jack. She was clear about one thing: "I want revenge for the killing and want him to either be executed, tortured, or put in jail for ever. If the criminal justice system won't do it, I will kill him myself," she said. The counselor saw this vituperative anger as a good sign, as it suggested that she was in touch with the anger and rage that consumed her within the depression and showed that she had some potential to override her depressive feelings.

Donna's initial bereavement period was in accord with much of the literature. She felt the irretrievable loss described by Fish (1986) and the guilt described by Rynearson (1995) and others. She continued to blame herself for Jack's unlawful behavior and the murder. She saw the death as punishment for all of the wrongs she had committed and as an outgrowth of her behavior when Jack was young. There was no moving her from this interpretation.

Donna continued to idealize Jack for months. Rynearson and McCreery (1993) accurately described this facet of bereavement. Early on in the counseling, she said, "Jack was basically a good boy and had been as he grew up. It was not in his nature to do bad things but he got into a bad group and they influenced him." A bit later in her counseling, Donna also began to wonder whether Jack had been influenced by his alcoholic father to do illegal things.

This externalization of Jack's behavior was a consistent theme and suggested that Donna was not able to acknowledge that Jack was responsible for any of what happened to him. In the early stages of counseling, this denial is to be supported, as the griever is not able to take in a different interpretation that challenges his or her denial or belief structure. Placing responsibility on Jack for his own behavior was a step that Donna was unable to take at that time.

As the counseling progressed, Donna detailed more and more of her history. Donna seemed to need to explain herself; surely she was exploring the past to see where "she went wrong that Jack was so messed up." Her exploration had almost a cathartic quality, as she went through some periods during the first 6 months of counseling in which she was less depressed than at other times.

It was not until almost 1 year after counseling began that she was able to express her anger at Jack for "his stupidity" and "arrogance." "What was he thinking?" she lamented. The acknowledgment that Jack's risky behavior played a role in his death was an important step as it allowed Donna the ability to shift blame off her—facilitating the easing of her depression—and onto Jack.

In addition to her anger about Jack's behavior, she began to more fully explore some of her guilt. She wondered what had made Jack behave as he did and one conclusion was that she had influenced and tacitly encouraged some of his behavior. She verbally would tell Jack that what he was doing was bad and that he must stop, but there was a part of Donna that loved expensive things. Some of the costly gifts and jewelry that Jack had given her for her birthday or as a holiday gift were things that she had been deprived of all her life. She wondered if this could account for his actions. In the counseling, a dual dynamic was employed: to allow the venting of guilt without passing judgment while urging Donna to see that Jack ultimately made his own decisions. This was intended to diminish legitimizing her speculation and guilt while pushing her to see Jack's participation in his destiny. The mourner does not easily disclose feelings at this level, especially of it paints him or her in a very negative light. The counselor has to be seen as fully trustworthy for the griever to be so exposed. Donna must have felt the trust.

An additional complication for Donna, which was not described in the literature, involved her shame. She was concerned that people would diminish the loss since Jack had been dealing drugs and was in the midst of a major drug deal when he was murdered. She said, "I don't want people thinking he deserved what happened to him or thinking badly of him." She was especially concerned that his criminal behavior would affect the decision of the judge and jury at the murder trial and that the feeling would be that "he got what he deserved." She also worried that those who were attending the trial, in an effort to show support to Donna, might hear things that would turn them against Jack and subsequently Donna. She even told friends not to attend the trial out of fear of abandonment. This was a new arena in the counseling, and to address these feelings, the counselor needed to reiterate to Donna to see Jack as responsible for his actions. Nonetheless, she was not relieved and eventually entered the courtroom with an additional burden.

As the trial date loomed, approximately 1 year after the murderer was apprehended, she became increasingly agitated and worried. Her need for revenge was consuming her. The trial lasted 2 weeks, which were "hellish" according to Donna. She felt exposed and vulnerable. The underlying fears were that she would be seen as an unworthy mother and that the murderer would go free. The counseling at this time was aimed at trying to hold Donna together by allowing her to vent her rage and fears. She desperately wanted to make certain that the accused murderer would receive the maximum sentence. She spoke of wanting pure revenge. Donna was told that these violent feelings were expected. She was more anxious and cried more during that time than at any other time during her counseling. The counselor, wanting to show additional support for Donna, attended some of the trial and made a special effort to be there when Donna read her impact statement at the conclusion of the trial.

In her impact statement at the hearing before sentencing, she said, "From the moment a woman learns that she is pregnant, she loves and cherishes this child. I cherished Jack. He may have been taken from me, but he will walk beside me in spirit and heart eternally." The murderer was convicted and sentenced to 25 years to life. She felt that "justice had been done" and that Jack's death was vindicated.

With the trial behind her by a few weeks, Donna stated, "I am beginning to take baby steps to join the living." These steps were halting, at best. The relief experienced by the ending of the trial and subsequent sentencing of the murderer was short lived. Donna resumed her work life and was able to maintain the hours and commitments there, but she was not engaged in any other aspect of life. The relationship that she had had with her boyfriend ended rather abruptly after the trial. In Donna's eyes, he was staying with her for the duration of the trial and was biding his time until he initiated a breakup. She experienced his departure from her life as another loss despite the distance that had grown between them over the months since Jack's disappearance.

This additional loss created a bereavement situation for Donna that Kastenbaum (1969) described as bereavement overload in the literature. In this situation the griever is so emotionally depleted or physically exhausted that he or she is unable to mourn the current loss. Although Donna was upset about the breakup of this long-term relationship, she described herself as "numb to any more pain" and felt "...so defeated that it did not matter that he was gone." At this point in her counseling, on the basis of the level of depression and emotional dissolution, the counselor suggested that Donna consider antidepressant medication. She was open to this suggestion and consulted a physician for a prescription that she filled and began taking. The medication became effective after 10 days and she experienced a slight elevation of mood that was welcomed.

In counseling, Donna was encouraged to air her despair. As the year passed, Donna was helped by the medication and she continued in counseling mainly for supportive work. At the 1-year anniversary of Jack's death, Donna, although more functional (able to navigate her work and nondemanding friendships), experienced a difficult and sad period. She withdrew from some of her social commitments for a span of time and there was tension in her relationship with her daughter.

Since the disappearance and murder, Donna's relationship with her daughter vacillated between being very loving and very volatile. There were times when her daughter blamed Donna for what happened. In counseling this was addressed frequently, with the counselor repeating that no one controls the behavior of another to that extent. There was some discussion of having a joint session between Donna and her daughter to ease the tension and relieve an area of stress for Donna, but the daughter refused.

Donna has remained in counseling. It has been 18 months since the murder was discovered. Donna struggles with her grief; sometimes it is more pronounced than at other times, but in general she is able to engage more in life. She sometimes slips into a denial mode in which she pretends that Jack is still alive and that soothes her for the moment. She can mention his name and not cry, which she feels is a major accomplishment. She says that she "cannot imagine that I'll never see him again." As a mother, she will always feel incomplete but has slowly begun to taste life again; some days are easier than others.

Issues for the Counselor

The pain expressed by Donna was extremely potent. Frequently, it was "emotionally taxing" (Brice, 1991, p. 9) to be in the room with such anguish. The urge to fix her situation and soothe her pain was heartfelt but could not be acted upon. The knowledge that she had to express and feel her pain guided the work but the feeling of powerlessness was difficult to manage. There were times when it was tempting to extend session time, lower fees, and call after a session, but the blurring of some of these boundaries would have created a dependency on the counselor rather than on those in her world. In hindsight, it might have been better to suggest medication earlier in the counseling to ease some of Donna's pain, but it seemed better to have her go through the pain rather than to blunt it.

As Parkes (1993) pointed out, for the counselor "the sheer enormity of the outrage that has been committed against them (the bereaved parents) may be hard for us to bear and it is tempting for us to distance ourselves from their suffering" (p. 53) and, at times, that was the case. What was equally true was the desire to jump into Donna's life and hold her and protect her from the pain.

There was also the tendency for the counselor to overidentify with the circumstances of the bereaved mother. As a female counselor, and a parent, the recognition of the depth of the loss and what it would or could mean for the counselor made empathy readily available and fear close behind. To be able to do this type of counseling in which death is ever present and pain and sadness are an accompaniment, the counselor sometimes must simultaneously join and distance from the client. The joining helps with empathy and the ability to more readily engage with the circumstances and pain, but the distance from the counselor's reality also has to be stressed. If the counselor loses his or her objectivity, acting as though it were his or her situation, the needed distance to be steady and more in control and focused is jeopardized.

It was very gratifying to watch Donna begin to emerge. Slowly, she began to rebuild her life and expand herself after months of extreme constriction. To imagine her as whole and fully engaged in life is an unrealizable expectation; to actually see her eased and gently touching life is rewarding. In bereavement work, that is major growth.

CHAPTER

Bereavement After Miscarriage: The Man's Experience

The Case—Mario

When Maria announced she was pregnant, Mario was ecstatic beyond words. It had finally happened; they had been trying to get pregnant for so many years. Maria (24 years old) worked in the local school cafeteria and Mario (25 years old) was a custodian in the same school. They had been saving money for a baby since they were married 6 years ago in Puerto Rico. They planned to start a family soon after they came to the United States, but Maria had not been able to conceive. There had been a lot of anguish and some tension between them about this, but it all vanished the day she returned from the doctor with her news. Actually, they had bought a pregnancy test kit that showed she was pregnant but they still wanted the final confirmation from the doctor. Maria and Mario both called their parents in Puerto Rico to tell them their wonderful news.

The plan was for Maria to work as long as possible because every bit of money would be needed for the baby. They agreed that the basement apartment they rented would be fine for a while but they assumed that by time the baby was 2 years old, they would have to find a larger place to rent. Things were going well; all went according to plan until the 20th week. By then Maria thought she had begun to feel the baby moving around, and they had a sonogram done and they knew they were having a son. They were thrilled. But then Maria started spotting. She and Mario went to the doctor immediately and Maria was examined; they were told that she might be having a miscarriage and that she should go home and stay in bed for a few days. She did as ordered.

For the rest of that week and over the weekend, Maria barely moved from the bed, but every time she did, the spotting would recur. On Monday she stood to go to the bathroom, felt a stabbing pain and a rush and within moments was bleeding profusely. Mario carried her to the car and they went to the local emergency room, where they were told that the pregnancy was over and that she would need a dilatation and curettage to stop the bleeding and to remove any fetal tissue from her uterus. The procedure was done that afternoon and Mario took her home from the hospital the following evening. Maria was no longer pregnant and their hopes and dreams were shattered.

While in the hospital, Maria cried almost constantly; Mario stood by her and also cried. But a strange thing happened to him just before they were to leave the hospital. He experienced what is known in the Latino community as an *ataque de nervios* (attack of nerves). He felt light headed, and he fell to the ground and suffered a series of convulsive bodily movements. The attack lasted maybe a minute, and Mario got off the floor, not sure what had happened. Maria watched as Mario had his attack; she had seen her grandmother in Puerto Rico have such an attack and although she was unsettled by it, she decided to let it pass.

After they arrived home, Mario helped Maria settle in and it happened again. This time, Mario's ataques de nervios lasted several minutes and Maria became frightened. Despite being weakened from her hospital procedure and miscarriage, she struggled to help Mario get up and decided that she would call their family doctor, a second cousin who had been in the United States for many years. He suggested that Mario might benefit from some counseling, that perhaps the stress of the past few days had been too much for him. Maria insisted that Mario see a counselor, which he reluctantly agreed to do. She did tell him that she would be glad to join him after he talked to the counselor alone.

Relevant History

Mario was a hardworking man. He was educated through high school. His family was large—he had three brothers and two sisters—and they had lived in Puerto Rico in a poor, working-class area. He had learned some English while in high school but his first language was Spanish. He met Maria while in high school, and they married soon after graduation. The young couple moved to the city and struggled to find jobs. The impetus to leave Puerto Rico was the lack of jobs but the decision to leave and come to the United States had been difficult for him. He was leaving all of his family in Puerto Rico and he felt very tied to his parents and siblings. Maria had two sisters and a few cousins in the United States who were comfortably settled, so the decision to emigrate was easier for her.

Mario was the oldest of his siblings and he felt a strong connection to them. He felt a keen sense of responsibility to care for his parents. This sense of responsibility by the oldest son is consistent with his heritage. However, there were few jobs in Puerto Rico and the promise of employment in the United States was a powerful incentive. Maria's insistence to leave, as she was eager to join her sisters and cousins, was also a compelling factor. As a dutiful son, Mario called his family frequently and would have liked to be able to fly home more often for various family occasions, but the couple had pledged to save for a house and family, and money was tight.

As a Latino, Mario had been exposed to the machismo (maleness) of his culture: there was the imperative to be strong yet sympathetic, caring, loving, and emotionally restrained. The traditional aspect of their marriage was culturally consistent, with Mario assuming the male tasks of repair, heavy lifting, and car maintenance, and Maria assuming the more domestic tasks. He was happy with Maria even though his temper sometimes erupted. It did not happen often but, as he said, "When I get angry, I blow up and then feel sorry soon afterward. But, Maria knows I love her."

Conceptual Issues

The two parallel influences of culture and loss due to miscarriage need to be explored to fully understand this bereavement experience.

Cultural Influences

The influence of Puerto Rican and Latino culture and its view of death is a consideration in this case. There is an underlying acceptance of death in the Puerto Rican culture. As a cultural norm, Puerto Ricans envision the dead in an invisible world inhabited by spirits. These spirits have influence over the living (Garcia-Preto, 1982). Death is not seen as an end to one's existence but rather as an opportunity to enter another dimension with the deceased while being given an opportunity to serve God and the community (Paulino, 2000). Despite this belief system, Puerto Ricans experience death as a powerful loss and mourn deeply. In a study, for example, comparing grief reactions of 50 Latino and 50 Anglo individuals to sudden unexpected death, Latinos scored significantly higher grief intensity scores than the other groups (Grabowski & Frantz, 1992).

Typically, the Latino family meets together when there is a death to comfort each other and pray for the dead. The physical and emotional support of the family and the community provides nurturance for the bereaved. Religious rituals, masses, rosaries, and novenas are said to help the dead and the living. The funeral can be a highly emotional affair with crying, screaming, and ataques (Garcia-Preto, 1982). Heart palpitations, gasping for breath, and screaming may occur in the deeply bereaved. These are accepted as natural expressions of grief because in most Latino cultures, emotional states are not conceived as separate from bodily reactions. At the same time, there are those who will experience the death and funeral of a loved one in very contained and controlled ways, with stoic resignation and acceptance. This response is equally acceptable and frequent (Falicov, 1999).

Ataques de nervios—what Mario experienced at home and in the hospital—is a culturally specific behavior of Latinos. The term is used to describe a broad range of reactions and is seen as an expression of strong emotion. "Latino mental health professionals have argued that the ataque de nervios is a culturally recognized and sanctioned expression of emotion which should be understood as a form of communication. ...Ataques de nervios communicate particular types of distress about powerlessness and anger" (Guarnaccia, DeLaCancela, & Carrillo, 1989, pp. 49–50).

In summary, the Latino expressiveness concerning death can range from a muted response to a powerful emotional expression concerning the loss. The acceptance of death permeates the experience of loss whereas the belief that the deceased is influential in the lives of the living is central. In some respects, this makes a death more acceptable and keeps the memory of the deceased as a vital influence.

Miscarriage—The Man's Experience

Miscarriage, or spontaneous abortion, is the natural termination of a pregnancy before the fetus is considered viable (20–24 weeks) and occurs in as many as 15% to 20% of pregnancies (Al-Fozan & Tuloulis, 2003). When miscarriage occurs, the typical response of most people is to be concerned for and sympathize more strongly with the woman; it is unusual for the male partner's response to the miscarriage to be considered in any substantive way. This obscuring of the male response is not surprising considering the extent of the physical involvement of women relative to men (Johnson &

Puddifoot, 1996). When the experience of men has been discussed it is usually in relation to that of the woman, with the man's role defined as being supportive of the woman. However, recent existing research suggests that the grief response for the male partner equals, and in some instances, exceeds that of the woman.

As an area of concern and subsequent research, the reaction of the partner to a miscarriage began to be studied in the 1990s. Several studies point to a variety of findings. Johnson and Puddifoot (1996) studied the responses of 126 men whose partners had miscarried prior to the 25th week. Using the Perinatal Grief Scale (Toedter, Lasker, & Alhadeff, 1988) and the Impact of Events Scale (Horowitz, Wilner, & Alvarez, 1979), they found high levels of grief for the partners, similar to the grief norms observed for the women. Number of children premiscarriage was not statistically significant nor was previous experience with miscarriage for men or women as a factor in the intensity of the grief experience. The longer term of the pregnancy was predictive of greater levels of grief for the men. These findings—that partners experienced high levels of unrelieved grief—were explained by the authors, who noted that the men found that they received little or no institutional or social support from friends or colleagues; many friends simply avoided the subject. The suggestion within this research is that levels of social and institutional support could help to mitigate partner grief.

Beutel, Wilner, Deckardt, Von Rad, and Weiner (1996) studied the responses of 56 couples at three stages after the miscarriage—immediately after, at 6 months, and at 12 months—to try to determine whether there were any differences in the grief patterns of the men and women over time. Initially, the women were assessed as grieving more intensely than their partners; men cried less, felt less need to talk, and were not pained when seeing another pregnant woman. For both men and women, the grief response waned over time and the giving up of their personal hopes, expectations, and fantasies about their unborn child was a struggle. In a study of 19 couples (Alderman et al., 1998), gender differences emerged, with women reporting more grief and stress than their partners, but the men's level of grief was very high. The explanation offered by the researchers was that women not only experience the pregnancy loss but also experience a physical trauma. In both of these studies, although the gender differences are noteworthy, what is more important is that the grief scores for the men were high although not as high as for the women. The bereavement needs of the unseen and underacknowledged male griever need to be addressed.

Conway and Russell (2000) studied responses to miscarriage of 39 women and 37 partners immediately after the pregnancy loss and 2 to 4 months later. Scores on the first administration of the Perinatal Grief

Scale showed that, in contrast to previous studies, initially the partners scored significantly higher than the women and on the second administration, months later, the men again scored higher levels but the difference was not statistically significant. This higher score for the men was noteworthy. The researchers concluded that miscarriage has to be seen as a significant event, with the majority of women and partners still experiencing feelings of loss up to 4 months afterward.

A very interesting finding (Johnson & Puddifoot, 1996; Puddifoot & Johnson, 1997) is the impact on the grief experience for the men who saw the ultrasound of their baby. "The contemporary routine use of ultrasound monitoring has drawn many men into the institutional aspects of the process much earlier and has provided a tangible image of the developing child to both partners" (Johnson & Puddifoot, 1996, p. 315). The authors speculated that the viewing of the scan and the ability to determine the gender of the baby contribute to the grief experience.

This brief overview of studies points to the fact that men are often deeply affected by miscarriage, and whether it rivals or equals that of women seems unimportant. This underacknowledged cohort suffers and this suffering has to be acknowledged.

Suggestions for Intervention

In this section I discuss the intervention strategy from the perspective of individual counseling for the man, and couples and group counseling, as each has its place and is effective with this type of bereavement situation.

Individual Counseling for the Partner

What became apparent through the cited research is that men experience the miscarriage as a profoundly emotional event with reaction levels at or near that of the women. For both parents, the pregnancy loss turns a self-enhancing event into a time of emotional upheaval and potential devastation (Canadian Paediatric Society, 2001). Although the grief experience is shared, the women suffer with the loss as well as with the physical manifestations of the miscarriage. Initially, this casts the partner in the role of caregiver and caretaker for the woman. The woman may be sedated, in pain, physically weary, and in a generally compromised physical condition needing care. Emotionally she may be devastated, exacerbated by hormonal changes, and feel guilty, blameful, and despairing. The natural helping effort is usually toward her, leaving the partner bereft without much support.

Although the grieving may be intense, it generally abates over time for both the partner and the woman, so that extended counseling would generally not be warranted. Counseling would be warranted if the grief seems to overwhelm functioning and profound depression occurs. If counseling is suggested or there is a felt need—by the woman, her partner, or the couple—there are certain guidelines that underlie the helping effort.

Generally, men are more reluctant to discuss feelings than women, especially if they feel that they should be caring for the women, disregarding their own needs at the time. Men and women deal with feelings in different ways; often men will sublimate feelings into work to deny their anguish. There is also the social expectation that the main role for the partner is to be there for support, that the man has to be strong for his partner and in control of the situation, and that he is expected to comfort the woman because she experienced a traumatic event (Abboud & Liamputtong, 2003). This support role for the man may be very difficult to articulate if he is grieving as the research suggests. This strain must be acknowledged in the counseling effort.

If the male partner is seen in individual counseling, the initial effort must be to recognize and legitimize the loss. Parental grief is facilitated when those people who surround the parents, especially the partners, honor the fact that a significant loss has occurred (Nichols, 1989). Specifically the counselor should be engaging the partner in a discussion of the events leading up to the pregnancy (how long had they been trying to conceive, were there any previous gynecological problems) of the progression of the pregnancy (were there any difficulties with eating or throwing up, how long had she been pregnant, did they know the gender of the baby) and of whether they had an ultrasound, selected a name, arranged space in the house for the new life, and so forth. If this is the first miscarriage, the partner may be more optimistic that the miscarriage is an isolated event, but if it is a repeated episode, there may be a deeper level of despair. The counselor should ask the following questions: How did you manage the first (other) miscarriage? What did you tell the other children, parents, in-laws? Were they supportive?

If this is the first miscarriage, questions include the following: What happened during this miscarriage? How did it feel to go through this with her, to realize that the pregnancy was over? How did your life and plans change with this event? What were you feeling as the miscarriage unfolded? Have you been able to express your feelings to others? Have you cried?

Although some of the questions may be difficult to respond to, talking about the pregnancy in detail, articulating the hopes, expectations, and dreams about the new life, helps the partner to express his emotions about the lost pregnancy and the losses that accompany the event.

Engagement around issues of guilt and blame needs to be aired. Often the partner blames the woman for the miscarriage but is constrained from admitting it. It could be that she was a smoker or did not eat right—or something along these lines—that the partner feels was a contributing factor. Sometimes the partner wants to blame the medical establishment for not offering the right advice or care. The reality of the blame is secondary to the need for the partner to express his feelings about causality.

Although the men do not suffer the physical pain, one man in the Johnson and Puddifoot (1996) study made a very valid point. He said, "We don't have the physical pain of the death like the women, but let me tell you, we have it worse, because the physical pain for women helps them through the psychological pain. We are just left with it going round and round in the head" (pp. 322–323). The counseling effort has to relieve the partner of what is going "round and round" in his head: the sadness, the disturbed view of the immediate future, the concern for the woman, and concern that this could happen again. Keeping the focus on the partner and his feelings while not obscuring the pain that the woman is experiencing and his reaction to it is important.

Many men feel useless and unable to deal effectively with the anguish the women are experiencing. Normalizing of the emotional reaction of the woman can be relieving to her male partner, and stressing the need for him to be supportive while urging him to share some of his emotions with her is important. Explaining to the partner that sadness is appropriate to the situation may help the man make peace with his current role.

Couples Counseling and Groups

As this is a situation that affects the couple, the counselor often suggests that a couple be seen together. The focus of this effort may be to help the couple explore differences in their responses to the miscarriage. Questions that should be explored include the following: How have you each responded to the other? Have you been supportive and helpful to the other? Are there discrepancies in emotional expression? Could you each be doing more? What can we learn from each other that can make this bereavement period easier? As a couple, how have you handled disruptive events in the past or handled other losses? The counselor should discuss the meaning that the pregnancy held for them as a couple, define the unique personal meaning that the pregnancy loss carries for each of them, and develop a strategy for nurturing of the other. For some couples, just being able to air their emotional differences and expectations is helpful; having a place to discuss this with professional guidance is often a very liberating and facilitating step (Black, 1991).

Groups for couples or individuals who have had pregnancy loss provide emotional support and information. Often these groups are offered by a hospital; referral to a support group is a viable option for the parents individually or as a couple. Counselors need to be aware of what group opportunities exist in their community to be able to refer a couple or individual to them. A specialized group for those experiencing miscarriage can offer critically needed support and validation of their experience by connecting with others who share the same loss. The group members can provide hope to other members who may be at a different point in their grief journey. Members may enhance their self-esteem through helping others through the grief experience. Couples' groups allow both members of the couple to express their emotions, thoughts, and feelings in a safe environment encouraged by the support of others; couples are often spurred by the revelations of other members. This can promote a strengthening of the couple's communications and relationship. Sometimes counselors need to suggest a group experience and urge individuals or couples to consider this option.

Major Issues in This Case

Mario was reluctant to seek any form of help for his reactions to the miscarriage. Culturally, this was not a place for a Latino who is expected to handle all things with equanimity and control. However, Maria had insisted that he seek help, and the two ataques de nervios that he experienced made it impossible for him to refuse Maria's insistence.

Mario, who came for counseling a week after the miscarriage, began by saying that he was basically OK with the miscarriage and that he thought that it was an isolated event and that they would start trying to conceive another child very soon. He presented a confident exterior. He added that he really did not want to be in counseling and that he was doing this for Maria. When he was asked a series of questions that brought him closer to the event—What were your reactions when you found out that Maria was pregnant? How did you feel looking at the sonogram? Did you want a son? When you knew the gender of the baby what was your reaction?—some of his confidence and detachment began to dissolve. In the initial session with Mario, the counselor reassured him that many men find this a very difficult experience, that they are supposed to be strong for the woman, but that it is usual for men to be very sad and upset when they lose a baby. He almost had to be persuaded to face some of the emotions related to his loss.

Mario admitted that he felt very sad when he thought about "the son who was supposed to be here" and acknowledged he had really wanted their first child to be a boy: "I was so excited when I saw the sonogram and the doctor told us it was a boy." Now, he did not know what would happen. He admitted that he was worried about Maria and had been scared to death when he saw all the blood on the day of the miscarriage: "I rushed into the bathroom and there was blood everywhere," he said, "and I grabbed a towel and grabbed Maria and we rushed to the car. I thought that she was dying." The hospital stay was a blur to Mario, as was his ataque de nervios. He had heard that people had these attacks but he could not imagine that it had happened to him; he was also a bit embarrassed to admit that it had occurred.

Consistent with cultural beliefs, Mario felt that their unborn son was going to join others in his and Maria's family and he took some comfort from that belief. He mentioned that he was angry with God and that he had been praying daily, even before Maria got pregnant, that they would have a healthy son. He felt that he "couldn't trust God anymore."

When he spoke of Maria, he said that he was not sure how he was going to deal with her, "as she seemed so upset, unable to talk a lot of the time and she didn't seem interested in him or anyone or anything." He admitted that he was struggling not to lose patience with her. He said, "I am trying very hard to be a comfort and take care of the house and things but she seems not to notice." Here, again, was an opportunity to educate Mario regarding what Maria was going through and normalize her behavior for him. As Mario really did not know what to expect, he thought that something very terrible was going on with Maria. He also felt that she was being very abrupt with him and sometimes her moodiness made him feel that she was angry with him and not the situation. Mario, in other words, was trying to do everything for Maria and make it better but Maria did not seem any better and Mario was feeling rejected and frustrated. This dynamic made it hard for Mario to express his own grief to Maria.

The trajectory of Maria's bereavement had to be explained to Mario because he was feeling his not doing enough was the explanation for her moodiness. He seemed somewhat relieved to be able to understand Maria's experience, and he acknowledged that he "did not have much experience with this sort of thing and did not know exactly how it should be handled." He also said that he had very few people to talk to about the experience as most of the men he knew "stayed away from these sort of discussions and all they would say was that they should start again soon to make another baby."

Mario did not stay in counseling long; there were five sessions, two in the first week and then once a week for 3 weeks. The focus of the sessions was on his reactions, with each session probing further into his grief feelings. Maria, of course, was a major concern, but by the end of the first month, she began to pick up the pieces of her life. Because Maria seemed to be gaining her equilibrium, couples counseling was not pursued. Mario, consistent with some of the literature, had much unexpressed feeling about the event; surely the loss of the baby was prominent but he stated that he had been "even more afraid that Maria would die and that would have been unimaginable." Each session sought to explore his feelings and even to educate him to the frequency and normalcy of them. When we parted, Mario was very appreciative and suggested, "If our next child is a girl, I want to name her after you." Perhaps they did.

Issues for the Counselor

The sadness of this man was very potent. In responding to him, what was noteworthy was the contrast between the exterior and interior man. It was crucial to be able to understand the impact of culture on his bearing and emotional receptivity, as beneath the cultural veneer was a very emotional person.

The length, breadth, and depth of the bereavement over miscarriage differ depending on a variety of factors. These factors include the age and stage of the parents, whether there are other children or the couple or mother is childless, whether the pregnancy was planned or unplanned, how many miscarriages the couple has sustained, how long they had been trying to become pregnant, the degree of physical trauma to the would-be mother, whether there were problems in conception, and the emotional mettle of the couple. Each of these factors must be considered and evaluated when developing an assessment as to the degree and potency of the grief. It requires that the counselor be attuned to any and all of these nuances and factors in the loss experience. Much of this content can be assessed early with the bereft, and the work of legitimizing the loss and supporting the grief can ensue.

Issues of life-experience overlap may be a factor for the counselor. As miscarriages occur in such a high percentage of pregnancies, there is the possibility that the counselor may have been touched by this experience and is reliving it through the bereavement of the client(s). As well, the counselor could be struggling with personal issues related to pregnancy and childbirth. Boundary issues must be attended to in order to be able to respond fully to the client(s).

The imperative of cultural awareness, always a theme in our work, is especially important for a full understanding of the impact of the miscarriage loss. In many respects, it explains much of what Mario was experiencing and helps the counselor offer culturally appropriate suggestions. Working with a machismo male can pose some conflicts and struggles in terms of attitudes toward women and their role and treatment. As with any cultural difference, it is to be respected and not necessarily challenged. Although strongly machismo, Mario was able to reveal the soft side of himself, the side that was in pain and anguish over his and his wife's loss. It was very touching; it was impossible not to be touched by his grief despite the fact that he healed fairly quickly. Maria's sadness lasted much longer, perhaps because she had felt the child developing within her.

I hope that Mario and Maria have realized their dreams.

Bereavement in Wartime

The Case—Alice

When Steve (19 years old) enlisted in the army, Alice and Dan were confused. Their family had always been on the liberal end of political thinking, they voted Democrat, they were essentially antiwar, and they thought that they had instilled a pacifist mind-set in their two sons. So Steve's decision to enlist after graduating high school was a source of surprise. Steve said that he was not ready for college, that he might never want to go, that he could not decide what he wanted to do, and that maybe the army would give him a sense of direction. And if he decided later on to go to college, the army would pay for it. Respectful of their son's decision, despite a lot of heated discussion, Alice and Dan said their good-byes to Steve with trepidation and concern for his welfare.

He entered basic training in September, many months before the situation in the Iraq had reached war levels, and was shipped off to Europe after the first of the year. When the United States officially declared war on Iraq, his unit was ordered to a desert location, waiting to be deployed to the front. Steve was conscientious about writing to his parents and younger brother, Pete. They were a close family and this was the longest that he had been away from home. He seemed to like army life and wrote to his parents that he was not scared of being in battle should he see active combat in a war with Iraq. Steve wrote to his family about life in the desert, the endless daytime heat and nighttime cold, the nonstop winds with sand covering everything, some of the other soldiers, having seen many Iraqi citizens, and how terrible, but plentiful, the food was. Alice and Dan cherished the letters from Steve and found themselves reading them several times over. They missed Steve and, of course, were worried about him.

He had been in Iraq for several weeks when war was declared. His unit received orders to head to Baghdad and they began the trek north, encountering almost no resistance or active combat.

Alice (51 years old) was a librarian and Dan (53 years old) was the manager of a car dealership. They had been married for 29 years and lived comfortably in a suburb. They had many friends and were active in a number of organizations in their community. Although their external lives seemed to go on with no apparent change after Steve left, both Alice and Dan were edgy, anxious, and upset as the war effort became more serious. The daily news briefs found Alice, Dan, and Pete glued to the television, hungry for details. The son of one of their neighbors also was stationed in Iraq and the families swapped news stories every evening.

Steve was the 10th soldier to die in Iraq. It was the fourth day of official fighting and his unit had been moving steadily north toward the capital. The call came from a central office in Washington, D.C. The details were sketchy but snipers had assaulted Steve and three other men. Two of the men died and two were seriously injured. Steve became a casualty of war. But a casualty of war is not just a dead soldier; add to the casualty list all family members and loved ones of the slain. Alice, Dan, and Pete also became casualties of war when Steve fell.

Steve's body was returned to the United States within days, and a full military funeral was performed. Throughout the days of waiting for the body and during the time of the funeral, Alice, Dan, and Pete held together. The community, for the most part, showed their respects, with some notable absences of friends they thought would have visited or noted Steve's death. When some of the activity of the death began to subside—family from out of town departed, the funeral and wake had been performed—Alice became "unglued," to use her word. She had been stoic and brave throughout the funeral period but was unable to continue, as she lamented that "my heart is broken, my son is dead, and for such a stupid reason."

She went to see the pastor of her church with the hope of gaining some perspective, as her anger and sadness were becoming too much for her to bear. He was soothing but did not really help, and she asked him to refer her to someone who could do bereavement counseling with her. She was terribly conflicted, she knew, as she had not wanted Steve to go into the army and "blamed him for what happened even though it is not rational." She also was depressed, frightened, and frozen. "I can't seem to find any energy to go to do anything," she exclaimed. Dan was not interested in counseling. "He was withdrawing but that was his way," explained Alice. Two weeks after the funeral, Alice entered counseling.

Relevant History

Alice was adopted as an infant. Her mother was a teenager and had decided to put her baby up for adoption. The adoptive parents were very loving; Alice had grown up in a home with another adopted girl whom she regarded as her sister. The family had moved around the country because her father was transferred frequently due to job changes. By high school, the family had moved five times and with each move Alice resolved that if she ever had children she would stay put in one place for life. Despite the moves, the family provided a stable emotional environment and Alice felt loved, cared about, and good about herself as she grew up.

Her college years were spent at one out-of-state university where she graduated with a bachelor's degree in library science. She met Dan 2 weeks after she took a job in the university library. He was attending the business school, studying for a master's degree in management. They began dating and married upon his graduation. They settled down to a comfortable life, waited several years to have children, as they wanted to solidify their professional lives and save some money. They were active in their church, and the boys soon became the center of their lives.

Alice prided herself on her children, marriage, and professional life, in that order. She had no history of depression or other emotional problems. Periodically, over the years, she had wondered about her birth mother but felt no desire to search for or know her. Basically, Alice was content in her marriage and the various roles she articulated. She was looking forward to retirement which would happen at age 60 and hoped someday she would have several grandchildren to take care of. When Steve announced his interest in joining the armed forces, she felt a sense of foreboding that, sadly, was realized.

Conceptual Issues

As a form of bereavement, wartime death has received almost no attention. This is an odd omission, as war has been part of the lives of all of us at some point in our history. The few studies that have been done focus on the reaction of parents; no studies are available about spouse or partner reactions.

Despite this limitation of available literature and studies, I offer an explanation as to why this form of bereavement can be so difficult. Wartime death carries a certain level of complexity beyond the "usual" for a variety of reasons. War is controversial and, within the debate, attitudes about participation and killing are woven into the bereavement experience. I describe the few empirical studies that have been reported in the literature.

The Complexity of Wartime Bereavement

Whenever there is a death of an adult child, the parents, spouse, or partner is going to suffer traumatic grief. When the death is related to war, it becomes magnified, as it is a vivid reminder to all that the world is not a safe and orderly place. For parents the death is experienced as untimely as children are not supposed to predecease their parents. In addition, the various stages of development have been traversed and adult-to-adult relationships with the children have been created that make the loss even more painful (Archer, 1999).

There are a variety of factors that affect the wartime bereavement experience. The service person's and mourner's philosophical agreement with war in general and the specific reasons for this war are a strong predictive factor in the bereavement experience. If the family or service person is philosophically against the war effort, a level of bitterness may enter the bereavement experience. If the family is supportive of the war effort and the service person is not, acrimony about participating in the war may be present (Beder, 2003b).

Wars have special meaning in that a cause is fought for and the responses of the bereaved may reflect particular strongly held values about fighting and killing. The response of mourners may be especially bitter if they perceive the death as having no point, as serving no purpose or a purpose they cannot support (Raphael, 1983). This also speaks to the general attitude within the country regarding the war effort, the political climate, and degree of support (Beder, 2003b). Rando (1993) noted that the extent of support for the mourner is always a buffering aspect of any bereavement situation. If there is general support for the war effort, deceased heroes are celebrated; if the war is not supported, deceased heroes are denied adequate recognition and the bereavement may be affected in a negative way (p. 521).

For the mourner, the service person's attitude about going to war may be a factor in the bereavement. Did the service person volunteer or was he or she drafted? Either way, it may influence the survivor's feelings about the death. The type and circumstances of the death are also important, as the mourner is left with a legacy of imagining how the deceased experienced his or her last moments.

These factors, above and beyond the usual anticipated responses in a death, can influence the bereavement trajectory for the wartime survivor.

Wartime Bereavement—What Is Known

War death and the ensuing bereavement have received minimal attention in the bereavement literature. This gap in the literature suggests an area for further study that would be a welcome contribution to extant knowledge. Next I discuss the existing studies and their findings.

The self-concept of 29 parents who lost sons in the 1973 Yom Kippur War in Israel were compared with the self-concept of 29 Israeli adults, with the finding that the bereaved ranked poorly in self-concept, with a higher tendency toward depression and a high frequency of somatic complaints (Gay, 1982). A few years later, Rubin (1989–1990) compared 42 Israeli parents who had lost sons in a war an average of 9 years before with a group of parents who had lost 1-year-old children around the same time. The bereaved parents of the soldiers showed higher current levels of grief and higher levels of recalled grief than parents who had lost a young child. The findings suggest that the ability to produce another child may modulate the grief experience, as those parents who had lost young children had the capacity to produce more offspring whereas the older parents who had lost adult children did not. This study suggests that wartime bereavement is a more powerful experience than losing a young child. Rubin's (1991–1992) second study included 102 parents who had lost sons in war 4 to 13 years before the study. These bereaved parents showed higher levels of grief and anxiety than did a control group of 73 nonbereaved adults despite the length of time since their loss. This study suggests that grief does not necessarily abate over time.

Fifty-two couples who had lost sons in combat were compared with 50 couples who had not experienced the death of a son either in wartime or in any other way. The bereavement deaths had occurred from 2 to 11 years before. The bereaved parents experienced less meaning and purpose in life compared with the nonbereaved parents; the bereaved couples, as a cohort, experienced poorer health status. The researcher concluded that the study demonstrates the devastating and long-lasting nature of wartime death (Florian, 1989–1990, p. 100).

The most recent study looked at long-term grief of 29 older parents, ages 60 to 87 years, whose sons were killed during military service in Israel. The length of bereavement was 11 to 33 years. The researchers documented that grief continued along the life span unaffected by other developmental processes or life events; the inner attachment to the deceased child was never relinquished (Malkinson & Bar-Tur, 1999).

These studies document the devastating and lifelong struggle experienced by those parents bereft because of war.

Suggestions for Intervention

Worden's (2002) task model is most appropriate in addressing the needs of individuals, parents, and family survivors of wartime bereavement. The strength of this model is that it asks the mourner to take steps on his or her own behalf to begin the process of healing with the understanding that grief resolution is not a linear process but a number of sometimes very small steps. The utility of the model for the counselor is that it creates a path and planned approach to follow and helps to locate the mourner in the bereavement process. The model is especially useful when applied to those struggling with sudden, unexpected death.

The model's four tasks for the survivor are as follows:

Task 1: To accept the reality of the loss
Task 2: To work through the pain of the grief
Task 3: To adjust to a new environment in which the deceased is missing
Task 4: To emotionally relocate the deceased and move on with life. (Worden, 2002, pp. 27–37)

Accepting the reality of the loss, the first task, requires the mourner to drop any defenses or denial about the death and face the fact that the deceased will never return and that reunion is not possible. Many people can accept the finality of death on an intellectual level but will not embrace their loss emotionally. This is very difficult for those who are grieving, as they are afraid of the emotional toll and the overwhelming feelings that accompany acceptance. For some people, the funeral ritual begins their acceptance. In wartime bereavement there often is no body to bury or it may take a long time for the body to be shipped home from a faraway place. This delays the funeral rituals and may delay the acceptance of the death, allowing the denial to remain in place. Kalish (1985) commented on denial as it relates to death, stating that it is the mind's way of insulating the individual from knowledge of the death and the loss. If the service person has been gone for a period of time, it is possible to pretend that he or she is still away fighting the war. In the counseling effort, the strategy is to keep the mourner talking about the deceased, to ask questions about the deceased, and to use his or her name to try to bring the deceased into the counseling room and give him or her a reality.

The second task, working through the pain of the grief, involves experiencing the pain of the separation, the sadness and emptiness that the death has created in the life of the survivor. Sometimes the pain is excruciating and may seem unbearable as the mourner comes to terms with the reality that he or she will never see or touch the deceased ever again. The counselor has to normalize the pain and allow it to surface by being supportive, present, and available during this phase. It may mean seeing the mourner more frequently so he or she knows that the counselor is a stable support system. The counselor may have to encourage the expression of these emotions as a way of easing the intensity of the feelings. The counselor has to question the mourner about his or her emotional reactions and has to ask what he or she anticipates life will be like without the deceased, what will be missed most, and what was special about the deceased. These questions force the mourner to give voice to his or her thoughts and feelings about the loss. This task is seen as crucial, as the negation and nonexpression of these feelings may lead to long-term emotional consequences.

Society's reaction to the war effort may be a factor in completion of this task. If society is generally in favor of war, then the fallen service person will be seen as a hero and support may be more forthcoming; if there is disdain for the war effort, there may be a withdrawal of support. If the war effort is prolonged and there have been many deaths, the societal support may be limited with less social support being forthcoming. When social support is not forthcoming, grieving parents tend to feel isolated and the pain of their grief is intensified.

Adjusting to the environment in which the deceased is missing is the third task. With this task, the survivor must make three levels of adjustment—external, internal, and spiritual. The external adjustments are the day-to-day roles and responsibilities that have to be assumed in the absence of the deceased; the internal shifts require a new self-definition as either a widow, a widower, or a bereaved parent, which requires a more complex adjustment; the final area, spiritual, requires the mourner to make peace with a revised view of the world in which equity and linearity are not necessarily the norm. The external adjustments may be easier for the wartime bereaved because they have had to accommodate to the absence of the service person, assuming they have been away for an extended period of time.

The final task of emotionally relocating the deceased and moving on with life may never occur. As the studies have documented, the bereavement of wartime deaths seems to last much longer than other types of death and the ability to move on and reinvest in another life is limited. In the counseling, the effort should be in helping the bereaved find a secure spot for the deceased in their emotional lives while fostering the capacity to go forward. This occurs when the bereaved are secure that the deceased will always be a part of their emotional world. The mourner has to be reassured that moving ahead does not mean moving away. This is accomplished by making a statement such as "Moving away from sadness and death does not mean you have forgotten the deceased" or "You will always remember Steve no matter what; the goal of bereavement is for you to be able to remember Steve and feel less pain." These types of reassuring statements have to be made repeatedly to help the mourner let go of the deceased and begin the process of reintegrating into his or her world without fear of losing the memory of the deceased.

Worden's (2002) paradigm provides a template from which the counseling work can proceed. I have to reiterate that the bereavement trajectory is not necessarily linear or smooth with completion of each task in a sequential order. Tasks can have degrees of completion and will surely overlap; the healing will be slow as wartime death, as noted, has many levels of complexity.

Major Issues in This Case

Alice was new to counseling, having never sought the help of a mental health professional, and she carried some stereotypical attitudes that affected the initial engagement. Alice appeared depressed, somewhat unkempt, edgy, nervous, and sad at the first interview; she said that she had never "done this before" and felt embarrassed. She hoped that she would not see anyone she knew when she came into the office. When reassured that many people seek help for difficult situations, that essentially we would be talking with each other about her reactions (when she was ready), and that beginnings are usually difficult, she was able to relax somewhat. She explained that her son had been killed in the early days of the Iraq war and that she had not been able to feel much other than anger. When she was asked to detail who she was angry with, she said mostly herself and then Steve. Why herself? She said because she felt this was a "crazy war with no purpose other than a political agenda" and "I know that killing is wrong and I should have stopped Steve from enlisting. So while I am angry at him for being so stupid, I am more angry with myself because I knew this was a bad decision."

In assessing Alice along Worden's tasks, the counselor thought that Alice's anger was keeping her from accepting the reality of the loss, suggesting that she was at the beginning of the bereavement process. Two sessions were spent with Alice articulating her anger at Steve, Dan, the government, uncaring neighbors, the political system, and so on. Through these angry tirades, Alice was able to connect with the counselor and appeared to begin to feel that she could trust the helping process.

Alice tentatively began to accept Steve's death during the third session, after the counselor pointed out to her that "Steve was 19 years old when he made his own decision. He was aware of the risks and something in him accepted them." With this intervention, the decision to enlist was placed firmly on Steve, exonerating Alice and Dan from the decision-making process. The counselor hoped that this would begin to clear the way for Alice to move the anger to the side and allow other feelings to surface. It seemed to work, as Alice was able to let go of some of the anger that she was directing at herself. The timing of interventions can sometimes make the difference between a griever standing still or moving ahead. Some aspects of timing are intuitive and are being developed as we proceed in the work and become more skillful. Sometimes the timing is a matter of luck, with the griever being more ready than expected to be responsive. In general, if the counseling relationship has been developing well, if the counselor is demonstrating consistent empathy and responsiveness and is supportive and intuitive, and the griever is seen to be opening up more and more with each counseling session, creative and sometimes challenging interventions can be made and successfully converted into insight and relief.

Sometimes in the counseling, it is necessary to guide the bereaved toward his or her feelings and emotional side. The counselor's gently moving the focus away from the denial toward the feeling level can do this. Questions about feelings can be worded in the following way: "What does it feel like when you think about Steve being gone?" or "Are you in pain when you think of Steve?" or, in a more educational vein, "Sometimes anger covers other emotions; what do you think your anger is covering?" These interventions are designed to lead the individual into being able to articulate and experience some of his or her emotions. The underlying premise is that unexpressed emotions can create a more complicated, potentially pathological bereavement experience. The answer to the question of whether the underlying premise should be explained to the griever rests on the counselor's assessment of the intuitive capacity of the griever: if fairly sophisticated, then sharing the premise may be helpful. The suggestion to not share the premise is based on the fact that many grievers can give intellectual recognition to concepts without feeling the emotions. If a griever thinks he or she should be doing something, he or she might do it without the necessary attendant affect and emotion. This would defeat the effort.

Alice responded to the question about anger covering emotion, and she slowly allowed some of her pain to surface. She became a grieving mother at that point, more responding to the loss of her son irrespective of the circumstances. And the floodgates opened; she adored her child, he was the essence of her existence, he defined her more than any of her other roles, and she could not imagine that she would never see him again, never run her fingers through his hair, never hug him when he left the house, and never see him at the dinner table. All of these images and more washed over her, and she wept copiously.

Following Worden's suggestions, the counselor's strategy for keeping the denial at bay is to have the mourner talk about the deceased, to bring the mourner into the counseling room and almost make him or her alive so that he or she can ultimately be relinquished. Alice was asked to tell the counselor about early memories, favorite stories, and Steve's quirks, manner, good points and bad points, and so on. This prepares the mourner to enter the second task of working through the pain of the grief. Alice was quick to talk about Steve and some of his habits and ways. As she did this, she cried a lot, especially when thinking and talking about the early years before Pete was born and Alice had put Steve into the center of her world.

With the second task, the impact of wartime attitudes can be felt. In Alice's case, not all in her community supported the war effort; indeed, Alice and Dan themselves had not supported the war. The church community was generally supportive and helped the family go through the rituals of grief. Other friends, who shared the pacifist view of Alice and Dan, were somewhat more reserved; one friend was so taken aback when Steve enlisted that she stopped calling Alice for several weeks and they had only begun speaking again just before he was killed. Alice concluded, "People can be very peculiar. I have lost my son and that is all that matters. He was not a bad boy or did anything wrong. Just because we did not agree politically and some of our friends don't agree with the war, is no reason to forget that our son died." At this juncture, it would have been easy for Alice to go back to the anger mode and be able to cover her pain again, thus providng the nonlinear aspect of the bereavement experience. But the counseling proceeded, with a short step back, by subsequently asking Alice what she will miss about Steve, was she able to imagine life without him, were there things she wanted to say to him that she had not been able to say. Alice alternated between staying with the emotional feelings of the pain of grief and shifting back to her anger. This was to be expected and did not signify a serious setback in the task sequencing. The anger was safer and Alice was not one who stayed with emotions for a long time. Throughout the counseling, she knew the emotion of the grief was there and that she would use her anger to avoid feeling. She had articulated and experienced her emotions and would spend the rest of her life touching this grief at intervals when she was able.

The three areas of adjustment in task three are external, internal, and spiritual. The external adjustments for Alice, although significant, were manageable. She had anticipated that Steve would leave home to go to college and had been preparing herself for that for several years. Although staying put and being near home were core issues from her history, Alice had expected that Steve would "leave the nest" after high school. She was very surprised, however, when Steve decided to leave home for the army.

Aligned with external and internal adjustment is the shifting of roles within the household. Internal adjustment suggests a new self-definition. In Alice's case, and with a tremendous amount of pain connected to it, she had to acknowledge that her role of mother had shifted and that she was mother to only one child now rather than two. She still was a "mother" but it felt completely different to her. She questioned her ability to be a parent—"What kind of mother would let her son go to war?"—which became a struggle for her. The spiritual side of the adjustment, the recognition of a changed view of the world, found expression in Alice's commitment to her faith. She found herself questioning God and her lifelong religious beliefs. Many people who are bereaved find themselves questioning spiritual and religious beliefs (Talbot, 2002). Alice said that she "could not attend church and put my faith in a God who took innocent young men for foolish reasons." She began missing Sunday service and found herself feeling detached from her religious practices and beliefs. This caused something of a rift between Dan and Alice, as Dan believed that sanity for him was in being able to put his faith in a supreme being who had a plan for the world and his family.

During the first few months after Steve died, the relationship between Alice and Dan went through some changes and struggles. Although Dan was grief stricken, he appeared better able to negotiate his anger and emotions. He began to stay longer at his job at the car dealership and worked more weekends than ever before. It seemed that Dan was trying to obliterate his grief through work. Alice wanted Dan to come with her for counseling so they could both begin to address their grief together but he had refused. As a couple, they felt distant from one another for the first time in their marriage, and Alice talked about this but felt that they "would eventually find their way back to each other." If Alice had conveyed the sense that her marriage had been troubled, distant, or weak before the death of Steve, the counselor most probably would have put more effort into exploring Dan's response and how Dan and Alice related as a couple over Steve's death. But, in this case, Alice conveyed solidness about her marriage and seemed to want to explore her own bereavement issues with the confidence that the marriage was stable and supportive and that she needed to look at Steve's death on her own.

Alice may eventually accomplish the final task, moving on and detaching, but it is doubtful. This almost seems impossible for a parent to fully achieve, as a child is such an integral part of a parent's self-definition and being. Alice had to be reassured that letting Steve go in her thoughts did not mean that he would be forgotten. At best, Alice will be able to give to her other son Pete in a wholehearted manner, and although Steve will always be in her thinking, she will be able to draw closer to Pete and continue being drawn back toward Dan.

Issues for the Counselor

This case was especially challenging not so much for the bereavement issues but because of the counselor's personal feelings associated with the war. It would have been very easy to side with Alice in her disdain for the war effort and engage her at that level but this would not have furthered her in any way. Nonetheless, the temptation was there. Conceptually what is being said is that there are times when we want to take up the causes of our clients and join with them in either their anger or their actions but we must be constrained from doing this. Although the professional understanding is there, the counselor still found it difficult to remain uninvolved in this part of Alice's struggle.

Following Worden's template was helpful in keeping focused and staying within a framework. Whenever there is overlap between the life of the client and the counselor, it usually triggers some form of reaction that has to be acknowledged. In this case, there was overlap in that the counselor is the mother of two sons and could so easily imagine her own feelings if one of her own had fallen in battle. This has to be monitored. Using the task model kept the counselor within needed boundaries.

There was some consideration of having Alice participate in a group but there were no bereavement groups available that specifically dealt with wartime experiences. The counselor decided that she would not respond well to a group with mixed bereavement issues. This meant that the helping would all have to emerge from the individual sessions, despite the belief that Alice needed more support than was forthcoming from her community. Not being able to find ancillary services to support clients is a frustration that happens fairly frequently.

Wartime death highlights some aspects of life that we try to obscure: that there is a fundamental inhumanity that at times prevails and that decisions are frequently made that cause lives to be taken. A wartime death highlights the lack of control that we all endure and it becomes a challenge to contain the feelings around this within the counseling relationship. However, the counselor's joining the client in his or her feeling of lack of control can serve to highlight the griever's feelings in an unnecessary way.

Many of the situations that are presented to us in counseling are in areas in which we may have no experience or have not even imagined. However, as I discussed in this chapter, the counselor will find guidance and success in relying on a framework such as Worden's task model for cases such as this one.

10
CHAPTER

Bereavement After the Death of an Identical Twin

The Case—Kaisha

Kaisha, or is it Karen? That was the comment wherever the girls went. As identical twins, it was almost impossible to tell them apart; in certain situations, even their parents had difficulty. Kaisha and Karen (Black women, 17 years of age) grew up in a middle-class suburban community. Their twinship was always a source of community conversation and private delight for the girls. They had two other siblings, an older brother and a younger sister, but it was the twins who got the most attention. For one thing, they were strikingly beautiful and the impact of their likeness was equally striking. In addition, they were bright and engaging and both were musically talented. Karen played the piano and Kaisha played the viola, and both girls won prizes for their musical ability. They both graduated from high school with honors, a year early, and made the decision that they would attend the same upstate college, as they both had been offered generous scholarships. "This is how it sometimes is with twins," explained Kaisha. "We really didn't want to be apart from each other when we had to go to college." They did decide that they would not room together but were in the same dorm. Kaisha majored in music whereas Karen was drawn to psychology.

It was Christmas break and Karen and Kaisha were planning to go home for the extended vacation. The drive home was about 4 hours, and their car, a small SUV, was equipped for driving in the snow. They left after Kaisha's last class, late in the afternoon, expecting to be home for a late dinner. It was snowing lightly when they left but as they headed south, the snow became heavier, making it difficult to see. Karen was driving. Apparently the weather forecast had been wrong, as they had predicted that the snow would not begin until much later. But it was not even 4 o'clock and the snow was coming down very heavily. They decided to stop for a break, grabbed a burger, and when they got back into the car, the visibility had become even more compromised but they felt that it would be best to keep on driving as they were just about half-way home. In the months to come, Kaisha would think back on that decision with pain and anguish, despite the fact that they had both agreed to continue their trip.

After the break, they headed back toward the interstate. The access roads were very slippery but the four-wheel option in the car kept them from slipping and sliding. A professional driver who claimed to have a lot of experience driving in the snow drove the truck that hit them. What the truck driver, who was driving parallel to the twins, was not able to prevent, despite his experience, was the small sports car that skidded in front of him; this caused him to slam on his brakes that resulted in a 40-foot skid that plunged his truck into the driver's side of the twins' car. Karen, who was driving, was hit broadside and was crushed, almost instantly, against the wheel, although somewhat cushioned by the air bag, and side of the car. Kaisha was jostled by the impact but was protected by the air bag that deployed almost instantly. She was hurled against the door and sustained a sprained right arm and lots of cuts and bruises. Karen was unconscious when the ambulance arrived and both women were taken to a nearby hospital. Kaisha was alert but in pain, and called her parents as soon as they arrived at the hospital. Karen was taken to a special trauma unit. Kaisha was told that Karen had extensive bleeding and internal injuries. Despite all efforts to staunch the bleeding and address the internal injuries, Karen died about an hour before her parents arrived at the hospital. Kaisha had been allowed to come into the room just before Karen expired and was there, holding her hand, when she took her last breath.

Kaisha described that moment as "the worst moment in my life. I experienced a blackness that surrounded me, a darkness with no light anywhere, and a pain in my chest that felt like a knife going into me." When her parents arrived, Kaisha crumbled into their arms and her sobbing and keening began. It would not end for days. One week after the car crash, after being evaluated by a psychiatrist for antidepressant medication, which she rejected, Kaisha was referred for bereavement counseling.

Relevant History

Kaisha was seen as the more ethereal, free spirit type; Karen, the more realistic and grounded twin. Kaisha was known as being more temperamental and was more emotionally complex in some of her reactions than her twin. Both women were gifted with different talents but all who knew them saw them as easygoing, fun, and bright. Kaisha would often go into what she referred to as "quiet periods" when she would just want to be alone and either read or listen to music or practice her viola. Sometimes she felt that she just wanted to be by herself. She thought that these quiet periods—which happened every few weeks and lasted for less than a day—were because of her being a twin and always having her twin nearby.

Kaisha had had several boyfriends in high school and was considered popular. Her transition to college had been smooth, probably eased by Karen's presence in her dorm, and basically she was happy and future focused, with everything going well in her life. There was no history of any psychological problems or major life upsets. Her adolescence had been the usual tumultuous time with no overly remarkable fissures between Kaisha and her parents. In sum, Kaisha was a well-adjusted young woman entering an exciting and fruitful period of her life.

Conceptual Issues

To grasp the depth of this bereavement experience, I must explore the experience of being a twin. We have all been, at times, fascinated by this compelling twist of nature. How and why twins occur is still not fully understood. Identical twins occur in about 3.5 of every 1,000 births (Wright, 1997). Twins can be either identical or fraternal. Most are fraternal twins—each twin develops from a separate egg and sperm. Fraternal twins each have their own placentas and amniotic sacs. Identical twins are more rare. They occur when one fertilized egg splits early in pregnancy and develops into two fetuses.

The identical twin bond is one of the most powerful bonds known in nature. This is explained in a number of ways: identical twins have similar genetic and constitutional beginnings, the impact of the environment and parental style is felt uniformly, and the same experiences are shared. These unified experiences serve to establish very early in the twins' lives what has come to be called the twinning bond. The bond involves experiencing oneself as part of the other person with a sense of self that is shared or distributed between the two people. The identification between twins is usually mutually felt and of equal intensity. The need for the other twin is described as different from the need for the mother or other siblings. Twins seem to share a closeness with each other that would be hard to create in any other relationship (Schave & Ciriello, 1983).

"An identical twin may be the best source for most types of assistance for which we would normally rely on other people, such as emotional sustenance or investment decisions. This is because, generally speaking, helping an identical twin is like helping oneself, i.e., helping one's own genes to survive" (Segal, 1999, p. 101). Identical twins are similar in general intelligence, personality, and physical appearance and appear to form a powerful cooperative bond with each other.

It seems that the bond between nonidentical twins is strong, but the bond between identical twins goes even deeper. The death of a sibling can be a traumatic bereavement; the death of an identical twin, based on the "twinning bond," creates a bereavement situation for the remaining twin that knows no boundaries.

Death of an Identical Twin

The death of a twin is a topic that has been almost completely overlooked in grief studies and literature (Archer, 1999). The few studies that have been done, however, show a remarkable consistency of findings: the death of an identical twin is a profound and wrenching experience. "Twinless twins" (Segal, 1999), those who have lost their twin, are truly an understudied population whose grief is often described as unimaginable. I describe the few existing studies that document the reaction to a twin death in chronological order, showing the progression of understanding of this phenomenon.

Woodward's (1988) pioneering work, based on her own experience of having lost a twin, involved more than 200 participants in the United Kingdom. The overall findings suggest that the loss of an identical twin is more devastating than the loss of a nonidentical twin.

Segal and Bouchard (1993), through the Minnesota Twin Loss Project, studied the grief reactions of 70 surviving twins, whose age at the loss of their twin was 15 years or older (this was to ensure that all respondents had shared the majority of their formative years with their twin). Surviving twins were asked to rate reactions to the death of the twin and reactions to the deaths of other relatives and acquaintances who had died during the twin's lifetime. Their hypothesis, that the bereavement experience is more devastating with increasing genetic relatedness, was borne out: the loss of an identical twin was experienced more severely than that of a fraternal twin and the loss of a twin is experienced more severely than the loss of other relatives, including a spouse, grandparent, parent, aunt, uncle, and cousin. In a follow-up study (Segal, Wilson, Bouchard, &

Gitlin, 1995), 279 participants, age 15 years and older, showed that the grief of a twin far exceeded that of nontwin individuals on the Grief Experience Inventory and that the grief of identical twins was greater than it was for fraternal twins.

A more recent study by Segal and Blozis (2002) looked at 245 surviving twins, 15 years old and older, who completed a retrospective Grief Experience Inventory (Sanders, Mauger, & Strong, 1985), which asked respondents to consider the first month or two following their loss. Significant findings showed that the level of somatic responses was high, the closeness of the twins predicted the level of grief, the younger the age at the time of loss were associated with increased grief and somatic symptoms and greater impairment in coping, and women reported greater levels of grief and somatic complaints than men.

A study (Tomassini, Rosina, Billari, Skytthe, & Christensen, 2002) using the Danish Twin Registry examined the differences between spouse loss and twin loss in a population of adults ages 50 to 70 years. The findings showed that there was an increased risk of death for the first year of bereavement in the lives of the surviving spouses and in the second year for the surviving twin. This effect was noted equally for men and women. This study suggests that the loss of a twin is experienced even more painfully in the second year of bereavement, another flag for those who counsel this group.

The conceptual issues point the grief counselor in the direction of heightened concern for the surviving twin. This loss is so powerful because of the shared identity, shared characteristics, shared past, shared experience base, and shared future that have been shattered. Research suggests that the second year postdeath may be even more upsetting than the first.

Suggestions for Intervention

Because of the unique issues relating to twin bereavement including the dynamics of the twin bond, identity issues due to overidentification, and centrality and the many social and emotional implications, bereavement counseling with a bereaved twin promotes a different level of expectation of healing and progress. The healing is generally slower and the progress is uneven (Wilson, 1995). Two core treatment issues that must be addressed in the counseling effort are fear of death, especially if the death is due to a genetic predisposition, and fear of the future.

Fear of Death

One of the earliest writings about identical twin death was a personal essay by Dr. George Engel (1975) in which he described his reactions to the death of his identical twin at the age of 49 from a fatal heart attack. Engel described the psychological and emotional adjustments to this loss and particularly made mention of his increased sense of physical vulnerability as he antici- pated his own heart attack, expecting that a genetic predisposition marked him as it had his twin. A year after his brother's attack, he had a heart attack and he stated, "My reaction to the attack was one of great relief... I no longer had to anticipate the heart attack; the other shoe had fallen, so to speak" (p. 25). Although the death under review is not from a genetic predisposition, there did emerge in Kaisha a sense of impending doom related to her twin's demise. This is a frequent response especially if this is a first experience with death.

Fear for the Future

As we mature, our use of denial as a defense mechanism against anxiety diminishes; lack of denial produces psychological distress (Fleming & Balmer, 1996). When a death occurs, especially in a young life, the sense of invulnerability that is characteristic of the young is challenged and an under- tow of fear for the self and for those they love enters their consciousness. Death becomes a possibility whereas before it was an abstraction.

Another aspect of the fear for the future is the unanswerable lament: How will I manage in the future without my twin? Whom will I depend on? The twin griever has to be reassured that there will surely be a time of reorganizing but that each person has many strengths and levels of resiliency that get him or her through such times.

When working with a young adult or a first-time griever, the counse- lor's stance is to be accepting of these fears and to be reassuring without being false. Both of these areas—fear for survival and for the future—are exaggerated with the death of a twin.

Identical Twin Bereavement

Wilson (1995) asserted that twins need more time to address their bereave- ment issues than nontwins and that the bereavement process will be pro- tracted. As such, when layering on the factors described previously, the likelihood of the bereavement experience being a "complicated mourning" (Rando, 1993) is to be expected.

Rando's (1993) schema of the six "R" processes of mourning to address complicated bereavement situations forms the basis for the approach to helping identical twins adjust to their loss. Rando's approach is particularly sensitive to the needs of a mourner who is experiencing a complex and protracted grief experience, an expectation when there is the death of an identical twin. The six "R" processes are divided into three phases: avoidance, confrontation, and accommodation.

In the avoidance phase, grievers must *recognize* the loss: acknowledge the death emotionally as well as intellectually, begin to feel the pain of the death, understand the context of the death, and experience the lack of meaning, orderliness, and predictability of life.

In the confrontation phase, grievers must *react* to the separation by experiencing fully the pain of the loss, giving vent and expression to the myriad emotions touched by the death (positive, negative, intense, and the unfamiliar), and identifying and mourning secondary losses (the interaction, validation, reinforcement, gratification) that the deceased offered. Within this phase, grievers must also *recollect* and reexperience the deceased and the relationship. The processes of recollection and reexperiencing help mourners to discover new ways of relating to the deceased, to alter the emotional attachments and investments in the loved one from those that were active to those that are remembered and internalized. In this "R" phase, the deceased must be remembered realistically, including the positive, negative, and neutral, and the beginning of untying of the many bonds must begin. The final process in this phase is to relinquish the old attachments to the deceased and to the safety and familiarity of the assumptive world that they shared.

In the final accommodation phase, grievers must *readjust* to move into the new world without forgetting their old existence by revising their assumptive views, developing a new relationship with the deceased, and adopting a new and different persona and way of being in this new world which incorporates new skills, behaviors, roles, and relationships. The final process, *reinvestment*, has mourners moving their emotional energy away from the deceased into a new attachment(s) that can provide them with some measure of emotional gratification (Rando, 1993, pp. 45–60).

Rando (1993) mentioned the revision of the assumptive world as one of the processes that the griever must resolve to move ahead. Some of the approaches that have been useful in helping an individual realign his or her assumptive world include reliving the trauma and relearning certain cognitive assumptions. This is a lengthy process and, in some cases, is furthered by participation in a group.

Major Issues in This Case

Kaisha and the family returned home from the hospital where Karen died. Karen's body was taken to a local funeral home and a service, wake, and burial were performed. To say that Kaisha's assumptive world had been altered is to minimize the sense of loss and devastation that she experienced; indeed, for Kaisha, her whole world had been shattered and she felt "destroyed." Kaisha was inconsolable. By the end of the first week, her parents began to be concerned that Kaisha was "having a breakdown" and took her to a psychiatrist for evaluation. The psychiatrist prescribed antidepressant medication, which Kaisha refused, but she did accept the suggestion of bereavement counseling. Kaisha was not eating, sleeping, or relating; it was as though she had climbed into a shell and could not or would not emerge. Contrary to some of the literature concerning fear of survival, Kaisha wished she could join Karen. On several occasions she said, "I want to be with Karen, that is where I belong" or "I know Karen waits for me, and I need to be by her side."

During the first counseling session, Kaisha was barely forthcoming with any emotion or information. It was difficult to understand the few words she spoke as she kept covering her mouth with her hands and looking in every direction but at the counselor. The first process in the direction of healing is, according to Rando (1993), for the griever to push into the avoidance phase and begin to feel some of the pain of the death. Kaisha was consumed with pain; all she felt was pain.

Early on, the counselor assessed that a group experience would not be the most advisable for Kaisha. This assessment was based on the level of her emotional pain and turmoil and the depth of her loss. Unless she was enrolled in a group for grieving twins, the group experience would have been experienced as unrelated to her loss. Kaisha would not have been able to avail herself of the support that a group could offer. A group experience was something that could have been considered after some bereavement work goals were addressed. The work had to first staunch her emotional pain to allow her to function, albeit minimally.

For the counselor to connect with an individual who is in such a painful state, the counselor must be accepting of the intensity of the emotion. In addition, one of the early tasks in a case as intense as this is to help the individual articulate his or her feelings rather than either withdrawing or crying constantly and not giving voice to the emotions. Asking simple questions that do not necessitate great thought but more of a spontaneous response can do this: Can you tell me some of what you have experienced—just the facts, feelings will come later? or Can you rate the intensity of some of these feelings? This operationalizes Rando's first step, to help survivors recognize their loss, by having them draw only on the concrete issues, sparing them the emotional side.

Rynearson (2001) suggested a strategy for working with loss that can be well used in efforts to engage: the retelling of the death. Everyone tells a story but Rynearson urged that great detail be urged while the focus is kept on the feelings and experiences of the griever; this moves the survivor into Rando's confrontation phase. This strategy was used with Kaisha who needed to tell, repeatedly, the events and circumstances of the day of the crash in detail. With Kaisha, this was ultimately what got her to open up and connect with the counselor. The details of what happened were initially difficult for Kaisha to tell, as she evidenced guilt in almost every sentence. However, after a few retellings, she was urged to tell the story with some of the guilt held back. The counselor hoped that ultimately this would be the version of the events that Kaisha would accept. This was a long-term goal, only partially accepted and realized by the time counseling ended; it should not be expected that this would be achievable early on.

Although the counselor is trying to engage the client, it is also important to be aware of the potential for suicidal thinking and planning. A client as depressed and depleted as Kaisha might consider ending her life. The counselor, through a series of questions, directly addresses the question of suicidality: Are you thinking of killing yourself? Depending on the answer, the following question is about plan: How would you do this? Then the means are to be questioned: Do you have pills/gun/razor? If there is intent, a plan, and means, the person's suicide risk is very high and action should be taken immediately, preferably having the individual hospitalized for his or her own protection. If the person is a minor, parents must be contacted and involved in the hospitalization. If older and the client does not acknowledge a suicide potential and will not go to the hospital, the counselor must initiate conscientious monitoring by making phone call check-ins, scheduling several additional sessions, and engaging social support systems, until the risk has eased. Although Kaisha wanted to join Karen, it was not a formulated plan but more of a wish, and the counselor determined that she was not at risk at that time.

Kaisha was slow to be engaged but she did agree to twice-weekly sessions. Slowly, very slowly, Kaisha began to open up. As the counselor accepted the emotional content and stayed with the stated feelings (and pushed a bit with every meeting), Kaisha began to say more and cry ever so slightly less. Pushing is to be qualified; it is gentle, attuned to the level of responsiveness, and eased if the client seems resistant. If the client remains resistant to some of the efforts at relating more content and feelings, the counselor can see this as a signal that the client is really not ready and stay with content that is more comfortable; waiting is sometimes the best approach. If waiting fails to facilitate further content, the counselor can articulate some concern that the client is "stuck" and suggest that perhaps "We need to look at some of the details from a different perspective, perhaps imagining how it could have been different," for example. A caution: If the client feels pushed too hard, he or she may decide that counseling is not what he or she wants to do as it increases stress rather than eases it and the client will withdraw from the counseling relationship.

As part of recognizing the loss, the client has to understand the death. For Kaisha that meant that she had to acknowledge that Karen had died because of an accident. Of course, Kaisha felt totally responsible for the decision to continue their trip but as she spoke about more and more of the details of the decision, it became clearer to Kaisha that Karen had been an integral part of the decision and had not been coerced by Kaisha; they had made the decision jointly. "But I should have said this is crazy," she wailed, "If only I had said no...." But she had not, and Karen had not either, even though Karen was the more grounded of the two. The counselor had to say this to her repeatedly and also had to state countless times that this had been an accident. Where Kaisha really got caught was that she had insisted on attending her last class; if she had cut the class they could have departed several hours earlier and they would have avoided most of the snow. There was no moving her from this belief.

Rando's (1993) second phase, reacting to the separation, occurs at all levels for the bereft. For a twin there are even greater depths to plumb and the areas of reaction are multiplied several times. Kaisha and Karen had not only shared a growing up but also the comfort of being known so fully by another: "Karen knew things even before I told her them, I knew when Karen was happy and when she was sad, I knew all her moods and moves. As far as I knew myself, I knew Karen."

Guiding the client through the minefield of her pain is grounded in the conviction that "...unacknowledged and unexpressed emotion is a major precipitant of pathology" (Rando, 1993, p. 47). This was the most difficult part of the counseling relationship for both Kaisha and the counselor. It required that Kaisha give words to her loss, say the feelings, and express them from her heart not her intellect: "Karen will never see me married or know my children. It hurts too much to think that"; "I am so angry, so angry that the driver walked away and she died"; and the most poignant, "How could she leave me?"

This part of the work went on for several months with periodic gains and setbacks. Gains were measured in terms of her ability to express facet after facet of the relationship she shared and would miss with Karen; setbacks were periods when Kaisha would become overwhelmed by her feelings, shut down, and sink back to the protection of the shell and wall she had established around her pain. The patience to shift with Kaisha's moods and hold to the therapeutic goal of articulating emotional pain was challenging for the counselor. There were frequent replays of the events that led up the accident, repeated life reviews of the closeness that the women had shared, and abject exclamations of pain over which a scab had not formed. Although Kaisha was so sad and bereft, there were signs that she was healing: she was less depressed, cried less frequently, was considering returning to school the following semester (many months away, not to the college she had attended but to a local university, which indicated future thinking), and was more responsive and forthcoming in the counseling sessions.

The adaptation around her loss and the restoration of Kaisha's assumptive world were only minimally realized. Kaisha may never have the worldview that she had before her twin's death; she may never trust that the world is safe and that things happen for a reason. As Kaisha stated repeatedly, "I have lost all my faith, in God, and in everything. The world stinks and there is no justice." She stated, at various times, that she felt vulnerable, that something else bad was going to happen to her or someone in her family. This had to be heard, not as a rational, reasonable assessment of the world but as a projection of Kaisha's feelings. Although they could be seen as temporary, and, in fact some of the edges of these feelings do resolve over time, they must be addressed in the moment. Grievers are to be reassured that these feelings of vulnerability are normal and that it may take time before they go away or are eased.

The accommodation phase, the period in the mourner's life when changes have to be made around the physical absence of the deceased, was especially difficult for Kaisha. The centrality of the closeness, the blended lives of the twins, the fact that they did almost everything together, mitigated accommodation to Karen's death. The attachment described in the literature and studies about identical twins suggests that the bond is the most powerful in nature; to imagine that accommodation to the loss could occur may be unrealistic. The wrenching of the twins from one another may ease and at times be manageable, but it is realistic to assert that this pain will follow through the life of the remaining identical twin. For Kaisha, even 2 years after the death—she was in counseling for more than 2 years—she found herself looking for Karen, sometimes having imagined conversations with her, and she was acutely aware that she cast the only shadow, not the two of them.

By 13 months after the accident, Kaisha returned to college, having decided to attend a local university rather than return to the school she and Karen had attended. She was still depressed but not acutely; more accurately, she was flat and minimally responsive. She had no interest in socializing with others and had enough energy to attend classes, but that was all. She stayed in her room a lot and had no interest in being with anyone, sometimes even closing out family members. She was still in counseling twice a week.

There were two key dates that were anticipated as being very difficult for Kaisha: the twins' birthday and the anniversary of the accident and death. In the first year, these dates were noted but did not produce any strong reactions in Kaisha, as she was still not very reactive. Consistent with the literature, the second year proved to be the more difficult as the inescapable reality of the loss was fully upon her. After the first year of counseling, she began to speak of the many ways, venues, and moments that her life had changed without Karen. She said, "I have difficulty making decisions at times and need her to help me" and "I want to talk to her about our father and his sadness but I can't" and "I sometimes go into her closet to smell her clothing and to feel connected and I cry and cry."

The guilt that Kaisha felt about the accident continued. She said, "I intellectually understand that it was a joint decision to continue in the snow but emotionally, I still blame myself. I should have insisted that we stay put and not go anywhere until the roads were plowed. And if I had cut my last class, we would have been able to leave earlier and that would have made all the difference." It may be safe to assume that an intellectual acceptance may be the best that Kaisha will ever achieve in easing her guilt.

After 2 years of counseling, the twice-weekly sessions were reduced to once-weekly sessions for 6 months. The length of time in counseling, always a difficult question for the counselor to determine, is based on how the client is faring in terms of healing from the loss. In this case, the counselor felt that Kaisha needed a transitional person to move her from reliance on Karen to reliance on the counselor and eventually to reliance on herself. The counselor became the bridge person (transitional object) on whom Kaisha could rely and depend. Transitional objects, as they are referred to in the psychoanalytic literature, are those that serve the function of allowing an individual to transition from one strong attachment to another. In this transitional phase, emotional energy is shifted from the primary relationship to a transitional person (the counselor) who carries the emotion, allowing a more realistic and, in some cases, less emotionally demanding relationship to begin with another person who is not the counselor. In cases of such profound loss, when the ties are so deeply seated, a transitional role is necessary for the client to be able to move forward in a new relationship. This addresses the readjustment phase described by Rando.

Because of the potency of Kaisha's loss, the counselor began termination many months before the actual date of the last session. This was done to ensure that there would be as nondisruptive a termination process as possible. In some respects this termination was planned to be instructive in how relationships can end in a planful, and not wrenching, manner. But it was difficult to say good-bye, as the relationship between Kaisha and the counselor was long and intense.

Kaisha may never feel whole again. She will always miss the part of her that was Karen. Nonetheless, by termination, which was agreed on by both parties, she was able to face her life with some degree of optimism and anticipation, but not without sadness. "To say farewell to one who is just like me is the hardest thing I will do; some part of me went with Karen but I know that some day we will be together again," she said.

Issues for the Counselor

This case was especially poignant: the depths of despair and torment that Kaisha experienced were truly painful to observe. What was compelling about Kaisha was the intense overlapping of the twins, which was such a determining factor in Kaisha's grief. The emotional overload that her despair brought was powerful and must be seen as a projected feeling from client to counselor. As grief counselors, we do not always absorb so much feeling from a mourner, and it is important to listen to the feelings that are provoked and understand.

An area of challenge with Kaisha was making an accurate assessment as to her potential for suicide. This was a very real fear and possibility for Kaisha, especially in the first few weeks after the accident. It became an issue for concern again as the anniversary date approached and she sank into depression. The role of the counselor is to confront these suspicions and not duck the potential that may be there. These are difficult moments because there is the possibility of misjudging the seriousness of the intent. There can be no room for error. It requires direct confrontation and a sense of clinical awareness about the client; these can be stressful moments for the counselor. The counselor has to be comfortable confronting these feelings in the client and not be hesitant to discuss them with him or her. If the counselor ducks this responsibility, the consequences can be serious. Even if the counselor's suspicions about the suicide potential of the client are misplaced, the questions have to be asked. If the counselor is wrong, so be it. If the counselor is right in these concerns, he or she may be saving a client's life.

Kaisha left counseling at an agreed-upon date. Perhaps she could have stayed longer, but the decision was made. It is hoped that she has been able to integrate herself with the Karen who is within her; she was well on her way.

Bereavement After the Death of a Therapist

The Case—Beth

Beth is a 40-year-old married mother of two children. She is a successful administrator in the legal department of a local hospital, married to a pediatrician. She lives comfortably and can be described as attractive, bright, and insightful. She is warm and personable and relates well to all. Soon after her children were born, she returned to her position at the hospital.

Beth had been seeing Dr. X for 6 years, twice weekly, for psychotherapy. She had entered treatment because she found that she was taking on too much responsibility for the care of others—family, children, colleagues—and was feeling overwhelmed and confused about several of her primary relationships. Over the course of the 6 years, she had explored long-ago history and family dynamics and had a good understanding of these forces as they related and affected her current functioning. In this period of time, she developed a strong connection to her male therapist and had worked through the nuances of her interpersonal relationships and work problems. She felt a growing need to terminate with the therapist as she felt that, after so many years, many of her concerns had been explored and that the therapy was not especially productive. The therapist was claiming there was more work to be done.

As a therapeutic style, Dr. X had built on Beth's ability to understand and develop insight into her personal struggles. Their work had been remarkably successful, albeit long term. When she got the call that he had been killed in a car accident, she was shocked. She wondered what would happen to her and how she would be able to manage her emotional life, and she thought about how she would miss the relationship that had been built up over the years. She felt lost and anxious.

Beth had attended a memorial service for the deceased but found little comfort in the experience. "I felt very out of place there and I saw, for the first time, several of the people he had referred to over the years, including his wife and two of his adult children. This was very uncomfortable for me," she commented. Because she knew another person in Dr. X's practice, she contacted her and they commiserated with each other about their respective psychological fates and their loss.

Beth felt that she needed to continue in treatment, and she began to search for another therapist. She felt a strong sense of abandonment and insecurity; she had invested a great deal in the relationship with Dr. X and was frightened that she would revert to old coping behaviors and habits. She had worked too hard and long to see the fruits of her therapeutic gains dissipate. She also felt an overwhelming sense of loss of connection to a significant person in her life. She was anxious, edgy, tense, and scared. She was referred to a grief counselor after consulting with some friends for a recommendation. She knew she was dealing with bereavement issues and that she needed to address these feelings as soon as she could; she also was looking for direction and support.

Relevant History

Beth and her older brother grew up in a poor, urban environment. Her father was a businessman and her mother stayed home to care for the children. Her mother suffered from profound mental illness and was unstable for most of Beth's growing-up years. The instability manifested itself in neglect of the home and children. Her father was verbally abusive and often inappropriate in his behavior. Beth attended private school and as soon as she was able, went away to college, met her husband, and married after graduation. Beth had struggled with issues of closeness from young adulthood on, and although she was very successful and well liked, at a very early age she began to rely wholly on herself and her resourcefulness. The paradox of her life was the degree of success in so many areas juxtaposed against her inner sense of low self-esteem.

Conceptual Issues

The death of a therapist can be a shattering experience. For many people, the relationship one shares with a therapist is more open, honest, and accepting than with others. The level of emotional attachment between client and therapist can be intense and, depending on the orientation of the therapist, can be used as a tool in the helping work. Although some therapists have an orientation that is more cognitive and stays with present-day concerns, many prefer to use the emotional history of clients to help release long-held memories and reactions, to help them see the patterns of their reactions, and to make changes based on the liberation from the past to be able to move into the future. To access this material, the client must unload a lot of emotions and release memories. This content is then shared with the therapist who also becomes a player in the relationship with the client. The emotional unloading is often painful and brutally honest, and it admits the counselor into places with the client that are very personal and often painful. Understandably, when the death of the therapist ends this relationship, especially if it is long term, the abrupt termination of such intimate sharing can cause a good deal of emotional fear, upset, and frustration.

These reactions are explained by the fact that unplanned termination does not allow the therapist and patient the ability to plan the phasing out of their relationship and to deal with the multiplicity of feelings that are provoked by ending. There is not the needed time to express the anger, pain, and feelings of rejection and desertion with the departing therapist and to explore options for further treatment. The therapeutic work may not have been finished, which can leave the client in a state of emotional turmoil.

With unplanned terminations of any type, the suddenness of the ending enhances the potential for complicated mourning reactions and pathological mourning (Dewald, 1965; Lehrman, 1956). Levin (1998) noted, "Unplanned termination is about the therapist leaving the patient. There is no forwarding address; there are no options for booster sessions or follow-up phone calls. The end of therapy is final and forever" (p. 43). As expected, there are numerous consequences for the client of unplanned termination whether by incident—a sudden move, sudden dreadful or debilitating illness—or through death.

The literature on unplanned termination due to therapist death is limited. The research points to several conclusions that form the basis for a conceptual understanding of the bereavement issues. Lord, Ritvo, and Solnit (1978) interviewed 27 individuals after the death of their therapists. Their findings suggest that those who experienced normal versus more profound or pathological mourning were those who had sustained fewer early losses in their lives. It was the loss of the therapist as a human being in his or her own right that seemed a powerful factor in the quality and duration of the mourning experience. The majority of those interviewed expressed angry feelings toward the deceased. There was no correlation between gender and age of clients, their reasons for seeking treatment and the character of the mourning reactions. It was the abrupt closing of the relationship that spurred the feelings of a breach of trust or betrayal (Shwed, 1980). In addition, not surprisingly, those who were going through simultaneous endings experienced greater levels of despair, anger, and abandonment (Garcia-Lawson, Lane, & Koetting, 2000).

Some of the feelings of abandonment are a result of the fact that the safety net that the therapist offers has vanished (Chwast, 1983). The irony of such a death is that the therapist, under other circumstances, would be the one to help the client make sense out of the loss. With the death of the therapist, the client has either to rely on his or her own devices and support systems or to seek another therapeutic relationship (Tallmer, 1989). The percentage of those seeking another relationship can only be guessed at, as findings in the literature are not informing. A conservative estimate would be that more than half of those who have experienced this type of loss would seek additional help. Some would say that starting over, risking oneself, and setting oneself up for another loss would preclude reengagement with someone else. Those who might want to start with someone new could be those who still feel a compelling need to have a therapeutic relationship or those who were not overly engaged with the deceased therapist and still want to continue their therapy. Either way, the starting over is difficult because history is revisited and engaging with someone new, under these circumstances, can be stressful.

The question of the level of transference and its impact on the bereavement is described in the literature. Transference is defined as the experience of feelings, drives, and attitudes toward a person in the present that are based on reactions and responses from a previous relationship(s). These reactions are a repetition of reactions originating in regard to significant persons of early childhood, unconsciously displaced onto figures in the present. The etiology of these reactions is not clear to the person experiencing them but it becomes a tool for the therapist as relationships between him or her and the client deepen. In psychoanalytic work (the form of treatment practiced by Dr. X), transference reactions are viewed as essential to the therapeutic experience in that their interpretation is believed to result in conflict resolution and personality change. These transference reactions can feel very real to the client who may not be able to differentiate between feelings toward the psychoanalyst and feelings from a previous time (Goldstein, 1997). In some instances, "...The transference refers to the extraordinary exaggerated sense of power and importance that the patient projects upon the analyst [therapist]. ...People project onto transference objects [the therapist] the power and ability to save and protect them from evil, fear, and anxiety... and then proceed to act toward these objects as if they really did have that power" (Liechty, 2002, p. 88). It would follow quite logically that in the event of the sudden loss of such a central idealized figure, the individual might experience a loss far greater than just the loss of the therapist (p. 89).

Janoff-Bulman (1992) contributed to the articulation of the concept of the assumptive worldview. She noted that we live in a world of assumptions about our world that ground us and help us to function maximally. These assumptions work along three basic dimensions: that the world is benevolent, that the world is meaningful, and that the self is worthy. These beliefs help direct us and lend order to our existence. When the assumptive world is broken through traumatic loss, the view of the world is shaken and a host of negative assumptions about safety and the self invades the inner life of the individual.

Liechty (2002) made an interesting link between the transferential relationship between therapist and client, and violation of the assumptive world. He stated, "Recognition of this transferential aspect in relationships with those significant others who constitute the assumptive world [one's therapist, for example] is an important key to deeper understanding of the range of emotional responses therapists find in their patients, especially responses that may seem extremely out of proportion to the situation" (p. 90). What Liechty is suggesting is that if there is a strong transferential component to the therapeutic relationship, if the therapist is seen as a powerful, nurturing, supportive person, then the death of that therapist would be sufficient to collapse the assumptive worldview of the client. Liechty cautioned the therapist who begins seeing a client who has a previous therapeutic relationship that ended in death to pay close attention to the magnitude of the role the dying or deceased person played in the assumptive worldview of the client. The loss of one on whom the client primarily relied for levels of support, insight, and understanding signals a higher likelihood of complication. This linking of the assumptive worldview and transference relationship is especially important in Beth's case.

As stated earlier, the literature on unplanned termination due to therapist death is limited. Consequently, the literature describing the impact of this unplanned termination for the succeeding therapeutic relationship is inconclusive and does not offer much direction to the subsequent therapist, but there are some suggestions from the literature. Barbanel (1989) noted that the attachments to the inheriting therapist are not as strong as to the deceased therapist and that comparisons between the deceased and current therapist are frequent. In addition, a form of splitting can occur in the client's mind in which the deceased has a presence in the new relationship and is a companion cotherapist, even though he or she is not present. Several authors (Flesch, 1947; Shwed, 1980) commented on the constant referrals to the deceased by the client, both the angry and tender expressions, which may be difficult for the inheriting therapist to manage.

An added dimension for the client's bereavement experience is the lack of social support. This form of loss, in which there is a remarkable lack of social support, is what Doka (1989a) referred to as disenfranchised grief. Doka noted that people need social validation and recognition of a loss. This lack of recognition leaves the bereaved in a situation in which they do not receive the support of family, friends, and others who potentially could help ease the pain and help to buffer the loss. Doka believed that this happens because the relationship is not based on traditional kin ties or does not have traditional status as a substantial loss or is not socially sanctioned. Within each society, there are grieving rules that define and in some ways limit the role of the griever, making each form of death more or less acceptable (Doka, 2002b). The death of a pet and the death of a coworker are examples of disenfranchised grief; the death of a therapist is surely another.

Typically, in situations of disenfranchised grief, the mourner is "embarrassed" to express grief both publicly and in some public forums as well. The embarrassment seems to stem from the client's not wanting to look foolish to others who might judge him or her as overacting or "being silly" because there might be an easy replacement of the deceased object or the deceased object does not warrant such a reaction. There are other instances of disenfranchised grief that are more pointed. In the early years of the AIDS epidemic, for example, some who mourned deaths from AIDS risked stigmatization through association.

The practical impact for the disenfranchised griever is that the griever experiences the bereavement more alone than not. This societal lack of social support can be particularly painful as the person mourns alone. For many, the emotional isolation is particularly powerful, as the availability of support and lack of receipt of it is worse than complete unavailability. This isolation tends to increase secondary loss and intensify shame, victimization, anxiety, guilt, and social withdrawal.

Those who have identified and written about disenfranchised grief have captured an important aspect of the grief experience. It has been borne out in many cases that social support is essential in the healing of bereavement and its absence makes a difficult time even more protracted and painful. It is hard to imagine a mourner losing someone dear and not having caring, responsive people there to ease the pain; even worse is when their support is superficial and lacking in sincerity, as they deem the loss not as important as the mourner does. This was the case for Beth.

Suggestions for Intervention

The decision to treat this client as someone who is in mourning is central to the initial engagement process. This decision is based on the length of time and the level of attachment the client expresses regarding the previous therapist and the level of expressed and behavioral upset provoked by the death. Clients who are grieving will talk about their loss, their feelings of vulnerability and anger, and their sense of disorientation provoked by the death of their therapist. The clients' need for offerings of comfort and consolation are direct responses to the pain and emptiness they are experiencing.

It is reasonable to assume that the client is experiencing some degree of disenfranchised grief (Doka, 1989a). The counselor must work toward enfranchising the mourner by legitimizing the loss and helping him or her articulate the importance and uniqueness of the relationship and by offering as much support as possible (Rando, 1993). It may be helpful to suggest to the griever that family members be apprised of the extent of the upset over the loss and encourage the client to express his or her loss more freely to gain much needed support and validation.

The counselor must have an awareness and acceptance of the displacement of rage and disappointment felt toward the deceased that is carried over into the new counseling relationship. This expression is to be expected and explored. It can be punishing at times, but the most favorable stance is for the new therapist to be as understanding and sympathetic as possible.

For the client who is not expressing feelings of loss and grief, the assumption should not be that the patient is fully resolved and has managed the grief reactions fully. The client may need the new therapist to help facilitate the expression of grief and attendant anger. Often the underlying feelings of vulnerability, disappointment, and disorientation are more difficult to express and time and trust are needed with the new therapist before these feelings can be explored.

Picking up the therapeutic pieces with these clients can test the mettle of the new therapist. It is in this unique inheritance situation that the therapist is forced to begin a new relationship while the old relationship is a major force in the treatment, often with many unresolved threads still present (Beder, 2003a). The new therapist must be able to sustain having a cotherapist in the room who has no life but has a huge presence; the ego-strength of the new therapist will surely be a factor in his or her ability to be compared with the deceased, especially if the relationship had been long and satisfying.

Major Issues in This Case

Beth had a very difficult time accepting and adjusting to the loss of Dr. X. After 6 years of twice-weekly sessions, her connection to the deceased was profound. Despite her wish to begin terminating, she had been deeply tied to Dr. X and she missed the praise and support he offered and the closeness of their connection. Because of this conflict, she experienced guilt feelings about his death. She was not blaming herself for his death; she more felt guilty that she had wished the relationship to end, but not in such a final way. She had some fears for herself but at the same time felt that she was "cured" and had internalized the many years of work with Dr. X. Beth did not feel that there were any major areas that needed work, yet she felt anxious. The counselor decided to see Beth and work with her, keeping the focus on bereavement issues. The rationale for that approach was that there was not much that the new counselor would be able to address with Beth that had not been addressed in the previous therapeutic relationship. In addition, anticipating that she had suffered a substantial loss and a violation of her assumptive worldview, bereavement work was warranted.

Beth cried many times during the first few months and lamented her loss. The paucity of closeness in her background could have accounted for her ultimate reliance on the relationship with the deceased. Of note in her history was Beth's resourcefulness and her ability to "appear very together while suffering internally." This quality had seen Beth through many difficult situations, but she was surprisingly shaken and overwhelmed by Dr. X's death and was admittedly not handling it well. She was able to continue working, but she was having disturbed sleep and renewed feelings of anxiety.

In the first few weeks of the new relationship, Beth explained some of her history and how Dr. X had helped her to understand the impact of the past on her present-day life. She described her family, how they lived, and some of the remembered stories of her youth. She also spoke of her present life: her husband, children, and work life. She appeared to be very bright, well tuned into her dynamics, and essentially well adjusted. But the trickiness of the assessment was that all of these relationships and systems were functioning well with the addition of Dr. X in her personal equation. Without Dr. X in her life, several of these relationships did not appear as solid or as sustaining. In other words, some of what she was receiving from the therapeutic relationship was keeping these other parts of her life that worked well in a balance. With Dr. X gone, Beth began to question the degree of closeness with her husband and the quality of her relationships at work and within her family.

Slowly, past information was explored and the beginning of a connection forged. The anger she felt initially toward Dr. X began to dissipate. This new counselor was a woman and Beth felt that she was more able to relate to her and feel understood. On a number of occasions, she said that she had become too attached to Dr. X and wondered whether he was too attached to her. Within these questions of attachment she thought that perhaps Dr. X was having more difficulty than she was when considering termination. Despite this line of thinking, there were many nostalgic comments about their relationship. "I miss the attention he gave me, he would compliment me frequently," she said. Often, she would preface a statement with "Dr. X always said that ..." or "Dr. X picked up on...." As necessary as this was for Beth to express, it was difficult sometimes for the new counselor to absorb this additional presence in the counseling sessions.

Personal reactions on the part of the counselor are sometimes difficult to manage. In this case, it would not have been appropriate to ask the griever to not make these comparisons, especially in the early phases of the work and when trying to make a therapeutic connection. Sometimes it can be informing to the new counselor to help in understanding what the client feels he or she needs and finds valuable in the counseling effort. After the therapeutic alliance has been forged, there might be instances when the counselor could raise the issue of comparisons to the former therapist by way of asking for an assessment of how the relationship seemed to be progressing. But, surely, early on with Beth, it might have sounded defensive and even aggressive to her bruised psyche.

The focus of the bereavement work, especially in the first few months, was to forge an alliance with Beth by accepting her grief over this loss. Her grief had been handled by those around her in what she felt was a "perfunctory way. Many of the people in my life, those who knew of my long-term relationship with Dr. X, kind of dismissed his death saying that I would find a new therapist. They did not realize that that is not such an easy thing or that he was so replaceable." This lack of support, a facet of disenfranchised grief, made it especially difficult for Beth, as she felt isolated in her pain. Fortunately, she knew of another of Dr. X's clients and they had been in contact soon after his death. This tie helped Beth as she and this other client were both searching for a replacement for Dr. X and both were struggling with issues of legitimacy of loss. By accepting and legitimizing the loss, the new counselor was hoping to facilitate Beth's ultimate ability to pull her emotional energy away from Dr. X and move it into another therapeutic relationship. Much of bereavement work has this goal—the moving of emotional energy from the deceased to the living or the self, or both.

In contrast to the literature, Beth did not begin with the new therapist with a lack of trust. The anger toward the deceased was prominent but it did not appear to affect the next connection. In fact, Beth was very complimentary to the new counselor and seemed glad that there "was such a good fit."

The inheriting counselor's therapeutic goal was to move Beth more into her relationships to gain the closeness she needed and had received previously from Dr. X. The counselor suggested that Beth endeavor to spend more time with her husband and to rely more on him. She was urged to allow him to see the weaker side of her emotional life. Beth did not immediately accept this approach, and in hindsight it may have been a premature area to mine. Beth was still grieving and was not yet ready to open herself up to any more pain.

At an anniversary juncture—4 months after Dr. X's death—Beth was especially tearful and upset. The ambivalence of missing him while questioning his intractable stand on terminating with her was hard for her to bear. She lamented, "What was he thinking as he kept prolonging the therapy? Why did he not want to let me go?" She felt angry and confused by his stand. The double meaning of termination may have been a factor in these feelings: Was she angry that she and Dr. X did not begin a formal, planned termination or was it the ultimate termination that was angering her so? She could not distinguish what she was more upset by.

After 6 months, Beth was beginning to rely less on the new therapist. Initially she had asked to be seen twice a week but by the 6th month her visits were down to once a week, at Beth's suggestion. The counselor saw this as a significant milestone. In a subtle way, Beth was moving away from the necessity of twice-weekly sessions that had been the pattern with Dr. X for 6 years. The new therapist supported this, as it spoke to progress in terms of both bereavement work and Beth's developing independence. She was still struggling with memories and thoughts of Dr. X and missed some of their interaction, but much less so. She had considered terminating with Dr. X after a few years in favor of a woman therapist, wanting the comfort she imagined a woman could better supply. She commented that she felt more comfortable with the new therapist, that "the lack of sexual tension is liberating," and she noted that she had been able to speak of some material that was never discussed with Dr. X.

To say that her bereavement is complete is not accurate, nor is it a situation of pathological mourning. It is more accurate to state that she experiences bereavement as sadness that does not affect her ability to function. She has been able to incorporate the gains she made with Dr. X, has mourned his loss, and has moved ahead. At the year mark, Beth made the decision to end the counseling. This was based on her not feeling "like a patient any more." She said, "I will always think of Dr. X and our years together, the work we did and the gains I made. But, I am not unstable or unhappy. I want to see what it feels like to go it on my own." The counselor agreed, and after a few sessions she focused on the work of termination. Good-byes were said. The termination experience was especially important in that Beth had not experienced a "good termination" but rather had had an aborted ending with Dr. X. In planned termination there is usually a review of gains, time to reflect on the quality and intensity of the relationship, and time to express the anger and fears associated with the ending of the therapeutic relationship. It is also a time in which the bittersweet aspect of endings can be reflected on: the agreement that the client can stand on his or her own, which means saying good-bye to the helper.

During a checkup call a few months later, Beth said that she was doing well but might want to call for an appointment some day soon. She felt good knowing that this would always be an option for her.

Issues for the Counselor

The bereavement issues in this case were difficult to assess. Beth was a high-functioning individual who had built a relationship with the deceased that satisfied many of her needs for closeness and support. The loss of this relationship created a void that the new therapist could not fill. It was, therefore, essential that the counselor manage this case as a bereavement case and acknowledge all of the needs of someone in mourning. Because Beth was grief stricken, her grief was equivalent to having lost a central person in her life. Her need to talk about the deceased was ongoing for the first months, and this was sometimes difficult as it was a struggle to "compete with a ghost." Indeed, the inheriting therapist must have a strong ego to be able to listen to the patient as feelings are discussed about the deceased therapist (Garcia-Lawson et al., 2000). There were moments of personal doubt for this counselor as the depth of Beth's connection to Dr. X was revealed through Beth's description: Was Beth going to like me as much as she did Dr. X? Would anyone ever be able to replace Dr. X? Was this an irreplaceable loss? In time, as Beth began to heal and the counselor was able to assert herself and her style, new bonds began to form. But there were many instances when the counselor would have preferred not having another against whom she was measured. Therapeutically, it was important for Beth to be able to give voice to these feelings, partly to be relieved of them and because there was the goal of enfranchising this loss for her (Beder, 2003).

An additional struggle was trying to gather relevant case information from someone who was grieving while knowing that complete areas of Beth's life had been explored repeatedly over the 6 years of therapy. If this were a client new to therapy or one who had made a switch for any other reason, this struggle would not be as clearly present. As the focus of the case was bereavement, it was easier to stay clear of some of the past that had been examined with Dr. X, but bereavement work has to consider the client's history of loss and loss management, so some venturing into the past was necessary. Keeping the focus with Beth, therefore, was difficult at times. In praise of Dr. X's work, Beth was able to relate emotional history and feelings with facility, was able to see them as events of her past, and was able to explain them with the needed perspective.

At times, the therapy room contained the new therapist, Beth, the deceased therapist, and grief. Sometimes, it was too crowded. In time, Beth was able to negotiate the new relationship and to do some meaningful work and ultimately say good-bye and thank you to Dr. X for all the good work they had done together.

12

Bereavement After the Death of a Divorced Spouse: A Double Loss

The Case—Hannah

Hannah (24 years old) and David (27 years old), both observant Orthodox Jews, had known each other for only a few months when David proposed marriage. Both Hannah and David were nearing the age when they wanted to be married and begin a family, and they were married soon after the proposal. After a short honeymoon, David returned to his job as a hospital administrator and Hannah returned to her teaching job. They took an apartment in an Orthodox Jewish community near David's parents and continued the religious observances learned in their homes of origin. This included an active religious life, Sabbath and dietary law observance, and, for David, daily synagogue attendance. It also dictated a way of life that is governed by *halakhic*, an authoritative law originating in the Bible (Torah) which has been updated and expanded by rabbinic authorities as modern life and its changes affect religious observance (Wolowelsky, 1996).

Hannah became pregnant within 3 months of their wedding and the pregnancy was welcomed. The birth of their son was a glorious time for Hannah and David. They both wanted a large family and the first birth was especially fulfilling. When the second and third pregnancy followed within 2 years of each other, Hannah and David purchased a home in a suburban Orthodox community, about 1 hour from David's work. With three children younger than the age of 5 years, Hannah "had her hands full" and the demands of David's work and additional commute left Hannah struggling with myriad responsibilities, some of which she did easily although "many things slipped through the cracks." Fortunately, financial concerns were not a major issue.

David spent more and more time at work, often arriving home well after 10 p.m., only to get up early the next morning to begin his workday. Hannah and David began to grow apart and although Hannah would always say that David "tried to be a good father," he was gone most of the time, leaving all home and child care responsibilities to Hannah. The Sabbath is a sacred day for Orthodox Jews in that they are expected not to perform any work responsibilities and time is spent in prayer and as a respite from secular concerns. Sabbath begins on Friday at sundown and is observed as a family. As soon as Sabbath is over on Saturday evening, regular activity can begin. As a matter of routine, after Sabbath ended and after he had gone to synagogue, David would go to his study to prepare for the following week. He would spend most of Sunday in his study, effectively keeping Hannah and the children from him.

Over time, as the little annoyances of the marriage became magnified, David grew more remote and Hannah more disillusioned. There were arguments and heated disputes that ended with both Hannah and David feeling more and more estranged. In Hannah's eyes, David became entranced by his work and did not want the additional responsibility of wife, home, and family. He was remote and cool to her. Needless to say, she was angry, disappointed, and frustrated by his behavior. David could not "put up with the constant battles and demands" made by Hannah. This is what Hannah believed was the basis of David's request for a divorce. The option of divorce had been discussed between them in both calm and heated moments.

After attempts to mend their relationship failed, David served Hannah with a *get* (the first step in securing a divorce in the Orthodox Jewish tradition). David claimed that Hannah was not sympathetic to his rigorous work life and Hannah maintained that David had abandoned her and the family. After the *get* was served, the legal details of the divorce were worked out with a lawyer and David and Hannah began living apart. The impact of the divorce within their community was strongly felt, as divorce is not common and Hannah and David had been viewed as a model couple and family with traditional Jewish values. David arranged to visit the children every other week and to spend the Sabbath with the family once a month. There was minimal contact between David and Hannah except as it related to the children.

Hannah was in a state of shock over the divorce that lasted for a few weeks. It was compounded by a subtle lack of community support.

Hannah soon realized "that life was really not much different after the divorce than before." Initially the children were upset but because David spent such a limited amount of time with them, his absence was not devastating. David fulfilled his financial and visitation responsibilities to Hannah and the children. A year went by with minimal friction between Hannah and David. Hannah grew mildly anxious when she thought about her long-term future and how she was going to manage as a single parent with three children.

Hannah stayed in the house that she and David had bought and although the children had periods of difficulty and struggle, as did Hannah as a single woman, Hannah "managed." David quickly began to pull away from the Orthodox way of Jewish life and dropped some of the religious observance of his marriage and family upbringing. He joined a conservative synagogue (less observant than the Orthodox), much to the chagrin of his parents and Hannah. Hannah was concerned that David's changed religious orientation would create tensions between them especially in the area of religious practices with the children. He seemed to have become indifferent to the opinions of Hannah, his parents, and others.

Almost seven years to the day of their first date, and about 14 months after their divorce, David, 34 years old and unmarried, had a massive heart attack. Hannah was called to the hospital by David's family and informed of the severity of his condition. He lingered in a coma for a week, then died. Despite the enmity between Hannah and David, the shock of his death sent Hannah into a depression. Hannah's internist, concerned about her sudden weight loss and lethargic state, recommended counseling, which she began a month after his death.

Relevant History

Hannah had been raised in an observant Orthodox Jewish home. She was the youngest of six children. She and her siblings had all been *yeshiva* (a Jewish school) educated and religion and strict observance of Jewish law was all Hannah knew. Her dating life had been somewhat limited. She had been active in the Hillel (Jewish social organization) of her college and dated a few men before being set up on a date with David. Her religious values included dedication to home and family and she thought that David shared these values and was pleased when their relationship began to deepen.

Hannah's mother, a recent widow, moved to Israel soon after Hannah's father's death, 6 months after Hannah and David were married. Hannah was not the type of woman "easily thrown," but she had known periods of depression, especially in her adolescent years, when her grandfather and maternal grandmother died. She had managed the death of her father quite well, in part because she was devoting her energy to her marriage and pregnancy.

Conceptual Issues

To fully understand the bereavement reaction of a spouse to the death of a previous marriage partner, we must see the divorce as a potentially unresolved traumatic event. Depending on the length of time since the divorce, the divorce itself can be seen as a form of loss with bereavement issues that are unresolved. In many situations, as in this case, cultural concerns also become an integral aspect of the bereavement picture. The impact of the divorce, culture, and death will be explored as they influence the bereavement experience.

Divorce as a Traumatic Event

Marriages fail. Sometimes people believe that they have fallen out of love, turn on each other, and become strangers; the decision to divorce is almost always infused with some degree of emotional pain. Divorce is ranked at the top of the list of stressful life events. For each partner, there is the dread of negative repercussions, of an uncertain future, and of painful losses. Although divorce often ends up as a mutual decision, at the early stages there is usually one person who is the initiator and one who is initially unaware of that desire. Leavers and those left have different feelings throughout the process of the divorce. The partner who initiates the divorce may feel guilt and anxiety about the welfare of the partner who did not want the divorce. Despite outcome differences, what both partners share is the end of the marital relationship. For some partners, this is a welcome relief from a bad decision; for others, there are long-lasting feelings of ambivalence and anguish.

With divorce comes several challenges: relinquishing the dream to "live happily ever after"; changing roles, such as becoming a single parent who dates; adjusting to income and property shifts; facing the challenge in meeting physical and intimacy needs; and dealing with the potential assault to one's self-esteem. As one author noted, "Divorce is an event tailor-made for feeling bad about oneself" (T. Martin, 1989, p. 165). Many have described the pain of divorce as a form of grief.

Although divorce is a painful life transition, for many couples it does not signify the complete end of their relationship, especially if there are children involved. There are financial obligations, ongoing material and emotional needs, visiting situations that must be arranged and abided by, and holiday occurrences. Special life events such as graduations, school activities, and vacations involve negotiations between the divorced parents.

When a divorced spouse dies, several factors dictate the degree of upset and anguish of the survivor: the level of ambivalence and upset over the divorce, whether the spouse was able to move into a new life, whether there was adequate support for the person who was left, and whether the person was an active or passive agent in initiating the divorce. The perceived desertion and levels of anger and guilt are also factors to be considered (Raphael, 1983). These aspects of the divorce process will all come into play when counseling those grieving after the death of a divorced spouse.

Divorce in the Orthodox Jewish Community

The importance of divorce in the Orthodox Jewish community cannot be understated. Judaism regards marriage as a special relationship between a man and a woman that begins with a holy bond and a contract called the *ketubah*. Under Orthodox Jewish law, a divorce is accomplished by writing a bill of divorce (*get*) that is served by the husband to the wife. Either husband or wife may initiate the process but the husband is the spouse who serves the *get*; this gives the husband ultimate control of when the marriage ends. The *get* is written by a scribe and presented to the wife in the presence of a rabbi and qualified witnesses. It is important to note that a civil divorce is not sufficient to dissolve a Jewish marriage; as far as Jewish law is concerned, a couple remains married until the woman receives the *get*. Without the *get*, any children borne by the woman would be considered illegitimate, the woman's second marriage would be considered adulterous, and her children would be considered *Mamzerim* (bastards). Marriage in the Orthodox Jewish tradition is for life; divorce is not encouraged and the process of divorcing is protracted and complex.

Death of a Divorced Spouse

There is a significant dearth of literature regarding this bereavement experience. In light of the astoundingly high divorce rates in the United States, this gap in bereavement knowledge is surprising. Scott (1987, 2000) and Doka (1986, 1989b) documented the limited research informing this type of bereavement.

Doka (1986) studied eight surviving ex-spouses and their attempts to explore the issues related to the impact of their former partners' death. Most of the people studied experienced a major sense of loss at the time of their divorce. There was an inverse relationship between the degree of impact of the divorce and the impact of the subsequent death of the ex-spouse; if the divorce was described as a major loss, the impact of the subsequent death was minimal. When the impact of the divorce and the loss connected with the divorce had not been resolved, strong affective responses to the death of the ex-spouse were noted and reactions were intensified. Emotions such as guilt and regret were particularly prevalent. One ex-spouse had fantasies about reconciliation that were shattered by the death.

Doka (1986) commented on the social dislocation that can complicate bereavement when death follows divorce, noting that the "...ex-spouse has an ambiguous role. There was and perhaps still is, a significant relationship with the ex-spouse. Yet they are no longer married" (p. 445). How do family, friends, and the community respond to this type of loss? Many participants reported a lack of social support and a surprising sense of disconnection from those close to them.

Scott's (1987) initial research used 75 participants who responded to a questionnaire about reactions to their ex-spouse's death. Three quarters of her sample reported a definite grief reaction following the death of their ex-spouse. Seventy-five percent of those reporting an overwhelming grief reaction had been divorced fewer than 5 years; the shorter the time between the divorce and the death, the stronger the grief reaction was Scott theorized that this might be due to the survivor not having had enough time or not being able to complete the necessary emotional detachment following divorce, or both. In terms of social support, almost half of the respondents received little or no understanding or sympathy from friends and people in their social circles.

Scott's (1987) study also analyzed cause of death and severity of the survivor's grief reaction. Sudden heart attacks, fatal accidents, and suicide accounted for 67% of all deaths reported and 92% of the severe grief reactions. The suddenness and realization of the finality of the loss of the relationship were mentioned by some of the participants as negative factors in their grief reactions. Scott also examined role ambiguity, especially at the time of the funeral; 60% of the participants attended the funeral and 45% felt uncomfortable there. Scott did not describe after-funeral rituals.

Scott repeated and expanded her 1997 study in 2000 with 79 respondents. In the earlier study, 77.5% reported a grief reaction and answered affirmatively to having had a grief reaction. In both studies, respondents noted that the shorter the time between the divorce and the death, the stronger the grief reaction. In the second study, 35% of the respondents admitted increased use of drugs, alcohol, and tobacco in the first year following the death of the divorced spouse. The author concluded, "A variety of factors influence the grief reaction... the length of time divorced, the degree to which the survivor has accomplished the 'emotional divorce,' role ambiguity during the funeral rituals, lack of understanding from family and friends... and in the event of remarriage, uncertainty of the response from the current spouse" (Scott, 2000, p. 218).

Orthodox Jewish Rituals in Death

Death in the Orthodox Jewish community is viewed through the lens of extensive ritual as dictated by *halakha*, the operative laws and concepts that define behavior within the religious community. As noted by one of the seminal texts describing guidelines for the Jewish way of managing death, "Thousands of years of our rich tradition provide us with direction during these moments of crisis. The accumulated wisdom of the ages is a source of great consolation" (Lamm, 1969, p. 3).

Halakha prescribes procedures for handling the dead body for funeral preparation, formal burial, and postburial activities. After the moment of death, the laws for formal mourning known as *keriah* go into effect. These rituals include having a group of very pious men and women called *Chevra Kadisha* stand vigil with the body until its burial, which takes place 24 hours after death. Traditionally, the *Chevra Kadisha* prepares the *mit* (deceased) for burial by carefully following the rules of purification called *taharah*. The preparation includes placing the body on a plank and washing it with large quantities of water from head to toe. The mit is formally dressed in special burial clothing—a white linen or cotton shroud, trousers, a long smock, and skullcap for men—and is placed in a simple, unlined casket made of wood with a bag of earth from the Holy Land. The body in the coffin is never left alone until burial. Orthodox Jewish tradition does not permit the viewing of the body. This is done as recognition of the finality of death. No cosmetic treatment of the body is allowed (Getzel, 2000; Lamm, 1969).

Lamm (1969) described five stages of traditional mourning: (1) *aninut*, the period of the most intense despair, which occurs between death and burial; (2) the 3 days following burial when the mourner does not respond to greetings and remains at home and visiting is discouraged; (3) *shiva*, the 7 days following the death when the mourner is encouraged to speak of the loss and, while remaining home, expresses grief to visitors; (4) *sheloshim*, the 30 days following burial, when the mourner is encouraged to leave the house and slowly rejoin society; and (5) the 12-month

period during which things return to normal, with the pursuit of enter-
tainment and amusement curtailed. In summary, Lamm saw that in this
"…graduated process of mourning an ancient faith raises up the mourner
from the abyss of despair to the undulating hills and valleys of normal
life" (pp. 78–79). The tradition regulates a time that could otherwise be
chaotic. The tradition creates a structured response to death that can be
very helpful during an otherwise chaotic time.

Suggestions for Intervention

There are several areas of intervention that must be considered in dealing
with clients bereft from the death of an ex-spouse. This form of grief is not
generally recognized by society and a bereaved ex-spouse may even hold
the belief that they have no right or reason to grieve. The counselor must
help the client recognize that he or she has experienced a real loss and that
grief is a normal subsequent reaction. Having the ex-spouse examine the
responses, both emotional and physical, to the news of the loss can facilitate
the legitimizing of the loss. Many ex-spouses have limited social support and
may need help and encouragement to verbalize and explore their responses
to this event. This can be done in the nonjudgmental atmosphere of the
counseling relationship.

The counselor also is listening for any ambivalent, angry, or unresolved feelings toward the ex-spouse and the divorce that can be revived
by the death. The ex-spouse must examine whether there are any remaining emotional ties that exist (Doka, 1989b) and begin the process of withdrawing emotional energy from them and redirecting it either to self-care
or to others. In the main, the survivor needs to be reassured that he or she
is experiencing a normal grief reaction to the death of a significant person
in his or her life (Scott, 2000).

Another area to explore is the ways in which the death of the ex-
spouse will affect the current life of the client, including financial implications, changes in the patterns of the lives of the children, and so on. The
ex-spouse must examine whether there are any remaining emotional ties
that exist (Doka, 1989b) and begin the process of withdrawing emotional
energy from them and directing it to self-care and to others.

Each one of these areas must be explored with the griever to understand where intervention and support is needed. It is safe to make the
assumption that if an individual seeks counseling, there are sufficient
unresolved issues and areas of concern that plague the survivor. These
areas have to be identified for the work to begin and to be accurately
focused.

Major Issues in This Case

There were two parallel and simultaneous forces and struggles in this case that had to be considered: the emotional impact of the death of Hannah's ex-husband and the cultural and religious implications of the death for Hannah.

Hannah, fully aware of the traditional religious management of death, was in a quandary when David died. Her instinct was to follow the tradition to the fullest but where should she insert herself into this process and where did she belong? As noted in the research by Scott (1987, 2000) and Doka (1986, 1989a) Hannah's role ambiguity was pronounced in this case. David's parents, from whom he had become somewhat estranged when he joined a conservative synagogue, were equally confused. The collective instinct—Hannah's and her former in-laws—was to follow the traditional route of burial, to take charge of the process. But only the most religious Jews, from whom David had turned away, follow these traditions. Fortunately, the rabbi of David's new synagogue intervened and felt that because David had moved away from the most traditional ways his ideological shift should be honored. David would not have chosen to have a traditional Orthodox burial. The pain that this decision caused for Hannah was profound. "It violated something fundamental in me," she said. As a woman steeped in the tradition of Orthodox behavior, she felt that this was shameful to her and her family and all that they stood for.

Another area of confusion was where David was to be buried. David's family had burial plots, as did Hannah's. Had they remained married, Hannah and David would have been buried in her family's plot. However, since the divorce, it was not clear where he belonged. Ritual suggests that, "If a man and woman were separated in marriage, they may nevertheless be buried alongside one another. If one of the partners, however, stipulated that he be buried separately, the request must be followed" (Lamm, 1969, pp. 68–69). Hannah felt strongly that David should be buried in her family plot and David's parents agreed, but not easily and not readily.

Hannah struggled with whether she should "sit shiva." As the ex-wife, should she be in mourning in the traditional manner? Guidance came again from David's rabbi who, while leaving the decision up to Hannah, told her that as a divorced mate she need not observe any of the mourning laws and was exempt from even attending the funeral, if she chose to not be there (Lamm, 1969). Hannah felt like a grieving widow and initiated the requisite Orthodox procedures for the mourning period. She reasoned that he was the father of the children, and Hannah felt an obligation to honor that relationship by observing the prescribed rituals.

The role of community in mourning is very important. "Mourning becomes a societal activity not simply in that it is done in public but that it is experienced interactively with the community. The comforters are not merely individuals; they are operative participants in a community activity" (Wolowelsky, 1996, p. 473). For Hannah, this meant that dozens of community members and friends were there to offer support, comfort, and tangible help in the form of preparing meals, taking care of the children, shopping, and so forth. Although very helpful and supportive, this help posed a paradoxical situation for Hannah, casting her more as the stricken widow than as the divorced wife whose ex-husband had recently died.

One theme that permeates much of the religious observations around death in the Orthodox Jewish community is that the inner turmoil of the mourner be given objective and controlled expression. As such, there is a ritual of tearing of the mourner's clothing as an expression of the inner anger over the death. "Mourning becomes a societal activity not simply in that it is done in public but that it is experienced interactively with the community. The comforters are not merely individuals; they are operative participants in a community activity" (Wolowelsky, 1996, p. 473).

Within the counseling relationship, the initial concerns that Hannah raised were management issues: did she do the right things with funeral ritual and burial, where did she belong in relation to her former in-laws, how should she handle the children, and so on. She seemed depressed but not immovable, and her depression was a mixture of sadness about David's death and anger at him and how he had managed to mess up his life, her life, and the lives of their children. From a therapeutic standpoint, the expression of her anger was a welcome sign. Depression has been described as anger turned inward so when clients begin expressing anger, they are apparently coming out of their depression and moving forward in their recovery. The counselor encouraged direct expressions of anger, and Hannah, once she got going, was vituperative and eloquent in articulating her feelings.

The counselor offered limited advice regarding management of Hannah's various life dilemmas. What was offered was that she should seek the guidance of people in her community. The hope was that as she sought guidance, she would also find support for her struggles around specific decisions.

Hannah's adjustment to David's death was marked by considerable emotional conflict and ambivalence. Although she had made "peace with the divorce" she nevertheless felt guilty for her alleged lack of understanding and impatience with David and blamed herself and her "neediness" for much of what had happened between them. The death brought forward all of the issues and upset surrounding the divorce as though it had just occurred. In her worst moments of despair, Hannah wondered whether his heart attack was a result of the divorce and the tensions that existed between them. This tendency toward self-blame and guilt was normalized as a reaction to a loss and Hannah was relieved that she "was not going crazy with these feelings."

Hannah had to deal with not only the finality of the relationship with David and of the marriage but also the finality of the relationship David had with the children and with her as an ex-spouse. It was the permanence of all of these changes that got to Hannah. Helping someone adjust to so many levels of change can be challenging: Where does the counselor start to help the person rebuild his or her life? Which finality is the most pressing? As often happens with people who grieve, Hannah was not able to see that her depression was obscuring her sense of capacity. Hannah had been living on her own for almost a year and managing her home, the finances, and her children with very little support and help from David. She had made some pivotal decisions about the children and their schooling, had managed some difficult periods of illness with the children, and had kept herself on an even emotional keel. What Hannah needed from the counselor was someone who could point out her accomplishments to strengthen and empower her. In general, a counselor has to be careful to not overemphasize capacity, as the griever may hear that as the counselor's not being able to understand his or her feelings of diminished self-esteem. If the griever feels that he or she does not have the ability to manage, the counselor has to gently suggest areas of competence.

In hindsight, one of the most helpful areas of the counseling was in justifying Hannah's position and the ambiguity surrounding it. It was understandably confusing that she did not know whether she had a place in David's death and the ensuing rituals. She commented, "I don't know where to put myself. I am not the widow, there is no widow, but I feel like a widow." By supporting the ambiguity, by saying that Hannah felt an understandable level of confusion, the counselor allowed Hannah to vent some of her anger toward David for "having put her in such a spot."

The additional aspect of David's religious shift further complicated her bereavement adjustment. She knew one way to act and observe a death. Hannah's torment in his death was that she had to abandon some of her religious practices in favor of David's newfound conservative views. This rankled and confused her. Here, again, she was reassured that this confusion was understandable and would have been experienced by anyone in her situation. She was simultaneously urged to see David's religious shift as a move away from her (and what she believed David had stood for) and as a pull in the eventual dissolution of the marriage.

In short-term individual counseling, Hannah was helped to simultaneously mourn her divorce and the loss of her ex-husband. Asking Hannah to recall the circumstances of the marital discord and difficulties that had been inherent in the relationship did this. It seemed that Hannah first had to come to terms with the dissolution of the marriage before she would be able to see David's death in the context of the separate life she had begun to develop after the *get* was issued.

In bereavement, recent loss triggers past losses and this was the case with seeing the divorce as a loss. The loss of the marriage, which had been masked by the anger and resentment she felt toward David at the time, was now unmasked and Hannah had to grapple with some of these issues for the first time. Initially, she presented the failed marriage as more her failing than David's, but as time progressed she was able to understand, through telling and retelling of some of the marital dynamics, that they were both responsible for the difficulties. Eventually, she shed any sense of responsibility for David's heart attack or for his turning away from his faith. Supportive counseling, with an intention to clarify and relieve guilt and misconceptions, guided the intervention schema.

Within a 6-month period, Hannah had returned to a level of functioning that left her feeling somewhat optimistic. She claimed that she better understood the forces that broke up the marriage and, although still struggling with single parenting and some financial concerns, she was hopeful that she might marry again. Her grief and anger at David had turned to sadness for him. She saw him as a man who was driven in ways that she was unable to predict or support. She confessed that if she met him today, she might still "fall for him as there were charismatic qualities about him, but the price for charisma was way too high."

Issues for the Counselor

This case was an excellent example of the need for a counselor to have some sensitivity to the cultural and religious traditions and rituals that can complicate a bereavement experience. If the counselor is not able to grasp some of the subtle forces that enter into the experience, much will be lost. "In all cultures, the rituals of funerals, burials, and post-burial rites are very important in attenuating the severity of grief reactions" (Parry & Ryan, 2000, p. xv). The counselor also must be sensitive to the disenfranchised quality of the grief of the ex-spouse. This is a segment of the population that receives little or no attention. More research needs to be done for counselors to fully understand the complexity and nuances of this form of loss.

Bereavement After Physician-Assisted Suicide: The Physician Ended the Pain

The Case—Marc

Marc and Judy were married for 18 years and were the parents of two daughters, ages 10 and 12 years. When Judy's illness was diagnosed as stomach cancer, the family was devastated. Despite the fact that Judy's father had died from the same cancer and a relative on her mother's side also had been a cancer death, the news was understandably shocking. For months before the diagnosis, Judy had been losing weight, had abdominal pain, was easily fatigued, and was not feeling "herself." The trip to the internist led to a CT scan and ultimately to the oncologist. The picture described by the oncologist—a friend of Marc's since high school—involved potent chemotherapy with a 15% chance of survival at 2 years. After a family meeting to discuss the options, Judy began chemotherapy treatment at a local hospital.

Judy had to give up her job as a schoolteacher to accommodate the chemo regimen and because she felt too weak to work. Marc owned his own printing business and was able to take her back and forth for treatment. The treatment days were very taxing on Judy. Although there are numerous new drugs that can help the chemo patient with nausea, they extract a toll in terms of fatigue. Judy lost her hair in the first month and began wearing a wig on the few occasions when she was feeling strong enough to leave the house.

Six months into the treatment, new scans were ordered and the oncologist told Judy and Marc that the treatment was not working; they were advised to stop the chemotherapy and were told that her situation was terminal. She could live as long as a year but her ability to function would become steadily compromised as time passed. The oncologist, as a family friend, wanted to continue to treat her and vowed to keep her comfortable and pain free.

As her condition worsened, Judy and Marc discussed end-of-life options. Judy was adamant that she did not want to be a burden and add to the anguish of her children and husband because of intolerable pain and the loss of her ability to function independently. She did not want them or herself to suffer endlessly.

In the next several months, Judy's condition spiraled downward. She was losing weight at an alarming rate and was so weak that she had to be carried from one room to another. Fortunately, resources were available for Judy to be cared for at home. The doctor—as physician and long-time friend—visited Judy on a weekly basis, en route from the hospital to his office. The initial manageable level of pain had been replaced by crippling spasms that began in her back and spread to her abdominal area. The pain medication was marginally effective but left Judy in "a place where she was unrecognizable." Marc's anguish was paralleled by Judy's depression. Often, she would scream out in pain that she wanted to die. In calmer moments, she made Marc promise that he would help her die either by direct means or by asking for the doctor to intervene. Marc was in an awful quandary: he was overwhelmed by responsibility and anguish on Judy's behalf, and he was very concerned about his children and was conflicted internally over his promise to help Judy die.

Another torturous month passed. Although hospice services and pain management had been initiated, the pain was unrelenting and in the rare lucid moments that Judy had, she renewed her pleas for Marc to help end her life. Marc spoke to the doctor, as a friend, and reluctantly the doctor complied by ordering adequate quantities of morphine tablets for Judy to be able to end her life. He explained to them both what dosage levels were needed. The doctor said that he was going beyond his medical orientation by supplying the pills, that it was a very difficult position for him, and that he was only complying with Marc's and Judy's wishes because of their friendship.

On one excruciatingly painful evening, Judy begged for Marc to give her the pills. In tears, and struggling with totally ambivalent feelings, Marc crushed the pills into some fruit and fed them to Judy. After a few minutes, he called his daughters into the room and Judy faded from them "in peace, at last."

Initially, Marc was relieved that Judy's suffering was over. However, within weeks after her death, he was assailed by feelings of guilt that he "may have done the wrong thing" by acceding to Judy's request and asking the doctor to help end her life. "Perhaps I acted out of my own selfish need to end my own misery and not have to see Judy suffering. ...Maybe I should have taken her for another opinion or to a major cancer center. ... I killed her!" he lamented. Marc's bereavement was heavily tainted by his sense of overwhelming guilt.

Marc sought counseling because of his depression. He was unable to resume some of his responsibilities after Judy's death and was not managing his emotions, which were "all over the place." He was new to counseling; initially he spoke mainly about his sense of loneliness and anguish over Judy's death. He cried often and wondered how he would be able to raise his daughters without his wife. It took several sessions for Marc to begin discussing, in detail, how Judy died through his and the physician's assistance. The information was haltingly conveyed; Marc was painfully conflicted over his participation in Judy's dying.

Relevant History

Marc was an only child, and his father had died from a brain tumor when Marc was 7 years old. Life without his father had been difficult both financially and emotionally. Marc had vivid memories of his father's loss of awareness and mobility as his illness progressed. He lived with his mother until he married Judy at the age of 27 years. Marc described his life with Judy as comfortable and fulfilling. As a father, he was close to his daughters. Marc had not had a sustained period of depression that he could remember. He stated that he "tended to see the dark side" in most situations and saw this as a lifelong pattern.

Conceptual Issues

Literature about bereavement after physician-assisted death is sparse. This paucity is understandable in light of the ongoing debate over legalization of physician-assisted death and the infrequency with which it occurs. Essentially, the debate over legalization pivots around patients' autonomy to control their lives (and deaths) and medical beneficence in relieving excruciating pain and suffering. Many claim that physician-assisted dying is equivalent to murder and puts the physician on an ethical and moral slippery slope. Others believe that self-determination is the core issue and that people should not have to suffer. We are kinder to animals, lament those in favor of physician-assisted death.

In 1997, after years of intense argument and spurred by the actions of Dr. Jack Kevorkian, the U.S. Supreme Court in a 9 to 0 decision refused to recognize a constitutional right to die by upholding New York and Washington state statutes criminalizing physician-assisted death. In a conciliatory or evasive posture, the Supreme Court invited state legislatures to examine the issue and pass legislation on their own, thus passing the venue of decision making about physician-assisted death from the federal to the state level. At this time, only the state of Oregon, as a result of a citizen-initiated ballot (Measure 16, passed in 1997) allows physician-assisted death under very restricted conditions (Fraser & Walters, 2002). The Oregon Death With Dignity Act applies to only terminally ill adults who have an incurable and irreversible disease that will probably produce death in 6 months. Repeated requests to die have to be made; the physician is then empowered to write a prescription for a lethal dose of medication. The act explicitly prohibits euthanasia (Bascom & Tolle, 2002; Kastenbaum, 1998). In Oregon, during the first 14 months of legalization, 15 persons—13 with cancer—have used the act to end their lives, an estimated 0.2% of those eligible (Fraser & Walters, 2002).

Physician-Assisted Death as Suicide

The unique aspect of physician-assisted death that affects the bereavement experience for the survivors is the unnaturalness of the death. Despite the popular support for physician-assisted dying—depending on how questions are worded and the types of choices offered, public support varies widely from 34% to 65%—many people are adamantly against the "taking of a life" and see the act as immoral (Emanuel, 2002). In essence, they claim, the deceased has committed suicide (with the help of the physician); the aftermath of suicide carries a particular burden for the survivor.

Several studies have attempted to assess the difference in bereavement for the survivor of suicide. An interesting finding in the research of Range and Calhoun (1990) was that those who lost a loved one through suicide were unique in saying that they lied about the nature of the death. The tendency to lie can be explained by the fact that suicide survivors experience higher levels of shame, stigma, and rejection as compared with other bereavement groups (E. Silverman, Range, & Overholser, 1994; Worden, 1982).

Anger and guilt also are observed in higher proportion in survivors of suicide. Many suicide survivors report feeling responsibility for how they treated the deceased and feel that they could have stopped the suicide. Although moderate guilt characterizes most mourning experiences, in "mourning after suicide, it is infinitely stronger and more persistent" (Rando, 1993, p. 526). It is especially difficult for some suicide survivors to get beyond the feelings of rejection and abandonment when they consider that the deceased has chosen death over life (Beder, 1998). The act of intentional self-killing is often seen as an act of desertion that threatens our own, sometimes tenuous, defense against experiences of nothingness and emptiness (Marrone, 1997, p. 61).

Individuals who have experienced a loss through suicide perceive themselves as treated differently by others, noting less community support than survivors from accident or naturally occurring death. An explanation for this apparent loss of support may relate to the potential for socially isolating behavior of the survivor based on feelings of guilt and shame (van der Wal, 1989–1990).

Physician-Assisted Death

Patients who think about physician-assisted death are usually exploring their options at the end of life. Some speculate that if faced with unbearable suffering, they want to know that predictable and expedient death is an option (Bascom & Tolle, 2002). In a study that surveyed attitudes of 100 terminally ill cancer patients, researchers showed that contrary to popular belief, unremitting pain and other somatic symptoms were not correlated to requests for assistance in dying. The strongest determinants of physician-assisted death attitudes were sociodemographic and religious attitudes (men and those with weak religious beliefs were more likely to entertain assistance in dying) and the desire to not be a burden to the family (Suarez-Almazor, Newman, Hanson, & Bruera, 2002).

The turmoil that precedes the decision to even request assistance in dying is profound. The level of distress, anguish, and perhaps exhaustion that promotes a wish to die is unimaginable. As Quill (1994) pointed out, patients who consider physician-assisted death are those for whom recovery is impossible and who face further disintegration of their personhood. They are people who do not want to die, necessarily, but who choose not to live under the circumstances they are forced to endure.

Having reached a decision, approaching the doctor is the next hurdle. Knowing that this is an illegal act, unless one lives in Oregon, makes approaching the subject with a physician a treacherous and very delicate interchange. The complexity lies in the fact that the patient or family is asking the doctor to facilitate an illegal behavior, which most doctors will not do. In essence, they are asking the physician to help murder the patient.

Bereavement Complications

Once the assistance has been accomplished, the family and patient have made peace with the decision, and the death has occurred, all parties involved in this action have entered into a collusion to keep secret the means of dying. If for no other reason than to protect the physician, a fabrication must be created. Secrets create shame (Bok, 1982); shame enters into the bereavement situation as an impediment to mourning. "Shame is closely allied to guilt. It is what people feel when they are in a situation in which they are not living up to their self-image" (Rando, 1984, p. 243). Shame and guilt are thus added to the constellation of feelings of remorse and loss.

An area of potential complication following physician-assisted death depends on the level of acrimony around the decision to seek assisted dying. If the decision to ask for assistance in dying is not held by both patient and family, the continued legacy of the survivors' questioning what they could have done to prevent the death could weigh heavily. If the patient wants to end his or her life and the family is unwilling, the level of added frustration for the patient can be alienating and enraging. If the family is supporting physician-assisted death and the patient is reluctant and wants to hold on, a message to the patient is conveyed about wanting him or her gone. This can greatly affect the mood and determination of the patient. Consider the situation in which the patient is in great pain, knows of the terminality of the situation, and wants to end the suffering and the family is adamantly opposed to assisted dying. Should that patient have to endure the suffering or should he or she be able to direct the dying and not consider the wishes of his or her family? Or the reverse: The family is coercing the patient to end his or her life when the patient still wants to hold on to whatever time is left. These are thorny ethical questions that touch values based on self-determination. Counselors are cautioned to be attuned to their feelings on this subject to be able to interact fully with families and family members who are engaged in this bereavement experience.

A final area of complexity, which is similar to unassisted dying, is the necessity to tie up loose ends before death. Within the emotional turmoil of impending death there is often the opportunity to deal with mending torn relationships and saying some of the things that need to be said as someone prepares to die. If the final days are spent trying to sort out the decision around physician assistance in dying, valuable time may be lost as energy and attention are used to arrange this form of death. Thus, it is crucial that the decision is well thought through before the patient is unable to interact and influence the process.

Unanticipated Occurrences

Mention must be made of the situation in which a physician-assisted suicide goes awry. This can occur when the amount of prescribed drugs is not adequate or administered in too protracted a length of time, or if the individual is stronger than anticipated. "Obviously, watching someone peacefully fade into death as a result of taking a physician-prescribed overdose is much different from holding a pillow over a loved one's face because the pills didn't work and both of these are different from securing a plastic bag over a significant other's head" (Werth, 1999, p. 251). These situations can occur, when the patient does not die and the assisted death goes awry, and the aftermath for the significant other, who was instrumental in arranging the death, can be extremely complex. In these instances, the hoped-for peaceful exit from life can turn into a situation in which the survivor is more involved and actively intervenes to accomplish the dying.

For many survivors, even if there is full accord from the suffering person, the levels of guilt, fear, and anxiety are heightened as the survivor(s) has had to play a much more active role in the dying than anticipated or wanted. With the help of intervention focused on reassuring the survivor that he or she was carrying out the wishes of the dying person, the additional burden of involvement can be eased or lifted.

Suggestions for Intervention

When counseling the survivor of a physician-assisted death, there are specific areas of concern that must be addressed beyond those of normal bereavement: shame, anger, guilt, abandonment, rejection, and the area of unfinished business (Rando, 1993).

The grief counselor must directly address shame and guilt. Whether religious orientation, cultural issues, or questions about the quality and extent of medical care obtained by the family are driving the guilt, there must be an attempt to normalize these responses. The fact that the decision to die was made by a terminally ill person who could no longer tolerate life as it was must be reinforced. The counselor must help the survivor see that regardless of what he or she did or did not do, they were not responsible for or in control of the choices of the deceased (Beder, 1998).

Anger, a powerful emotion in all bereavement responses, may be especially prominent in a physician-assisted death. The anger can be directed at the world, fate (God), the medical establishment, the doctor who complied with the suicide request, the patient who made this choice, other members of the family who may not have acted quickly enough in the face of the medical situation, and the self for not being powerful enough to save the patient from a terminal illness. The counselor must help the survivor to express and ultimately externalize the anger so it is not turned on the self (Worden, 1982).

Abandonment and rejection in particular are often common feelings experienced by the survivor(s) in a physician-assisted death. In an effort to assist the survivor to overcome these feelings, it is important to help the survivor understand why the deceased chose the option of suicide (Rando, 1995). The survivor is encouraged to play out different scenarios about the deceased's frame of mind, reasoning, and decision-making processes. Although the survivor may not agree with the deceased's decision, he or she may be helped to see that this was the deceased's choice and was the best option perceived at the time. The effort is directed toward having the survivor understand that the deceased had the right to end his or her life even if it was over the objections of family and friends (Beder, 1998) and to understand the emotions the deceased was experiencing.

One of the most remarkable areas of conflict for the bereaved survivor is the sense of relief experienced by the survivor. At last the patient is no longer suffering and has found peace and so has the survivor. But the survivor is constrained by society from expressing this sense of relief because of the illegality of the act. Counselors are urged to normalize the feeling of relief that comes with assisted death. It is acceptable for the survivor to feel relieved and still mourn (Rando, 1993). "Such emotions are not necessarily evidence of greed or a lack of compassion but rather may be a healthy expression of the opposite—a lack of a need for the deceased person to carry on for the client's sake and/or a feeling that the person is better off because his or her suffering has ended. For some (survivors) having positive feelings after a death may be confusing or disturbing so the (counselor) can help to normalize and assuage any guilt" (Werth, 1999, p. 246).

Major Issues in This Case

When Marc entered counseling he was consumed by guilt over his participation in Judy's dying. His guilt was preventing him from dealing with his mourning. He called himself a murderer, and indeed, he seemed to really believe that he had murdered Judy. He recounted, time and again, the events leading up to the day and time when he administered the morphine tablets. Rynearson (2001) suggested that retelling is an important part of bereavement work and it can have cathartic benefits. This recounting of the details of a death is a common response in all forms of dying. There is something therapeutic in the retelling in that it tends to normalize the event and helps the survivor accept the reality of the loss. In addition, with each telling, some of the content becomes less charged and the sharp edges of the experience are somewhat softened.

Marc said that the night before her death, Judy had been lucid and reiterated her wish to die. She felt that she could not endure another day of pain and humiliation. She told Marc that the burden of her care and the pain she saw on the faces of her daughters was too much for her to bear. Simultaneously, Marc wanted to hold on, as he had just found notice of a new treatment on an Internet site, and to end her suffering. Both Judy and he knew that by using the pills given to them by their doctor, they were engaging in an illegal act, but in the end Marc could not deny Judy this final wish.

Sadly and with a sense of resignation, Marc administered the pills to Judy. They embraced; she thanked him for ending her misery and told him that she loved him. He then went to get their daughters, and Judy, now getting very sleepy, told the girls that she loved being their mother and kissed each of them. She closed her eyes; the last sight she saw was her daughters and Marc beside the bed.

Along with the feelings of guilt for having done an illegal act, Marc felt shame. As a Jewish man, although not the most observant of Jewish lore, he was aware that it was a sin in his religion to take a life. This was not the most prominent area of shame, but it was discussed early in the counseling relationship as a concern. He felt that he had failed as a husband, a father, and a Jew. What the counselor interpreted to Marc was that perhaps he felt he should have been able to save Judy from her cancer. Tearfully, Marc agreed.

Another area of deep regret for Marc was the "misuse of time." "We had so little time together, not only as married people and parents, but in the last few weeks. In the end, all we talked about was medical stuff and when she was to get her shot, or when the hospice people were coming. We never had a chance to say good-bye. The girls were not really brought into this. I wanted to protect them." So many of Marc's reactions were understandable. He was carrying far too many burdens and for Marc to begin mourning his loss he needed to be relieved of some of his concerns.

The counselor must make every effort to reassure the mourner that the feelings of not having enough time are almost always present when there is a death, especially a death that has been protracted, and when energy has been used in caring for the ill person. The survivor invariably feels that he or she has not done enough, that if only there had been more time to say some of the things there was never a chance to say. One strategy in the counseling that is often effective in relieving the regret of things unsaid is to ask the mourner to say the unsaid things, to imagine telling the loved one all of what the mourner has thought about since the death. This puts the survivor's feelings into specific words, which, although the words will not be heard by the one they are intended for, allows the mourner to liberate some of the emotional energy being used to beat himself or herself up.

Not lost in the reactions for Marc was the history of his father's death. His father had suffered unmercifully in his dying from a brain tumor. Marc had been a young boy at the time, yet the memories of his father's pain and debilitation and his mother's anguish were still quite vivid. When Judy's disease had first been diagnosed, Marc prayed that she would not suffer the way his father had. After several counseling sessions, he was able to acknowledge that he had wished his father had died sooner so he and his mother could have been spared the last weeks of his life. Taking this admission further, the counselor suggested that some of what motivated Marc and allowed him to fulfill Judy's request was to help her avoid the pain and anguish of a slow and torturous death. This was reframed to Marc as an act of compassion rather than an act of aggression or unlawful behavior.

The counseling strategy was to normalize as many of Marc's feelings as possible. The retelling of the last moments and the decision-making rationale were important for Marc to repeat and retell. The retelling helped to ease the guilt Marc was carrying. Marc had a very hard time accepting that Judy had such a strong wish to die. He had hoped she would be able to endure longer until a new treatment or cure was announced. To address this concern, the counselor introduced the reality of medical knowledge that dictated that Judy's cancer, despite what might have been discovered, was too far advanced for treatment to be initiated or successful.

It almost seemed that Marc had been unable to accept that Judy's illness was terminal. He was still in denial, up until the last moments. His denial made the last act even more emotionally complicated for him. Had he been more emotionally aware of the progression of the illness—he was surely aware of the physical progression—he might have been more accepting of his actions on her behalf. This was explored with Marc and he acknowledged the duality of his denial as he said, "My brain knew what was happening with her, it was inescapable as she was becoming weaker, thinner, and more compromised in front of my eyes. But, my heart and soul ached when I thought of life without her and prayed every day that something would turn this horror show around."

The last area of concern for Marc, before being able to move into the anticipated bereavement issues of a widower, was his view of himself as a murderer. It seemed impossible for him to accept that Judy had wanted to die and that he had complied. He questioned what kind of person he was and how he, who was a moral, God-believing person, could have acted in this way. Meier and Morrison (2002) helped frame the counselor's response to Marc: "What is it that patients really want? Seriously ill patients want… relief from suffering, help in minimizing the burden on families, closer relationships with family members, and a sense of control" (p. 1088). Marc had to see that Judy wanted this, not to escape from her life but to end her pain. This recognition was the hardest hurdle for Marc to accept; he needed to accept that he had done an action that was relieving of Judy's pain but was excruciatingly painful for him and his daughters.

The bereavement issues for Judy and Marc's daughters were not exaggerated because of the circumstance surrounding Judy's death. The girls were not told of the fact that there had been assistance for her dying. The grief of the daughters was consistent with a "normal" loss of a parent. As described by Rando (1984), in children from ages 8 to 12 years, when the death is anticipated, the potential for denial is minimal and although the children have exhibited growing independence from the parent, there is the possibility of reawakening of feelings of childishness and helplessness while trying to put up a facade of independence and coping. Marc had to be encouraged in his own counseling to help his daughters express their feelings as he was struggling with his own grief. Family sessions were encouraged and on several occasions he would bring one or both of his daughters.

It was many months before Marc was able to forgive himself for his actions. He was unable to speak to his friend, the physician involved in the death, for 6 months despite repeated outreach from the doctor. The strongest push for reengaging with life was from Marc's daughters.

He was mending, slowly.

Issues for the Counselor

Physician-assisted death is extremely controversial. In working with situations in which this has occurred, the counselor is cautioned to be aware of his or her position on this issue. If the counselor has conflicted feelings, he or she may infuse them into the counseling and heighten guilt and shame reactions of the survivor. If the counselor is in favor of assisted death, he or she may have difficulty understanding the anguish and struggles of the survivor. The struggle to remain impartial over such a contested issue can be very challenging to the counselor.

The counseling effort with Marc was slow to show improvement, which is always a frustration in this work. Underneath all the anguish, Marc was a broken and lonely man. He was overwhelmed with concern about his daughters and frequently sought advice on how to handle their grief. There were several family sessions that were very therapeutic but painful to witness, as the girls were devastated by the loss of their mother. The 12-year-old, just hurtling into adolescence, was most hard hit by the death. The sense of loss expressed by each of the children was truly poignant and the urge to comfort them, even beyond the counseling relationship, was compelling.

Physician-assisted death continues as a topic of debate. Counselors are advised to keep current on the issues and determine where they stand. There will always be some form of assistance in dying, whether legal or not. Clarity on the issue will facilitate "cleaner" counseling.

It may be helpful to counselors to know what the code of ethics for their discipline says about their role in a physician-assisted death. The National Association of Social Workers, for example, has outlined ways that its members can be helpful in these circumstances: a social worker can be in attendance at a physician-assisted death but cannot be instrumental in providing the means. But the most reliable indicator of counselor effectiveness is his or her stance on the issue of physician-assisted dying. If the counselor has a strongly held position against this form of death, and is not able to monitor his or her feelings and responses, then the survivor should be referred to one who can be neutral about the survivor's decision and help the survivor make peace with the choices that were made.

CHAPTER

Bereavement After the Death of a Young Grandchild: A Triple Loss

The Case—Katherine

For Mark (62 years old) and Katherine (59 years old), both retired, the birth of a grandchild was a long awaited event. Both sons had been married for several years and the anticipation of the first grandchild was high. When the announcement of the pregnancy came, according to Katherine, she wept. She and Mark were at the hospital for the birth and from the moment she held the baby boy, she felt that her life had shifted. The depth of love that she felt for her grandchild Samuel could not be described; she just knew that this love was qualitatively different from any love she had experienced up until then. To Katherine, it felt more pure and more direct and was not diverted by the necessities of having to raise him.

The first few weeks were hectic for the parents, Dan and Sarah, as the baby and parents adjusted to their altered lifestyle. Katherine and Mark lived 20 minutes away from Dan and Sarah and called often and watched Sam whenever they could arrange the time. Sam was alert and by 3 months began to recognize his grandparents, much to their joy and delight. Sarah's parents lived in a distant state and were able to see Sam only on holidays and special occasions.

Sam talked and walked according to the normal developmental schedule and was a dear and engaging child. Katherine and Mark bought a crib and toys for their house and at least one weekend each month they would keep Sam overnight so his parents could get some much needed rest; they were always available to babysit whenever needed. Katherine, especially, developed a deep bond with Sam and never missed an opportunity to show off his pictures or tell a story about him to "whoever would listen." "He was the greatest joy in my life. I had a sense of fulfillment whenever I saw or thought about him," she said.

Sam started day care when he was 3 years old so that his mother could return to work as a schoolteacher. Often, Katherine would be at the house when Sam was dropped off from day care, allowing her daughter-in-law time to shop or relax. Sam seemed to adjust well to his new schedule but soon the absences began. Sam had stomach pains, Sam was throwing up, Sam had diarrhea and a fever. The pediatrician prescribed medication for symptom relief but after many weeks with little easing of symptoms, the pediatrician suggested an ultrasound of Sam's abdomen, followed by a CT scan. It was at that time that the term neuroblastoma, as a probable diagnosis, entered the lexicon of the family's world. A neuroblastoma is a cancerous tumor frequently found in children. It has some familial incidence and in many cases by the time it is diagnosed it has spread beyond the site of origin to the liver, lung, or bone. Standard treatment is aggressive with strong chemotherapeutic agents.

Immediately after the scans, Sam was hospitalized—the first of many such hospitalizations—and further tests were performed to confirm and further clarify the diagnosis of neuroblastoma. Sam was 3 years 7 months old when the medical world took over his life and the life of his family. The doctors were cautious in discussing Sam's prognosis. Neuroblastomas are aggressive and often lethal. Chemotherapy treatment would be harsh, necessitating long periods of hospitalization. After the tests were completed, Sam had his first chemo treatment and stayed in the hospital for 3 weeks. He lost his hair and became weak and listless but cried very little. Dan and Sarah were at the hospital as work schedules permitted (Sarah subsequently took a leave from her teaching) and Katherine and Mark were at the hospital every day. Katherine would hold Sam for hours, rocking him and reading his favorite books. Sam rallied somewhat after treatment ended and came home. This was the first of five hospitalizations spread over an 11-month period.

Each hospitalization left Sam more and more depleted. The treatment regimen was rigorous, and between treatments Sam's ability to regain strength was limited. Throughout the entire period, Katherine and Mark tried to be steadfast and optimistic. According to Katherine, in hindsight, she "felt that a light was going out within her."

Sam died in the hospital soon after the fifth treatment; Sarah and Dan were holding him and Katherine and Mark stood by. The cause of death was neuroblastoma. Sam was 4 and a half years old. He was buried in a family plot. All members of the family were beyond consolation, in a state of exhaustion and shock. Katherine plunged into depression.

Katherine's sorrow seemed boundless. She stated, "I almost feel as though I have no reason to live. I know this is crazy because I have Mark and Dan and Sarah and there will probably be other grandchildren but it feels as though a part of me died with Sam." The motivation for Katherine to begin bereavement counseling did not emanate from her; Mark insisted that she get help, that she had a responsibility to help Dan and Sarah get through this time without their having to worry about her.

Katherine began counseling, initially against her will, but once she began to talk, she seemed comfortable. She spoke of her loss in terms of "the unnaturalness of things: grandparents are not supposed to bury grandchildren," she exclaimed. She also berated herself and felt guilty that she was not able to be as supportive to Dan and Sarah as she wanted. "I am still Danny's mother and yet I cannot fix this for him." She felt that she was becoming a burden to Mark, who she "knew was going through his own anguish over Sam's death." In short, the triple abdication of roles—grandparent, mother, and wife—was overwhelming to Katherine.

Relevant History

Katherine's psychoemotional history was not remarkable. She had grown up in a middle-class family with close ties to both parents and grandparents. She had not known her maternal grandfather, as he died before her birth, but she had had a close relationship with both her paternal grandparents and maternal grandmother.

She described her marriage to Mark in positive terms. Her own parenting had been a very pleasurable part of her adult life. Mark had worked as a foreman for the water company in their community and Katherine felt that although he had been a supportive father and husband, he had the capacity to "emotionally shut down, like a lot of men, and was not always there in the hard times." Katherine had gone to college and had been a high school librarian for many years. She and Mark had decided to retire in the same year to be able to travel and, hopefully, tend to grandparent responsibilities. They had both been retired only a year when Sarah and Dan announced their pregnancy.

Katherine was a religious woman, a regular churchgoer. She was active in various parish activities. One day a week she and Mark volunteered at a soup kitchen. She and Mark had a moderately active social life and at least once a month they were engaged doing something social with their religious community.

In all, Katherine would not have been a candidate for counseling as she had reached a stage in her life in which she was comfortable within herself, doing what she enjoyed. She and Mark had planned and pre-pared well for retirement, so both were spared some of the dislocation and role upheaval associated with that time of life. Both she and Mark had many activities that they enjoyed together and separately and their weeks were always full. The missing piece in Katherine's life was grand-parenthood.

Conceptual Issues

To gain a conceptual understanding of the impact of the death of a grand-child, we must look at the life and developmental stages during which grandparenthood begins. Although the actual age of becoming a grandpar-ent has decreased over the years, with couples today typically becoming grandparents in their late 40s and early 50s (Gee, 1991), grandparenthood must be understood as a role shift with meaningful consequences. For some, the role of grandparent signals old age, a negative feeling in our youth-ori-ented culture; for others it may be too early, caused by a wanted or unwanted teenage pregnancy. When grandparenthood is "on time," the transition is typically viewed as positive and is likely to reinforce the connec-tions between the younger and soon-to-be born generation (Seifert, Hoff-nung, & Hoffnung, 2000).

Older adults take great pride in their grandchildren. Grandparents are in a unique position in the family system in that their participation and relationship with the younger generation is voluntary and is usually devoid of parental obligation (Ponzetti & Johnson, 1991). Kivnick (1983) noted that grandparenthood has a variety of personal meanings that con-tribute to the stage and experience. Grandchildren symbolize an exten-sion of personal influence that will endure beyond the life of the grandparent and help older adults to accept their own deaths as they see that some thread of their lives will persist into the future. In addition, grandparenthood offers an opportunity to pass on the wisdom and cul-tural heritage of their lives and provides a link from the past to the future (Newman & Newman, 1999). For older adults, the fun of watching, play-ing with, and caring for the young children is a great source of pleasure.

It is understandable that when grandparents have been involved inti-mately, or even less so, in the life of their young grandchild, and the child dies, grandparents are "...like bereaved parents of a second order" (Rando, 1988, p. 181). The grief of a grandparent can be crippling and life altering, but because of the circumstances and necessary attention paid to the parents, the grief of the grandparents is frequently overlooked. For the grandparents, not only have they lost their grandchild but they also have lost their own child to bereaved parent status. Many grandparents wonder why they could not have died instead, to save the life of their grandchild (Rando, 1988). It is a time of soul searching and profound anguish as grandparents grieve in a threefold sense—for the beloved grandchild, for their son or daughter who is the parent of the grandchild, and for themselves (Hamilton, 1978).

The dynamics of grief for the grandparent are marked by a variety of responses, some of which complicate the grieving process. The death of a grandchild is a death that occurs out of turn. There is a basic societal expectation that the old die before the young. This sequencing is undermined when a grandchild predeceases the grandparent and contributes to the sense of bewilderment and survivor guilt that permeates the experience. Societal reactions to the death of a grandchild are another dynamic that complicates the grieving process. "One of the most common problems grandparents experience is the perceived inability of the rest of the world to understand the depth of their despair..." (DeFrain, Jakub, & Mendoza, 1991–1992, p. 167). For parents and grandparents, the death of a child may be experienced as isolating and socially stigmatizing as other grandparents and parents are made anxious by the bereaved and feel the need to distance from them. For the nonbereaved, there is the recognition that this unnatural event could happen to them and their children or grandchildren. Bereaved parents and grandparents are often left without many of the social and emotional supports for coping that could facilitate the grief experience (Rando, 1985).

There are very few empirical studies that explore the particular bereavement reactions of grandparents to the death of their grandchild. This appears to be an area begging for further study, as our population is living longer and the average age of becoming a grandparent is going down. This means that there is a greater opportunity for older adults to be grandparents and even become great-grandparents.

Ponzetti and Johnson (1991) studied 45 grandparents in an attempt to understand some of the salient features of their bereavement experience. Participants were culled from a notice in a national newsletter for families who had lost children. The majority of deaths had occurred within the past 5 years. More than half of the grandparents reported feeling shock, numbness, or disbelief on hearing of the death of their grandchild. Many of the grandparents experienced physical symptoms attributed to the loss; most felt a need to talk about the grandchild after the death. Less than half of the sample found solace in their religious faith. Many grandparents noted that they felt pain for their children and feelings of closeness to them; grandparents appeared to grieve as much for their children's loss as for their deceased grandchild.

In a study of the psychological effects of sudden infant death syndrome on grandparents, DeFrain et al. (1991–1992) described common reactions of grandparents of disbelief, anger, guilt, anxiety, depression, concern for adult children and siblings, exhaustion, and bitterness. Of the 80 grandparents who participated in this study, half suffered flashbacks, a small percentage blamed themselves, and one third felt that their marriages had been strengthened by their experience of loss. A noteworthy aspect of this study is that the grandparents felt that grieving survivors need someone willing to listen to them without judgment, without platitudes, and without false assurances. The grandparents indicated the need to have others who would listen and just let them talk about the death.

Ponzetti (1992) attempted to study how different family members experience the death of a child, comparing the grief reactions of parents and grandparents. Findings showed that parents reported feeling shock, disbelief, and numbness significantly more than grandparents did; parents were significantly more likely than grandparents to mention a need to talk about the death of their child. The majority of parents mentioned that they felt or acted differently toward their surviving children, whereas only one third of grandparents noted any difference in their reactions to surviving grandchildren. In summary, the authors found, "The bereavement of parents and grandparents was different in that parents' reactions expectedly centered on their deceased child, whereas grandparents' concerns focused more on their children—the parents of the deceased child" (Ponzetti, 1992, p. 69).

A more recent study by Fry (1997) explored the reactions of 152 grandparents who had suffered the loss of a grandchild within the past 3 years. In this descriptive study, the authors noted several important findings. With the passage of time, more and more grandparents were able to come to terms with the death and were better able to cope with their grief. In the recovery process, more women than men experienced a strengthening in their beliefs about religion and spirituality. Grandmothers were more likely than grandfathers to search for an outlet for their grief and were eager to offer emotional support to others, which, in turn, fostered their own healing. Grandfathers, more so than grandmothers, sought an outlet through work. For grandmothers and grandfathers there was a marked change in beliefs about personal vulnerability, experienced as wisdom rather than as negativity, leading to more meaningful relationships within the family. Other themes that emerged in the study included a strong sense of survivor guilt among grandparents, a sense of helplessness and pain in not being able to protect their children from the loss of their child, and an expressed need on the part of the grandparent to realign relationships and patterns within the family (pp. 135–136).

Although each study presented different aspects of the bereavement experience for grandparents, several common themes can be cited: grieving grandparents felt the need to talk with others about their loss, many experienced survivor guilt, and they had an overwhelming concern for their children with a desire to address and staunch the pain they were feeling over the loss of their child. Guilt and self-blame also were noted in several of the studies.

Suggestions for Intervention

On the basis of the conceptual findings that there is a felt need on the part of grieving grandparents to talk in a nonjudgmental setting, a counselor could reasonably suggest that grieving grandparents participate in a group. The ideal group would offer mutual support as members deal with their grief and would offer the opportunity for grandparents to talk about their deceased grandchild to others in a similar situation. However, the reality of finding such a group might preclude this experience. To mix parents and grandparents in one group, even from different families, is not urged, as the issues for each are different. It seems that the parents are more focused on the loss of their child whereas the grandparents are striving to care for their grieving children.

In working with bereaved grandparents on an individual level, as in other bereavement situations, the counselor must legitimize the loss, as grandparents are often the forgotten grievers. The efforts of most grandparents to address and assist their children, the parents of the deceased child, to ease the pain of their grief should be encouraged, but at the same time support must be offered to the grandparents in their own expression(s) of loss. The grandparents have lost their hopes and dreams to see and nurture a grandchild into a new generation.

The age of the grandparent is an additional factor that must be acknowledged. If the grandparents are older—older than 70 years—the loss of a grandchild may be one of many losses that they have begun to experience. Many older persons (older than 70) no longer work, may have experienced a loss of some physical capacity, may have lost friends, may have been forced to relocate, and may have experienced multiple losses from which they struggle to recover (Kalish, 1987). The ability and resiliency of the older grandparent to rebound from the death of a grandchild may be limited. As such, helping the older grandparent to express sorrow for the present, past, and future is a necessity.

It is also essential to address the feelings of survivor guilt and self-blame. This may be facilitated by pointing out that we as individuals have little or no control of what happens medically in a life, that no one has the answers for why things happen. As grandparents, it is unrealistic that they could protect their grandchildren from harm and equally unrealistic that they could protect their children from their loss. The grandparent must be reassured that the lack of control over the life of another exists regardless of the depth of love and caring.

Intervention has to acknowledge that grandparents will continue to search for an explanation for what has happened and that there will be times when they will feel jealousy and bitterness toward those who have grandchildren, anxiety about the future, and a sense of vulnerability. Affective responses to these feelings are to be expected and encouraged.

Major Issues in This Case

Katherine was in counseling for 6 months. Initially, she was despondent and was unable to speak about Sam without intense emotion. Sam had had several hospitalizations and suffered throughout his illness, and this was all that Katherine seemed able to focus on. She could not understand why he was forced to suffer so; she was able to understand why he "was taken from us" but not why he had to have such pain and misery. In her view, based strongly on religious beliefs, God had decided that Sam was to be "his angel and serve Him." Her faith was shaken, as she was unable to incorporate the suffering from any vantage point. Contrary to the findings by Fry (1997), Katherine was never able to fully embrace her faith again. She said that she was "too angry with God to return to her level of religious observance and faith." This discrepancy between the literature and the actual situation with Katherine suggests an area of further research on the impact of grief on religious conviction that could add to the knowledge base on this facet of bereavement. In assessing Katherine, the counselor found that this expression of anger was supported with the underlying belief that these unexpressed feelings were contributing to her depression. Katherine was encouraged to verbalize as much emotional content as possible. The counselor would often say, "Tell me more about that," as sometimes Katherine would describe a feeling and then pull away from the expression of it or any further exploration.

Katherine struggled with her anger toward Mark, whom she characterized as "nonresponsive and not active in taking care of things." Although Katherine had mentioned this about Mark in earlier descriptions of their relationship, it appeared to have surfaced again during this very difficult time. Her criticism of Mark was seen as a projection of Katherine's inability to influence what had occurred for Sam and her frustration in not being able to affect the situation. The counselor reflected this back to Katherine, and she seemed able to ease up a bit on Mark and look more closely at herself and her own impotence in being able to influence Sam's health.

In counseling sessions, Katherine began to feel safe enough to speak about her anger and rage at the medical establishment, God, and the healthcare world. The counselor encouraged her to cry, wail, and kick the wall when words failed her. This level of expression was not something that she did easily, as her style was more self-effacing and withdrawn. She had never known such a gamut of feelings and she was surprised at their breadth, power, and depth. The counselor normalized this for her by telling her that she was not alone and that others would have responded in exactly the same way and by reassuring her that her emotional overload was within the range of a healthy and expected response. As she began to accept these feelings, she was able to be more and more expressive.

Within 6 weeks of entering counseling, Katherine had begun to be much more responsive to Mark, Dan, and Sarah. She said that she was "feeling terribly guilty about not being there for them" and she wanted to do something to rectify the situation. Katherine felt that she could ease the guilt she felt by being a bit "less emotional and more focused on the needs of others." It seemed that Katherine was beginning to emerge from her grief enough to see the hurt and pain of her husband, daughter-in-law, and son. The counselor urged Katherine to find her place in the family grief and to share her emotions with each of the family members. This would allow the family to pull together in their shared grief and be able to help each other.

An interesting twist occurred in this case. Katherine "righted" herself and realigned with the family fairly quickly. In the process of her healing, by 4 months after Sam's death, she declared that she wanted to do something for other families who struggled with lengthy hospitalizations similar to those that Sam and her family experienced. She decided that she would create a fund with which to buy holiday dinners for families who had a child hospitalized during Easter, Christmas, and Thanksgiving. The fund would go to buy the food that Katherine and her family would prepare and bring to the hospital on the holiday days. This idea fully engaged Mark, Dan, and Sarah in an effort to give to others to ease their struggle. This was not to suggest that Katherine's sorrow ended, but she was able to move away from the most active phase of her grief as she developed her idea to care for others.

Katherine's bereavement experience was relatively short term; the darkest time was from just after Sam's death until the 3-month point. She had already begun to see that her emotions were "normal" and her anger had begun to dissipate. Katherine was essentially a well-adjusted woman who had not experienced an extensive amount of loss and had both internal and external resources from which to draw to help stabilize her in her sadness. This facilitated a shorter active period of grief. Katherine and the counselor jointly decided to end their relationship 6 months after Katherine began counseling. She was well engaged in her hospital project and the family dynamics were quite well healed. She still was angry with God and was not ready to resume any church affiliation.

Dan and Sarah had another child 2 years after Sam's death. And Katherine and Mark have a "second grandchild."

Issues for the Counselor

In a case of this type, the level of identification with the bereft seems to be critical. Katherine was an easy woman to like and her struggles were easy to identify with. Depending on the stage of life of the counselor, layers of identification and overidentification can be an issue. In counseling, the notion of boundaries refers to an invisible line between client and counselor. This boundary line precludes the counselor from sharing extensive personal matters with the client despite similarities that may exist between the counselor and client.

The maintenance of boundaries often poses a problem for the bereavement counselor, as he or she may struggle with wanting to engage with the client at a certain level that potentially could alter the objectivity and effectiveness of the counseling effort. If boundaries are not adequately maintained, there is the tendency for counselors to overidentify with the struggles of their clients and to want to share their experience or fears. It is natural to empathize with the client and the empathy can be helpful in being able to relate more fully; bridging boundaries, however, goes beyond empathy and has the counselor telling personal material that can deflect the focus from the client. In this case, if the counselor was of grandparent age or had grandchildren, his or her maintaining of boundaries could well have been challenged by Katherine's grief.

This issue of identification was a prominent factor in Katherine's case. The counselor, herself the grandparent of a baby boy, was upset and frightened by Sam's situation. The struggle to not absorb Katherine's pain was strong but was eased as Katherine began to heal.

In Katherine's situation, another dynamic surfaced that had to be monitored. Although Katherine was struggling to emerge from her depression, the counselor had the tendency to want to push her along faster than she was able so that she could be more receptive to her son and daughter-in-law. The need for her to address the pain for Dan and Sarah was more the counselor's agenda than Katherine's. When she was able to help comfort her son and daughter-in-law more fully, Katherine and the counselor both "felt better," but this could easily have obscured underlying issues with the loss. In fact, Katherine was not that multilayered and there was not much hidden content being obscured. It took a bit of time to realize that and allow the process of healing to take place at whatever pace was necessary.

The idea of translating grief into a productive effort on behalf of others is often seen in bereavement work. It is almost as though there has to be some good that emerges from a loss. Indeed Katherine framed it that way by saying, "Sam's death has led us to do something for others. It will never bring him back but we will know that he did not die in vain." This compensatory behavior is a comfort to the bereaved and is to be encouraged. The struggle for the counselor is timing and whether the compensatory action will mask deeper bereavement issues that need attention. It is reasonable to assume that any compensatory actions may mask bereavement but the assessment is to determine whether this is furthering the client. The more knowledge one has about the client and his or her coping strategies, the better the counselor is able to assess this. If the client presents a history of avoidance through action, caution is indicated, but many people seem to welcome the outlet of wanting to help others in order to help themselves. This appeared to be the situation with Katherine and her family. Perhaps it was the religious imperative to help others that moved Katherine; her actions have helped many other families through a tough time and helped Katherine in her darkest moments.

15
CHAPTER

Bereavement After the Death of a Disabled Sibling

The Case—Nancy

It was not that Nancy was oblivious to Susan's disabilities; it just did not seem to matter to her. Susan was her sister and that was that. Nancy (26 years old) loved and adored her sister Susan (18 years old). Susan was severely challenged with a multitude of serious disabling conditions: she was unable to stand; she had very limited motor coordination which meant she was not able to feed, bathe, or clothe herself; her vision was slightly impaired; she could not speak; and she had very limited intellectual capacity. The problems had been diagnosed at birth and the doctors did not know what had happened that could have caused such profound disabilities. Her life expectancy could not be determined, as there were congenital birth defects as well.

Susan had lived in a residence for the disabled since she was 7 years old. She was very well cared for and her needs were attentively met. Each weekend Nancy or one of her other siblings picked Susan up and brought her home where she would spend the weekend with whichever siblings were around and partake, as much as she was able, of the household activity. She also was with the family on all special occasions and holidays.

Nancy and Susan were two of five children. There was one other sister and two brothers. All siblings, except Susan, were fully capable, highly functioning young adults. One of the siblings still lived at home with his mother, two were married, and one was a college student. The parents had been divorced for many years. Nancy had recently married and moved out of the house but kept some of her weekend time open to accommodate to Susan's scheduled visits.

The occasion was Easter, a time when the family, sometimes in shifts, went to church. Susan had been picked up the night before and Nancy and her younger sister had bathed and dressed Susan in preparation for going to church with her mother and brother. Nancy left to walk to church with her husband to attend the early service. As Nancy and her husband were leaving the church, they heard sirens and Nancy instantly felt that something was wrong at home. She and her husband ran the few blocks to the house and saw an ambulance and police car parked in front of the house. Nancy ran in and was told that Susan was injured. She raced up the steps and saw the medics pulling the sheet over Susan. Her mother was sobbing. Nancy was shocked by what she was seeing and was hardly able to take it in. Although it was expected that Susan would not live to be very old, she had appeared to be fine when Nancy left for church after helping bathe and dress her. Apparently, Susan had a seizure and had fallen; she had not regained consciousness and died moments after the fall. The medics had done all they knew to try to bring her back but it was futile. How could this have happened? She had never had a seizure before. No explanation was forthcoming then or subsequently.

As in most cases of sudden death, the death assumes an unreality and even though Nancy and her family all went through the ritualized behaviors of the funeral, wake, and burial, the reality of Susan's untimely death took some time to fully register. For Nancy, the depression and inability to stop crying hit about 2 months after the burial. Nancy was able to go through the motions of her work and school routine (she was taking classes toward an advanced degree), but whenever she was at home or when she was driving, she found herself crying. She also realized, especially when her new husband started to question her about why she was so irritable and why she was crying so much, that she was having a harder time than she realized. Counseling had been suggested but Nancy resisted until finally, 3 months after Susan's death, she agreed to speak with a bereavement counselor. The crying, irritability, and sadness had become too much for her and she knew that she needed to discuss this with someone. In addition, her husband and friends were beginning to be concerned, so with some trepidation, as she had never before been in a therapy situation, Nancy became a client.

Relevant History

Nancy came from a fractured family. Her parents had divorced when she was 10 years old; both parents had drinking problems. Nancy was the oldest and in some respects had been the "parentified child," the child who assumes the parental role in situations where the parents are unable to function fully in that capacity. As such, she was often in the position of having to make decisions in relation to her younger siblings and did not have a parent to whom she was able to turn when she was struggling with her own life situations. This aspect of her upbringing made it difficult for her to identify her own needs for support as she was consumed with having to take such good care of others, and it was equally difficult for her to ask for help as her life experience had taught her that the "buck stopped with her."

Despite some of the family patterns and history, Nancy had many friends, had had several serious love relationships before meeting her husband, and was professionally tracked in her field. She could be described as a warm, outgoing, and attractive woman who was fun to be with, with a tendency toward being intense. She spoke of her past as "difficult, but in many ways, it made me stronger and more accepting of difference and courage." No matter how hard she tried, she could not make sense of the death of her sister.

Conceptual Issues

Two sources of literature inform this bereavement experience: the impact of disability on bereavement and the impact on a young adult when a sibling dies.

Disability and Death

The term developmental disability encompasses a variety of physical and mental impairments. In the Americans with Disabilities Act of 1990 (ADA), the term was defined as "a physical or mental impairment that substantially limits one or more of the major life activities" (ADA, 1990, sec. 3/2). Developmental disabilities result in functional limitations in three or more areas of life activity: self-care, learning, mobility, self-direction, economic sufficiency, receptive and expressive language, and capacity for independent living (Begun, 1987).

The literature on parenting a child with developmental disabilities has gone through an interesting attitudinal shift from parents describing the experience in very pessimistic terms, as reflected in the observations of Olshansky, to parents fully accepting the disabled child and even feeling empowered by the experience, based on the more recent findings by Milo and others. Olshansky (1962) stated, "It has been suggested that the parent of a mentally defective child suffers from chronic sorrow. This sorrow is a natural response to a tragic fact" (p. 193). In 1987 Copley and Bodensteiner observed that many parents did experience the chronic sorrow described by Olshansky but noted that some parents were able to accept their situation and move forward with periods of sadness that lessened over time.

More recent work by Milo showed that when faced with the reality of having a developmentally disabled child, "...many families do not experience chronic sorrow. Many reported that they have found that parenting a child with a developmental disability, although unexpected and exhausting, becomes the single most defining experience of their family's lives. Some found the whole experience a blessing in many ways" (Milo, 2001, p. 114). Further corroboration by Turnbull (1993) suggested that families find meaning, power, and value in their experience of parenting children with disabilities.

Literature concerning the response following the death of a disabled child is scant, at best. Much attention has been focused on the reactions of parents when a child dies from an accident, suicide, or from illness or sudden death. And although the literature is replete with articles and studies that document the experience of parenting a child with developmental disabilities, virtually no research informs the death and bereavement experience for the survivors (Milo, 1997). Milo appears to be a pioneer in this area of research, documenting responses of both fathers and mothers to the deaths of their disabled children. However, there appear to be no research studies or literature that explore the grief and bereavement experience of the disabled child's sibling(s).

Wood and Milo (2001) studied the grief of eight fathers who experienced the death of their developmentally disabled child. Milo had done earlier research on eight mothers (not related to the fathers in the subsequent study) and the format and measures used in that study were mirrored in the study with fathers. In both studies, the Grief Experience Inventory (Sanders, Mauger, & Strong, 1985) was administered and data was gathered through semistructured and open-ended interview techniques.

In both studies, parents acknowledged the struggles inherent in raising and parenting a disabled child. Many expressed their anguish at the months and years of difficult parenting that preceded the death. Several of the parents had other children and felt the strain of parenting and giving to them, juxtaposed against the additional effort required of parenting the developmentally disabled child. Mothers generally felt set apart in their grief and felt that their loss was not validated by those around them. A common comment to the bereaved mothers by well-wishers was "It is for the best" or "She (or he) was such a struggle." The response of many of the mothers was the felt need to justify their love for this "unlovable" child both during the child's life and after the death. Mothers often were offered well-meaning but insensitive condolences such as "It is not as great a loss as it would have been if you lost one of your other kids" (Milo, 1997, p. 455).

The mothers in Milo's (1997) study refuted the earlier, more negative views regarding parenting children with developmental disabilities. Almost all of the mothers felt that although parenting a disabled child was the most difficult challenge they ever had faced, the positives far outweighed the negatives. Six of the mothers felt that they had managed to shift what could have been considered a tragedy into the most significant and powerful experience of their lives (p. 458). The struggle of managing a disabled child with other nondisabled children in the family was successfully negotiated in most cases, with several mothers speaking about how much the other children had gained from the experience. In general, Milo found that there was a uniformity of response from the mothers.

The findings in the study of grieving fathers did not exhibit the uniformity of response or consistency of experience described in the study of mothers. Nonetheless, some themes did emerge. Several fathers spoke of the double loss of disability and death and even articulated a sense of relief or freedom when their disabled child died. Many of the fathers wanted to take action and keep busy and occupied after the death as a means of coping with their grief. All men experienced isolation from family, friends, and colleagues; for most men, speaking of their sorrow regarding their disabled child and his or her death was extremely difficult and they felt poorly responded to by friends and work colleagues (Wood & Milo, 2001).

Similar to the findings in the study of mothers, findings in the study of fathers showed they made a great effort to include the disabled child with the rest of the family rather than protect the siblings and keep their activities separate. Regardless of how each father coped, they did not want their child forgotten and all fathers had made special memorials for their child. All of the fathers reported having reached a place of peace, in spite of struggles with anger, bitterness, and depression. In general, Wood and Milo (2001) found that fathers used action for coping with painful feelings of loss, that fathers felt isolated and a lack of social support, and that the grief of their wives, which was very painful, exacerbated their own grief (p. 658).

Milo and the work of her colleague help to bring understanding to the impact of the death of a disabled child on the parents and ultimately on the whole family system. The detailed experience for siblings awaits further research. One aspect of the bereavement process, regardless of whether it is the grief of parents or siblings, is society's reaction to this form of death: the death of someone who is devalued and marginalized by society. In such cases, others perceive the death as unworthy of significant sympathy and support. This apathetic and insensitive response can exacerbate an already very difficult bereavement situation. The devaluation becomes a theme in the management of the bereavement (Doka, 2002a).

Young Adult Sibling Loss

The bereavement of young siblings has been extensively explored in the literature but the paucity of research on sibling bereavement in the young adult years has precluded the development of a sound theoretical model to explain this form of loss (Sundar & Nelson, 2003). Although there is limited literature, some conceptual material exists and is related here.

"The sibling relationship is unique among human relationships. ... The death of a sibling marks an end to what is expected to be one of the longest and sometimes most intimate relationship of a lifetime" (Robinson & Mahon, 1997, p. 477). It can be experienced as a crushing loss to the sibling and the family. Based on the literature, studies of bereaved siblings document the potential for physiological, psychological, behavioral, and emotional reactions.

Sibling death occurs within the context of a family. As such, there are usually themes of sibling rivalry, close and intimate contact, or distant and formal contact. Irrespective of the quality of the bonds, it is important to understand that sibling relationships often are marked by deep levels of attachment and antagonism, caring and competition, and loyalty and lingering resentment. Competition for parental attention and affection also is present (Rando, 1988). The quality and intensity of the relationship between the bereaved and the deceased sibling can have implications in the bereavement experience. If the sibling relationship was competitive and conflicted, more complex reactions are possible, with unresolved and unfinished feelings lasting a long time. If the relationship between siblings was close and intimate, the loss may never be fully resolved.

The family context also speaks to the notion of a shared past, and although one sibling may not agree with the other sibling's perceptions of the past, the sibling was there and is able to recall incidents and events in ways that are shared. When a sibling dies, part of the history and past of the family dies.

Within the family context, the bereavement situation for the young adult griever is potentially complicated, as the need to comfort the parents may take precedence over his or her own needs. Birth order seems to have an impact on the bereavement experience, with older siblings taking on a parental role with younger siblings during the period of bereavement. Sundar and Nelson (2003) pointed out that bereavement for the young adult who has lost a sibling may be complicated because during young adulthood, separation and autonomy from parents is occurring and a death can bring the young adult back into the family network in ways that he or she has been struggling to break. Peer relationships also seem to be strained during the bereavement experience. Davies (1991) found that young adult surviving siblings felt somewhat estranged from their peers and perceived as trivial some of their activities and interests. Consequently, sibling survivors tended to withdraw from their peers.

There is another area of concern in being able to understand the grief journey of the young adult who has lost a sibling: the impact of the loss on the worldview and the need for the individual to reinterpret the ways in which the world works. As a young, emerging adult, logical and sensible explanations for the ways the world operates have been developed over time and an unexpected death potentially overturns all these beliefs. The bereaved young adult sibling must struggle to make sense of the world and answer some of the existential questions that emerge around death: Why did this happen? What kind of world is this that such suffering can be created? Why me? A death experience at this age also challenges developing notions of spirituality and faith around which a worldview has been developed. These beliefs and notions have to be redefined and reevaluated as the griever tries to make sense of what has occurred in his or her life (Sundar & Nelson, 2003).

Despite the intensity and challenges of young adult sibling bereavement, research has shown that many adolescents and young adults have been able to overcome their loss and be strengthened and enhanced by it. A study by Oltjenbruns (1991), for example, found that 95% of late adolescents identified at least one positive outcome following the death of a family member. Many cited a deeper appreciation of life as the most positive outcome; some noted that they were less afraid of death and others felt more independent and clearer about their priorities.

Suggestions for Intervention

The initial intervention goal in working with the young adult sibling of a deceased disabled sibling is to legitimize the death. As mentioned by several of the authors who studied the grief reactions of those related to the disabled, the societal devaluation and marginalization of the developmentally disabled that occur are detrimental to the bereavement experience by creating distance between the griever and the anticipated support system.

As a form of disenfranchised grief (Doka, 1989a), losing a disabled sibling often stands in opposition to the view held by the majority of society about the experience of having a family member who is developmentally disabled—that it is for the best that the disabled person died. This mitigates the sibling tie and the love, connection, and affection that could exist within the family. The counselor, aware of this dynamic, must make initial efforts to address this with the client and allow the griever to speak openly and freely about the loss. Neimeyer and Jordan (2002) referred to the process of "respectful recognition" (p. 102) that accords legitimacy and honor to the relationship between the survivor and the deceased as well as honoring the place the relationship had in the life of the survivor.

Wood and Milo (2001) noted in their study of fathers that several spoke of a double loss: the first loss was their having to accept that their child was developmentally disabled and the second loss was the actual death of the child. This notion of a double loss can be applied to interventions with the young adult: How did they handle the fact that their sibling was "not right" and needed additional time and care from all members of the family? What did it ultimately mean for them to lose this sibling? If they can remember, what did they feel when they learned that their sibling was developmentally disabled? Were they embarrassed or ashamed by their disabled sibling? How do they remember the impact that this had on their parents and how did it ultimately affect them? This area of discussion is best explored after the client feels that the loss is legitimized and feels confident that the counselor is able to accept that there might be ambivalent feelings that exist (or existed) toward the sibling.

The area of ambivalent feelings and guilt has been underacknowledged in the existing bereavement literature with this population. As in most cases of death, especially sudden death, it is inevitable that there be "loose ends"; life is not tidy and predictable, allowing us to do all of the things we know and hope will be effective. Perhaps there were hurt feelings between the deceased and the survivor, or perhaps the survivor felt he or she had not been patient or caring enough and feels selfish or bad. Guilt and loose ends plague most people who are confronted with a sudden death; with the loss of a disabled person, there may surface all of the frustration they might have experienced in the face of their disabled sibling, which can create a heightened sense of guilt during the bereavement.

For the young adult sibling of a developmentally disabled sibling there must exist instances when the sibling felt the loss of parental attention as it was, by necessity, given to the disabled child. These hurts and disappointments, even in the most favorable family situation, linger somewhere in the emotional history of the nondisabled sibling and can cause emotional anguish and guilt. These feelings need to be addressed and legitimized in the counseling process.

The grief reaction can cause a serious disillusionment with which survivors must contend. In addressing this rupture to the worldview of the young adult, the counselor might find a cognitive approach to be helpful. The underlying principles within a cognitive approach are that individuals actively construct their reality such that highly personal idiosyncratic meanings are attached to events, that cognition mediates affect and behavior, that cognition is knowable and accessible, and that cognition is central to change (Fleming & Robinson, 2001). In other words, how individuals think about an event is based on their personal construction that affects how they feel and behave. This personal construction is available for scrutiny and can be examined and changed. In practical terms, how does the survivor view the loss, what adaptations can be made regarding this view, what changes are necessary for the individual to feel some sense of control, and so on.

Ideally, through the counseling, the survivor once again is able to see the world and the self in positive ways as he or she incorporates the loss. This is accomplished through the development of new schemas or core beliefs, often by reordering priorities, changing one's goals, redefining relationships, and assessing critical areas of one's life. It ultimately requires that the griever transform some part of his or her identity so as to redefine the symbolic connection to the deceased while maintaining a relationship with the living (Neimeyer, 1998, p. 98).

Although not an option in the case under discussion, counseling the family together often is helpful. The life and death of a developmentally disabled child puts strain on the family system at many levels and is differentially experienced. In meeting with the family, the counselor may be able to assess how each member interacts and supports the others and where the gaps in emotional support exist. A concern to be noted is that the siblings' grief is not being eclipsed by the grief of the parents. When such a death occurs, most people will identify with the loss of the parents and the grief of the sibling(s) may not be attended to. Meeting with the family as a whole allows the counselor the ability to assess this and, if necessary, redirect energy toward the grief of the sibling(s).

Major Issues in This Case

Nancy began crying almost as soon as she was settled in the chair and the preliminary inquiries about why she had requested counseling were over. Although the death of her sister had occurred more than 3 months before, she was almost unable to control her crying adequately for her to be able to talk. In fits and starts, she tentatively began the retelling of the events of the day of Susan's death, from getting Susan up in the morning to dressing her and combing her hair and getting her ready so that Nancy and her husband would be able to attend church. She detailed what happened when she arrived at the house, the scene with the medics, and so on. She claimed that the days after the death were almost a blur and that she found herself going through the motions of the wake and funeral rituals.

When she was able to regain some of her composure, she described her current levels of functioning. Nancy said that she was struggling to concentrate at work and in her school studies; she claimed she was short tempered with her new husband and that she could not seem to "snap out of it despite the fact that the death had happened several months ago." It was very clear that the attachment between Susan and Nancy was powerful and sustaining for Nancy, as evidenced by the reality that much of Nancy's world had paled since Susan's death.

To fully understand Nancy's bereavement situation, the counselor needed to assess not only her functioning, which appeared to be seriously affected, but also her position in the family, her social supports, her worldview, and her level of guilt and ambivalence regarding Susan. When asked to describe her role in the family, Nancy explained that she was the mover in the family, she made things happen, and, especially in light of the alcoholism of her parents, she had been cast in the role of the "caretaking mother" to her younger siblings. She had not been responsible for Susan's care in the early years as they had household help to attend to her needs. When Susan was 7 years old, she moved to the residence. As Nancy saw her current role in the family, she said that if she did not suggest something—a family gathering, the need for something in the house—it would not be attended to. At the time of Susan's death, Nancy was newly married and was trying to extricate herself from the household to begin turning her energy to her new life with her husband. This would have been no easy task even without Susan's death, as she instinctively responded to and anticipated the needs of the family, but the death had cast Nancy back into many of her caretaking responsibilities and roles.

For Nancy to restart her efforts toward independence, some of the counseling effort had to go toward helping Nancy be aware that she was slipping back into habits of caretaking that she had worked hard to give up. Her pattern of taking over had to be held up to her so that she could see what she was unwittingly and instinctively doing. This could not be addressed initially as there were other more pressing issues confronting her, but it was not to be put off too long—no later than the fourth session—as she was backsliding too quickly.

Although Nancy had many friends, she said that she "felt quite disappointed in many of them, despite their attendance at the funeral and postfuneral rituals." She explained that many of them expressed the sentiments reported by Milo (1997) that Nancy and the family were better off that Susan had died as she was such a strain on the family. One truly insensitive comment, according to Nancy, was made by a friend she had not seen for some time: "Susan is better off dead as she was never going to be able to pass for normal in society." Although that was the most egregious comment, many of the people whom Nancy expected to understand the depth of her loss did not. The counselor must be attuned to this dynamic of marginalization of the deceased and be as reassuring as possible that this is a serious, legitimate, and deep loss of a sibling.

Nancy's view of the world had not been seriously affected by Susan's death. Nancy claimed that she had made peace with Susan's disabilities, that even as a young child and because of Susan she instinctively felt that her life was not fully secure and that she had to depend almost exclusively on herself. As a child of divorce, as a sister of a seriously disabled girl, as the child of alcoholic parents, Nancy believed and had accepted that there are inequities in the world. According to the conceptualization of Janoff-Bulman (1992), Nancy's worldview involving victimization, the belief in personal invulnerability, and the perception of the world as a safe and secure meaningful place had been shattered and rebuilt years before Susan's death. Having lived in a house with two alcoholic parents and a father who abandoned the family when she was 10 years old had helped shape Nancy into a well-defended, self-reliant young woman. What became clear after exploring the network of relationships in Nancy's family was that many of these adaptations had served her well through the years. Understanding how Nancy adapted to difficult family situations was a valuable part of her history and one that the counselor built on and referred to when Nancy was struggling to adjust to the loss.

Nancy claimed that she felt little or no guilt in relation to how she treated Susan: she never saw her as a burden, was able to look past the disabilities, had laughed with her and enjoyed her at whatever level that occurred, and felt very "proud of my family and how we related to her. When she came home for the weekends, it sometimes was the only bright spot in our week. But, it wasn't an effort and we [she and her siblings] did not think we were doing anything special. It was Susan and this was how we related to her."

What started to become clear to the counselor was that for Nancy, the relationships that she and her siblings had around Susan's care and needs had brought out the best in each of them and helped them feel close and united in an effort. With Susan gone, that cohesion was fractured and Nancy, based on her role in the family, felt that some of the repair of the family after Susan's death was her job. This was adding unnecessary pressure and anguish to her bereavement experience. What Nancy ideally needed to do was to relinquish parts of her role as family caretaker and transfer some of that energy to self-care.

When the counselor sees a situation clearly—Nancy's role in the family and need for self-care—how soon and in what way should that interpretation be shared with the client? Timing of interpretative interventions is a skill learned often by trial and error. In general, the offering of an interpretation that involves a recasting of the individual can be made when the counselor feels that the client is well engaged in the counseling and is able to hear the interpretation not as a condemnation but as a suggestion for exploration and ultimate change. If an interpretation is premature, a client could begin to feel challenged and respond defensively. The newly developing trust between the counselor and the client could be broken and the client may become guarded, evasive, or withdrawn.

In this case, if the interpretation were not offered, Nancy would quickly revert to her accustomed roles, would feel burned out and exhausted, and would not be attending to her own bereavement issues. By the third session, the counselor felt that Nancy was able to hear and accept a discussion of her role with an eye toward channeling energy differently. This discussion took an interesting turn: Nancy initially felt very relieved that she was "being given permission to let go of certain roles and responsibilities" but questioned how this "...could be done without feeling guilty." Several sessions were spent exploring how she might extricate herself from her sense of responsibility—her need to take care of her alcoholic mother, her younger sister (27 years old), her brother who was about to leave for college—and move that into her self and her marriage.

The counselor urged Nancy to imagine what might happen to her family if she were sent to Mars. What would happen to her mom and her siblings, and how would her brother get set for college? Nancy resisted this technique initially, as she was skipping into the role of organizer but she admitted, "Deep down I really don't want to be there and do all that with them. I want to be in my new apartment with my husband, doing our things." This approach seemed to work well and Nancy began pulling back.

After Nancy was relieved of some of her burden to take care of the whole family, she was able to speak of her own sense of loss, how she missed Susan and the times they spent together and how Susan had affected her life. Years before Susan's death, and soon after the extent of Susan's disabilities were known, Nancy had made the decision to work with developmentally disabled children. Now she felt an even stronger sense of resolve about her work.

Nancy stayed in counseling less than 1 year. The counselor felt that Nancy would need support to get through the 1-year anniversary of the death and the mass that was planned for that day. Nancy still played a pivotal role in the planning of that event and was central to many of the decisions surrounding the day, but she had done some significant work in relinquishing many of her caretaking roles. The counseling had opened up a new way for her to see herself and for this she was grateful to Susan on yet another level.

Issues for the Counselor

Initially, working with Nancy was troubling, as the counselor would have been one who imagined that the care, stress, ambivalence, and competitiveness of having a disabled sibling would have been relieved by her death. It was another reminder of the necessity for the counselor to refrain from expressing his or her own personal reactions and views, as they are unrelated and in this case would have been inflammatory to the client.

Nancy was easily engaged and brought openness to the counseling despite her sadness. When working with a motivated client, the counselor has the tendency to push the process of the helping a bit faster than might be best for the client. Keeping in mind that bereavement is a slow and often draining personal voyage, the counselor must conscientiously oversee the timing and pace. Despite Nancy's receptivity and willingness to relinquish the diverse roles that she played in the family structure, the counselor had to remember that there was secondary gain for Nancy from being so capable in that area. If she were to have given up all the roles, she might have gone through a difficult time as she redirected her energy to other places. Again, there is the need for careful pacing and timing. In our eagerness to help, we sometimes may do more harm than good. Experience is often the greatest modulator of those instincts.

Nancy gradually emerged from her grief. It was slow and there were some setbacks as the family wanted to pull her back into a caretaking role, but she was moving her venue of activity away from the family and toward her husband and self. Susan will always be there with Nancy, motivating her in her work and other pursuits. Nancy has found a successful way to use the love and energy she felt for Susan as she works with similarly challenged children. It was very gratifying to watch Nancy reclaim her life, her work, and her marriage.

The counselor was stopped short by her own attitudes and had to reevaluate her perceptions about the disabled. Thank you, Susan.

Appendix

Books

Baugher, R. (1996). *Guide to understanding guilt during bereavement.* Newcastle, WA: Caring People Press.
Blank, J. W. (1998). *The death of a child: A book for and about bereaved parents.* Amityville, NY: Baywood.
Bucholz, J. (2002). *Homicide survivors: Misunderstood grievers.* Amityville, NY: Baywood.
Faldet, R., & Fitton, K. (Eds.). (1997). *Our stories of miscarriage: Healing with words.* Minneapolis, MN: Fairview.
Klass, D., Silverman, P. R., & Nickman, S. L. (1996). *Continuing bonds: New understandings of grief.* Washington, D.C: Taylor & Francis.
Livingston, G. (1999). *Only spring: On mourning the death of my son.* New York: Marlow.
Peterson, L. (1997). *Surviving the heartbreak of choosing death for your pet.* Tempe, AZ: Greentree.
Rosenblatt, P. (2000). *Help your marriage survive the death of a child.* Philadelphia: Temple University Press.
Sife, W. (1998). *The loss of a pet: A guide to coping with the grieving process when a pet dies.* New York: John Wiley.
Sittser, G. (1998). *A grace disguised: How the soul grows through loss.* Grand Rapids, MI: Zondervan.
Smith, H. A. (1996). *Grieving the death of a friend.* Minneapolis, MN: Augsburg Fortress.
Spungen, D. (1997). *Homicide: The hidden victims.* Thousand Oaks, CA: Sage.
Talbott, K. (2002). *What forever means after the death of a child: Transcending the trauma.* New York: Brunner-Routledge.
Webb, M. (1999). *The good death: The new American search to reshape the end of life.* New York: Bantam Books.
Wolfert, A. (2001). *Healing a teen's grieving heart.* Ft. Collins, CO: Companion Press.

Scholarly and Professional Journals

American Journal of Hospice and Palliative Care
Prime National Publishing
Weston, MA 02493

Death Studies
Taylor & Francis Ltd.
Washington, D.C. 20005

Hospice Journal
Haworth Press
Binghamton, NY 13904

Illness, Crisis and Loss
Sage Publications
Thousand Oaks, CA 91320

Journal of Crisis Intervention and Suicide Prevention
Hogrefe & Huber, Publishers
Cambridge, MA 02139

Journal of Loss and Trauma
Taylor & Francis
Philadelphia, PA

Journal of Palliative Care
Center for Bioethics
Montreal, Quebec, Canada

Journal of Personal and Interpersonal Loss
Taylor & Francis Ltd.
Washington, D.C. 20005

Loss, Grief, and Care
Haworth Press
Binghamton, NY 13904

Mortality
Carfax Publishing
Levittown, PA 19057

Omega—Journal of Death and Dying
Baywood Publishing
Amityville, NY 11701

Suicide and Life-Threatening Behavior
Guilford Press
New York, NY 10012

Selected Internet Sources

American Association of Suicidology
www.suicidology.org

Dougy Center (for bereaved children)
www.dougy.org

GriefNet
www.griefnet.org

Hospice Foundation of America
www.hospicefoundation.org

Interactive Bereavement Courses
www.bereavement.org

Last Acts
www.lastacts.org

National Association of People With AIDS
www.napwa.org

National Organization of Parents of Murdered Children, Inc.
www.pomc.com

Pet Loss Grief Support
www.petloss.com

Project on Death in America
www.soros.org/death

Selected National Organizations

AMEND
(Aiding Mothers and Fathers Experiencing Neonatal Death)
Witchita, KS 67208
(316) 268-8441
www.amendinc.com

American Hospice Foundation
Washington, D.C. 20037
(202) 223-0204
www.americanhospice.org

American Sudden Infant Death Syndrome Institute
Marietta, GA
(800) 232-SIDS
www.sids.org

Association for Death Education and Counseling
Hartford, CT 06117
(860) 586-7503
www.adec.org

Candlelighters Childhood Cancer Foundation
Bethesda, MD 20814
(800) 366-2223
www.candlelighters.org

Children's Hospice International
Alexandria, VA 22314
(800) 241-CHILD
www.chionline.org

Compassionate Friends, Inc.
Oak Brook, IL 60522
(630) 990-0010
www.compassionatefriends.org

International Association of Pet Cemeteries
Ellenburg Depot, NY 12935
(518) 594-3000
www.iaopc.com

National Association for Home Care and Hospice
Washington, D.C. 20002
(202) 546-4759
www.nahc.org

National Center for Death Education
Newton, MA 02159
(617) 928-4500
www.mountida.edu

National Center for Victims of Crimes
Washington, D.C. 20036
(202) 467-8700
www.ncvc.org

National Organization of Parents of Murdered Children, Inc.
Cincinnati, OH 45202
(513) 721-5683
www.pomc.com

SHARE, Pregnancy and Infant Loss Support, Inc.
St. Charles, MO 63301
(800) 821-6819
www.nationalshareoffice.com

Sunshine Foundation
Philadelphia, PA 19124
(800) 767-1976
www.sunshinefoundation.org

Violent Death Bereavement Society
Seattle, WA 98199
(206) 223-6398
www.vdbs.org

References

Abboud, L., & Liamputtong, P. (2003). Pregnancy loss: What it means to women who miscarry and their partners. *Social Work in Health Care, 36(3)*, 37–62.

Ahrons, C., & Wallisch, L. (1987). *Divorced families: A multidisciplinary developmental view.* New York: W. W. Norton.

Albert, P. (2001). Grief and loss in the workplace. *Progress in Transplantation, 11(3)*, 169–173.

Alderman, L. et al. (1998). Bereavement and stress of a miscarriage: As it affects the couple. *Omega, 37(4)*, 317–327.

Al-Fozan, H., & Tuloulis, T. (2003). Miscarriage and spontaneous abortion. UpToDate on Line 2.1.

Americans With Disabilities Act of 1990, 42 U.S.C.A. § 12101 *et seq.*

Archer, J. (1999). *The nature of grief.* London: Routledge.

Archer, J., & Winchester, G. (1994). Bereavement following the loss of a pet. *British Journal of Psychology, 85*, 259–271.

Asaro, M. (2001). Working with adult homicide survivors: Helping family members cope. *Perspectives in Psychiatric Care, 37(4)*, 115–126.

Attig, T. (2002). Questionable assumptions about assumptive worlds. In J. Kauffman (Ed.), *Loss of the assumptive world* (pp. 55–70). New York: Brunner-Routledge.

Balk, D. (1996). Models for understanding adolescents coping with bereavement. *Death Studies, 20*, 367–387.

Balk, D. (2000). Adolescents, grief, and loss. In K. Doka (Ed.), Living with grief (pp. 35–49). Washington, D.C.: Hospice Foundation of America.

Balmer, L. (1992). *Adolescent sibling bereavement: Mediating effects of family environment and personality.* Unpublished doctoral dissertation, York University, Toronto, Ontario, Canada.

Barbanel, L. (1989). The death of the psychoanalyst. Contemporary Psychoanalysis, *25(3)*, 412–419.

Barbant, S. (2002). A closer look at Doka's grieving rules. In K. Doka (Ed.), *Disenfranchised grief: New directions, challenges, and strategies for practice* (pp. 23–38). Champaign, IL: Research Press.

Bascom, P., & Tolle, S. (2002). Responding to requests for physician-assisted suicide. *Journal of the American Medical Association, 288(1)*, 91–98.

Beder, J. (1998). Bereavement after a physician assisted suicide: A speculation based on theory. *Suicide and Life Threatening Behavior, 28(3)*, 302–308.

Beder, J. (2002). Mourning the unfound: How we can help. *Families in Society, 83(4)*, 400–403.

Beder, J. (2003a). Picking up the pieces after the sudden death of a therapist: Issues for the client and the inheriting therapist. *Clinical Social Work Journal, 31(1)*, 25–36.

Beder, J. (2003b). War, death, and bereavement: How we can help. *Families in Society, 84(2)*, 1–5.

Begun, A. L. S. (1987). *Sibling relationships with developmentally disabled people.* Ann Arbor: University of Michigan Press.

Beutel, M., Wilner, H., Deckardt, R., Von Rad, M. & Weiner, H. (1996). Similarities and differences in couples' grief reactions following a miscarriage: Results from a longitudinal study. *Journal of Psychosomatic Research, 40(3)*, 245–253.

Biller, R., & Rice, S. (1990). Experiencing multiple loss of persons with AIDS: Grief and bereavement issues. *Health and Social Work, 15(4)*, 283–290.

Black, R. B. (1991). Women's voices after pregnancy loss: Couples' patterns of communication and support. *Social Work in Health Care, 16(2)*, 19–36.

Bok, S. (1982). *Secrets*. New York: Pantheon Books.

Bolling, J. (2000). Guinea across the water: The African-American approach to death and dying. In J. Parry & A. S. Ryan (Eds.), *A cross-cultural look at death, dying, and religion* (pp. 145–159). Chicago: Nelson-Hall.

Bolton, S., & Camp, D. (1987). Funeral rituals and the facilitation of grief work. *Omega, 17(4)*, 343–352.

Boss, P. (1999). *Ambiguous loss*. Cambridge, MA: Harvard University Press.

Boykin, F. F. (1991). The AIDS crisis and gay male survivor guilt. *Smith College Studies in Social Work, 6*, 247–259.

Brice, C. (1991). Paradoxes of maternal mourning. *Psychiatry, 54*, 1–12.

Burton, L., & Devries, C. (1992). African-American grandparents as surrogate parents. *Generations, XVII(3)*, 51–54.

Cain, R. (1991). Stigma management and gay identity development. *Social Work, 36(1)*, 67–73.

Canadian Paediatric Society. (2001). Guidelines for health care professionals supporting families experiencing a perinatal loss. *Paediatrics and Child Health, 6(7)*, 469–477.

Carmack, B. J. (1992). Balancing engagement/detachment in AIDS-related multiple losses. *Image: Journal of Nursing Scholarship, 24*, 9–14.

Casper, L., & Bryson, K. (1998). *Co-residents grandparents and their grandchildren: Grandparent maintained families* (Working Paper No. 26). Washington, D.C.: U.S. Bureau of the Census.

Cherney, P., & Verhey, M. (1996). Grief among gay men associated with multiple losses from AIDS. *Death Studies, 20*, 115–132.

Chwast, R. (1983). The death of one's therapist. *Gestalt Journal, 2*, 34–38.

Conway, K., & Russell, G. (2000). Couples' grief and experience of support in the aftermath of miscarriage. *British Journal of Medical Psychology, 73*, 531–545.

Copley, M., & Bodensteiner, J. (1987). Chronic sorrow in families of disabled children. *Journal of Child Neurology, 2*, 67–70.

Cox, C. (2002). Empowering African-American custodial grandparents. *Social Work, 47(1)*, 45–54.

Dannemiller, H. C. (2002). The parents' response to a child's murder. *Omega, 45(1)*, 1–21.

Davies, B. (1991). Long-term outcomes of adolescent sibling bereavement. *Journal of Adolescent Research, 6*, 83–96.

Deck, E., & Folta, J. (1989). The friend-griever. In K. Doka (Ed.), *Disenfranchised grief: Recognizing hidden sorrow* (pp. 77–89). Lexington, MA: Lexington Books.

DeFrain, J., Jakub, D., & Mendoza, B. L. (1991–1992). The psychological effects of sudden death on grandmothers and grandfathers. *Omega, 24(3)*, 165–182.

DeVaul, R., Zisook, S., & Faschingbauer, T. (1979). Unresolved grief: Clinical consideration. *Postgraduate Medicine, 59*, 267–271.

Dewald, P. A. (1965). Reactions to forced termination of psychotherapy. *Psychiatric Quarterly, 9*, 313–316.

Doka, K. (1986). Loss upon loss: The impact of death after divorce. *Death Studies, 10*, 441–449.

Doka, K. (1989a). Disenfranchised grief. In K. Doka (Ed.), *Disenfranchised grief: Recognizing hidden sorrow* (pp. 13–23). Lexington, MA: Lexington Books.

Doka, K. (1989b). A later loss: The grief of ex-spouses. In K. Doka (Ed.), *Disenfranchised grief: Recognizing hidden sorrow* (pp. 103–113). Lexington, MA: Lexington Books.

Doka, K. (2002a). How we die: Stigmatized death and disenfranchised grief. In K. Doka (Ed.), Disenfranchised grief: *New directions, challenges, and strategies for practice* (pp. 323–336). Champaign, IL: Research Press.

Doka, K. (2002b). Introduction. In K. Doka (Ed.), *Disenfranchised grief: New directions, challenges, and strategies for practice* (pp. 5–22). Champaign, IL: Research Press.

Dubowitz, H. (1994). Kinship care: Suggestions for future research. *Child Welfare, 73(5)*, 553–564.

Dworkin, J., & Kaufer, D. (1995). Social services and bereavement in the lesbian and gay community. *Journal of Gay and Lesbian Social Services, 2(3–4)*, 41–52.

Emanuel, E. (2002). Euthanasia and physician-assisted suicide. *Archives of Internal Medicine, 162,* 142–152.

Engel, G. (1975). The death of a twin: Mourning and anniversary reactions. International *Journal of Psychoanalysis, 56,* 23–40.

Evans, I., & Carter, J. (2000). The lesbian perspective on death and dying. In J. Parry & A. S. Ryan (Eds.), *A cross-cultural look at death, dying, and religion* (pp. 131–144). Chicago: Nelson-Hall.

Eyetsemitan, F. (1998). Stifled grief in the workplace. *Death Studies, 22,* 469–479.

Falicov, C. J. (1999). The Latino family life cycle. In B. Carter & M. McGoldrick (Eds.), *The expanded family life cycle* (3rd ed., pp. 141–152). Boston: Allyn & Bacon.

Fehr, B. (1996). *Friendship processes.* Thousand Oaks, CA: Sage.

Fish, W. (1986). Difference of grief intensity in bereaved parents. In T. Rando (Ed.), *Parental loss of a child* (pp. 415–428). Champaign, IL: Research Press.

Flaim, D. (2002, August 25). Animal memorials. *Newsday,* pp. G8–G11.

Fleming, S., & Adolph, R. (1996). Helping bereaved adolescents: Needs and responses. In C. Corr & J. McNeil (Eds.), *Handbook of adolescent death and bereavement* (pp. 97–118). New York: Springer.

Fleming, S., & Balmer, L. (1996). Bereavement in adolescence. In C. Corr & D. Balk (Eds.), *Handbook of adolescent death and bereavement* (pp. 139–154). New York: Springer.

Fleming, S., & Robinson, P. (2001). Grief and cognitive-behavioral therapy. In M. Stroebe, R. Hansson, W. Stroebe, & H. Schut (Eds.), *Handbook of bereavement research* (pp. 647–670). Washington, D.C.: American Psychological Association.

Flesch, R. (1947). *Treatment considerations in the reassignment of clients.* New York: Family Service Association.

Florian, V. (1989–1990). Meaning and purpose in life of bereaved parents whose son fell during active military service. *Omega, 20(2),* 91–102.

Fraser, S., & Walters, J. (2002). Death—Whose decision? Physician-assisted suicide, dying, and the terminally ill. *Western Journal of Medicine, 176,* 120–123.

Fry, P. (1997). Grandparents' reactions to the death of a grandchild: An exploratory study. *Omega, 35(1),* 119–140.

Fuller-Thomson, E., & Minkler, M. (2000). African-American grandparents raising grandchildren: A national profile of demographics and health characteristics. *Health and Social Work, 25(2),* 109–118.

Garcia-Lawson, K., Lane, R., & Koetting, M. (2000). Sudden death of the therapist: Effects on the patient. *Journal of Contemporary Psychotherapy, 30(1),* 85–103.

Garcia-Preto, N. (1982). Puerto Rican families. In M. McGoldrick, J. Pearce, & J. Giordano (Eds.), *Ethnicity and family therapy* (pp. 164–186). New York: Guilford.

Gay, M. (1982). The adjustment of parents to wartime bereavement. In N. A. Milgram (Ed.), *Stress and anxiety* (Vol. 8, pp. 47–50). New York: Hemisphere.

Gee, E. M. (1991). The transition to grandmotherhood: A quantitative study. Canadian Journal on Aging, 10, 254–270.

Getzel, G. (2000). Judaism and death: Practice implications. In J. K. Parry & A. S. Ryan (Eds.), *A cross-cultural look at death, dying, and religion* (pp. 18–31). Chicago: Nelson-Hall.

Gibson, P. (2002). Caregiving role affects family relationships of African American grandmothers as new mothers again: A phenomenological perspective. *Journal of Marital and Family Therapy, 28(3),* 341–353.

Goldstein, E. (1997). *Ego psychology and social work practice.* New York: Free Press.

Gosse, G. H. (1988). Factors associated with the human grief experience as a result of the death of a pet. Unpublished doctoral dissertation, Hofstra University, Hempstead, NY.

Grabowski, J., & Frantz, T. (1992). Latinos and Anglos: Cultural experiences of grief intensity. *Omega, 26(4),* 273–285.

Guarnaccia, P., DeLaCancela, V., & Carrillo, E. (1989). The multiple meanings of ataques de nervios in the Latino community. *Medical Anthropology, 11,* 47–62.

Hamilton, J. (1978). Grandparents as grievers. In O. J. Sahler (Ed.), *The child and death* (pp. 219–225). St. Louis, MO: C. V. Mosby.

Harris, J. M. (1984). Nonconventional human/companion bonds. In W. J. Kay, H. A. Nieburg, A. H. Kutscher, R. H. Grey, & C. E. Fudin (Eds.), *Pet loss and human bereavement* (pp. 80–87). Ames: University of Iowa Press.

Harrison, L., & Harrington, R. (2001). Adolescents' bereavement experiences, prevalence, association with depressive symptoms, and use of services. *Journal of Adolescence, 24,* 159–169.

Hatter, B. (1996). Children and the death of a grandparent. In C. Corr & D. Corr (Eds.), *Handbook of childhood death and bereavement* (pp. 131–148). New York: Springer.

Horowitz, M., Wilner, B. A., & Alvarez, M. A. (1979). Impact of Events Scale: A measure of subjective stress. *Psychosomatic Medicine, 41,* 209–218.

Hughes, T., Haas, A. P., Razzano, L., Cassidy, R. & Matthews, A. (2000). Comparing lesbians' and heterosexual women's mental health: A multi-site survey. *Journal of Gay and Lesbian Social Services, 11(1),* 57–76.

Janoff-Bulman, R. (1992). *Shattered assumptions: Toward a new psychology of trauma.* New York: Free Press.

Jarolmen, J. (1998). A comparison of the grief reaction of children and adults: Focusing on pet loss and bereavement. *Omega, 37(2),* 133–150.

Johnson, M. P., & Puddifoot, J. (1996). The grief response in the partners of women who miscarry. *British Journal of Medical Psychology, 69,* 313–327.

Kalish, R. (1977). Introduction. In R. Kalish (Ed.), *Death and dying: Views from many cultures* (p. III). Farmingdale, NY: Baywood.

Kalish, R. (1985). Death, grief, and caring relationships (2nd ed.). Monterey, CA: Brooks/Cole.

Kalish, R. (1987). Older people and grief. *Generations, XI(3),* 33–38.

Kastenbaum, R. (1969). Death and bereavement in later life. In A. H. Kutscher (Ed.), *Death and bereavement* (pp. 89–103). Springfield, IL: Charles C. Thomas.

Kastenbaum, R. (1998). *Death, society, and human experience.* Boston: Allyn & Bacon.

Kastenbaum, R. (2001). *Death, society, and human experience* (7th ed.). Boston: Allyn & Bacon.

Katz, P., & Bartone, P. (1998). Mourning ritual and recovery after an airline tragedy. *Omega, 36(3),* 193–200.

Kauffman, J. (2002a). *Loss of the assumptive world.* New York: Brunner-Routledge.

Kauffman, J. (2002b). Safety and the assumptive world. In J. Kauffman (Ed.), *Loss of the assumptive world* (pp. 205–211). New York: Brunner-Routledge.

Keddie, K. (1977). Pathological mourning after the death of a domestic pet. *British Journal of Psychiatry, 131,* 21–25.

Kivnick, H. Q. (1983). Dimensions of grandparenthood meaning: Deductive conceptualization and empirical derivation. *Journal of Personality and Social Psychology, 44,* 1056–1068.

Kollar, N. (1989). Rituals and the disenfranchised griever. In K. Doka (Ed.), *Disenfranchised grief: Recognizing hidden sorrow* (pp. 271–286). Lexington, MA: Lexington Books.

Lagoni, L., Butler, C., & Hetts, S. (1994). *The human-animal bond and grief.* Philadelphia: W. B. Saunders.

Lamm, M. (1969). The Jewish way in death and mourning. New York: Jonathan David.

Lattanzi-Licht, M. (1996). Helping families with adolescents cope with loss. In C. Corr & D. Balk (Eds.), *Handbook of adolescent death and bereavement* (pp. 219–234). New York: Springer.

Lattanzi-Licht, M. (2002). Grief and the workplace: Positive approaches. In K. Doka (Ed.), *Disenfranchised grief: New directions, challenges, and strategies for practice* (pp. 167–180). Champaign, IL: Research Press.

Lee, D. (2000). The Korean perspective on death and dying. In J. Parry & A. S. Ryan (Eds.), *A cross-cultural look at death, dying, and religion* (pp. 193–214). Chicago: Nelson-Hall.

Lee, G. (1994). Death in the workplace. *AAOHN Journal, 42(12),* 590–610.

Lehrman, S. R. (1956). Reactions to untimely death. *Psychiatric Quarterly, 30,* 564–578.

Levin, D. (1998). Unplanned termination: Pain and consequences. *Journal of Analytic Social Work, 5(2),* 35–46.

Levinson, B. (1972). *Pets and human development.* Springfield, IL: Charles C Thomas.

Liechty, D. (2002). The assumptive world in the context of transference relationships. In J. Kauffman (Ed.), *Loss of the assumptive world* (pp. 83–94). New York: Brunner-Routledge.

Lindemann, E. (1944). Symptomatology and management of acute grief. *American Journal of Psychiatry, 101,* 141–148.

Lord, R., Ritvo, S., & Solnit, A. (1978). Patients' reactions to the death of the psychoanalyst. *International Journal of Psychoanalysis, 59,* 189–197.

Malkinson, R., & Bar-Tur, L. (1999). The aging of grief in Israel: A perspective of bereaved parents. *Death Studies, 23(5),* 413–433.

Margolies, L. (1999). The long good-bye: Women, companion animals, and maternal loss. *Clinical Social Work Journal, 27(3),* 289–301.

Marrone, R. (1997). *Death, mourning, and caring.* Pacific Grove, CA: Brooks/Cole.

Martin, J. L. (1988). Psychological consequences of AIDS-related bereavement and HIV-related illness on psychological distress among gay men: A 7 year longitudinal study, 1985–1991. *Journal of Consulting and Clinical Psychology, 61,* 94–103.

Martin, T. (1989). Divorce and grief. In K. Doka (Ed.), *Disenfranchised grief: Recognizing hidden sorrow* (pp. 161–172). Lexington, MA: Lexington Books.

Mawson, D., Marks, I. M., Ramm, L., & Stern, R. S. (1981). Guided mourning for morbid grief: A controlled study. *British Journal of Psychiatry, 138,* 185–193.

McGoldrick, M. (1989). Ethnicity and the family life cycle. In B. Carter & M. McGoldrick (Eds.), *The changing family life cycle* (2nd ed.). Boston: Allyn & Bacon.

Meagher, D. (1989). The counselor and the disenfranchised griever. In K. Doka (Ed.), *Disenfranchised grief: Recognizing hidden sorrow* (pp. 313–328). Lexington, MA: Lexington Books.

Meier, D., & Morrison, R. (2002). Autonomy reconsidered. *New England Journal of Medicine, 346(14),* 1087–1088.

Milo, E. M. (1997). Maternal responses to the life and death of a child with developmental disability: A story of hope. *Death Studies, 21,* 443–476.

Milo, E. M. (2001). The death of a child with a developmental disability. In R. Neimeyer (Ed.), *Meaning reconstruction and the experience of loss* (pp. 113–134). Washington, D.C.: American Psychological Association.

Neimeyer, R. (1998). *Lessons of loss*: A guide to coping. New York: McGraw-Hill.

Neimeyer, R., & Jordan, R. (2002). Disenfranchisement as empathic failure: Grief therapy and the co-construction of meaning. In K. Doka (Ed.), Disenfranchised grief: New directions, challenges, and strategies for practice (pp. 95–117). Champaign, IL: Research Press.

Neugebauer, R., Rabkin, J., Williams, J., Remien, R., Goetz, R., & Gorman, J. (1992). Bereavement reactions among homosexual men experiencing multiple losses in the AIDS epidemic. *American Journal of Psychiatry, 149(10),* 1374–1379.

Newman, B., & Newman, P. (1999). *Development through life* (7th ed.). Belmont, CA: Brooks/Cole.

Nichols, J. (1989). Perinatal death. In K. Doka (Ed.), *Disenfranchised grief: Recognizing hidden sorrow* (pp. 117–126). Lexington, MA: Lexington Books.

Nord, D. (1996a). The impact of multiple AIDS-related loss on families of origin and families of choice. *American Journal of Family Therapy, 24(2),* 129–144.

Nord, D. (1996b). Issues and implications in the counseling of survivors of multiple AIDS-related losses. *Omega, 20,* 389–413.

Olshansky, S. (1962). Chronic sorrow: A response to having a mentally defective child. *Social Casework, 43,* 190–193.

Oltjenbruns, K. A. (1991). Positive outcomes of adolescents' experience with grief. *Journal of Adolescent Research, 6,* 43–55.

Parkes, C. (1993). Psychiatric problems following bereavement by murder or manslaughter. *British Journal of Psychiatry, 162,* 49–54.

Parkes, C. (2001). A historical overview of the scientific study of bereavement. In M. Stroebe, R. Hansson, W. Stroebe, & H. Schut (Eds.), *Handbook of bereavement research* (pp. 25–45). Washington, D.C.: American Psychological Association.

Parry, J., & Ryan, A. S. (2000). Introduction. In J. Parry & A. S. Ryan (Eds.), *A cross-cultural look at death, dying, and religion* (pp. ix–xxvi). Chicago: Nelson-Hall.

Paulino, A. (2000). Death, dying, and religion among Dominican immigrants. In J. Parry & A. S. Ryan (Eds.), A cross-cultural look at death, dying, and religion (pp. 84–101). Chicago: Nelson-Hall.

Peach, M., & Klass, D. (1987). Special issues in the grief of parents of murdered children. *Death Studies, 11*, 81–88.

Pesek, E. (2002). The role of support groups in disenfranchised grief. In K. Doka (Ed.), *Disenfranchised grief: New directions, challenges, and strategies for practice* (pp. 127–134). Champaign, IL: Research Press.

Ponzetti, J. J. (1992). Bereaved families: A comparison of parents' and grandparents' reactions to the death of a child. *Omega, 25(1)*, 63–71.

Ponzetti, J. J., & Johnson, M. A. (1991). The forgotten grievers: Grandparents' reactions to the death of grandchildren. *Death Studies, 15*, 157–167.

Prigerson, H., & Jacobs, S. (2001). Traumatic grief as a distinct disorder: A rationale, consensus criteria and a preliminary test. In M. Stroebe, R. Hansson, W. Stroebe, & H. Schut (Eds.), *Handbook of bereavement research* (pp. 613–646). Washington, D.C.: American Psychological Association.

Puddifoot, J., & Johnson, M. A. (1997). The legitimacy of grieving: The partner's experience at miscarriage. *Social Science Medicine, 45(6)*, 837–845.

Quackenbush, J., & Glickman, L. (1984). Helping people adjust to the death of a pet. *Health and Social Work, 9*, 42–47.

Quill, T. (1994). Physician-assisted suicide: Progress or peril? *Suicide and Life Threatening Behavior, 24(4)*, 315–325.

Rando, T. (1984). *Grief, dying and death*. Champaign, IL: Research Press.

Rando, T. (1985). Bereaved parents: Particular difficulties, unique factors, and treatment issues. *Social Work, 30(1)*, 19–23.

Rando, T. (1986). Unique issues and impact of the death of a child. In T. Rando (Ed.), *Parental loss of a child*. Champaign, IL: Research Press.

Rando, T. (1988). *How to go on living when someone you love dies*. New York: Bantam Books.

Rando, T. (1993). *Treatment of complicated mourning*. Champaign, IL: Research Press.

Rando, T. (1995). Grieving and mourning: Accommodating to loss. In H. Waas & R. Neimeyer (Eds.), *Dying: Facing the facts* (pp. 211–243). Washington, D.C.: Taylor & Francis.

Range, L., & Calhoun, L. (1990). Responses following suicide and other types of death: The perspective of the bereaved. *Omega, 21(4)*, 311–320.

Raphael, B. (1983). *Anatomy of bereavement*. New York: Basic Books.

Robinson, L., & Mahon, M. (1997). Sibling bereavement: A content analysis. *Death Studies, 21*, 477–499.

Romanoff, B., & Terenzio, M. (1998). Rituals and the grieving process. *Death Studies, 22*, 697–711.

Ross, C., & Baron-Sorensen, J. (1998). *Pet loss and human emotion*. Philadelphia: Taylor & Francis.

Rubin, S. S. (1989–1990). Death of the future: An outcome study of bereaved parents in Israel. *Omega, 20(4)*, 323–339.

Rubin, S. S. (1991–1992). Adult child loss and the two-track model of bereavement. *Omega, 24(2)*, 183–202.

Ryan, C., Bradford, J., & Honnold, J. (1999). Social workers' and counselors' understanding of lesbian needs. *Journal of Gay and Lesbian Social Services, 9(4)*, 1–26.

Rynearson, E. J. (1978). Humans and pets and attachments. *British Journal of Psychiatry, 133*, 550–555.

Rynearson, E. J. (1984). Bereavement after homicide: A descriptive study. *American Journal of Psychiatry, 141(11)*, 1452–1454.

Rynearson, E. J. (1995). Bereavement after homicide. *British Journal of Psychiatry, 166*, 507–510.

Rynearson, E. J. (2001). *Retelling violent death*. Philadelphia: Brunner-Routledge.

Rynearson, E. J., & McCreery, J. (1993). Bereavement after homicide: A synergism of trauma and loss. *American Journal of Psychiatry, 150(2)*, 258–261.

Sable, P. (1995). Pets, attachments, and well-being across the life cycle. *Social Work, 40(3)*, 334–341.

Sanders, C., Mauger, P., & Strong, P. (1985). Manual for the Grief Experience Inventory. Blowing Rock, NC: The Center for the Study of Separation and Loss.

Schatz, B. (1986). Grief of mothers. In T. Rando (Ed.), *Parental loss of a child* (pp. 303–312). Champaign, IL: Research Press.

Schave, B., & Ciriello, J. (1983). *Identity and intimacy in twins.* New York: Praeger.

Scott, S. (1987). Grief reactions to the death of a divorced spouse. In C. Corr & R. A. Pacholski (Eds.), *In death: Completion and discovery* (pp. 107–116). Lakewood, OH: Association for Death Education and Counseling.

Scott, S. (2000). Grief reactions to the death of a divorced spouse. *Omega, 41(3),* 207–219.

Segal, N. (1999). *Entwined lives.* New York: Dutton.

Segal, N., & Blozis, S. (2002). Psychological and evolutionary perspectives on coping and health characteristics following loss: A twin study. *Twin Research, 5(3),* 175–187.

Ségal, N., & Bouchard, T. (1993). Grief intensity following the loss of a twin and other relatives: Test of kinship genetic hypotheses. *Human Biology, 65(1),* 87–105.

Segal, N., Wilson, S., Bouchard, J. T., & Gitlin, D. (1995). Comparative grief experiences of bereaved twins and other bereaved relatives. *Personality and Individual Difference, 18(4),* 511–524.

Seifert, K., Hoffnung, R., & Hoffnung, M. (2000). *Lifespan development* (2nd ed.). Boston: Houghton Mifflin.

Shapiro, E. (1994). *Grief as a family process.* New York: Guilford.

Sharkin, B., & Bahrick, A. (1990). Pet loss: Implications for counselors. *Journal of Counseling and Development, 68,* 306–308.

Shwed, H. (1980). When a psychiatrist dies. *Journal of Nervous and Mental Disease, 168(5),* 275–278.

Sias, P., & Cahill, D. (1998). From coworkers to friends: The development of peer friendships in the workplace. *Western Journal of Communication, 62(3),* 273–299.

Silverman, E., Range, L., & Overholser, J. (1994). Bereavement from suicide as compared to other forms of bereavement. *Omega, 30(1),* 41–50.

Silverman, P. (2002). Living with grief: Rebuilding a world. *Journal of Palliative Care, 5(3),* 449–454.

Sklar, F. (1992). Grief as a family affair: Property rights, grief rights, and the exclusion of close friends as survivors. *Omega, 24(2),* 109–121.

Sklar, F., & Hartley, S. (1990). Close friends as survivors: Bereavement patterns in a "hidden" population. *Omega, 21(2),* 103–112.

Sprang, M., McNeil, J., & Wright, R. (1989). Psychological changes after the murder of a significant other. *Social Casework, 70,* 159–164.

Stallones, L. (1994). Pet loss and mental health. *Anthrozoos, 7(1),* 43–54.

Stein, A. J., & Winokuer, H. (1989). Monday mourning: Managing employee grief. In K. Doka (Ed.), *Disenfranchised grief: Recognizing hidden sorrow* (pp. 91–102). Lexington, MA: Lexington Books.

Stroebe, H., & Stroebe, M. (1987). *Bereavement and health: The psychological and physical consequences of partner loss.* New York: Cambridge University Press.

Stroebe, M. S., Stroebe, W., & Hansson, R. (1993). *Handbook of bereavement: Theory, research and intervention.* New York: Cambridge University Press.

Stroebe, M., Hansson, R., Stroebe, W., & Schut, H. (Eds.). *Handbook of Bereavement Research.* Washington, D.C.: American Psychological Association.

Suarez-Almazor, M., Newman, Hanson, & Bruera. (2002). Attitudes of terminally ill cancer patients about euthanasia and assisted suicide: Predominance of psychosocial determinants and beliefs over symptoms distress and subsequent survival. *Journal of Clinical Oncology, 20(8),* 2134–2141.

Sundar, P., & Nelson, G. (2003). Moving towards resiliency: A qualitative study of young women's experiences of sibling bereavement. Currents: *New Scholarship in the Human Services, 2(1).* Available at http://fsw.ucalgary.ca/currents/purnima_sundar/sundar.htm

Talbot, K. (2002). *What forever means after the death of child.* New York: Brunner-Routledge.

Tallmer, M. (1989). The death of an analyst. *Psychoanalytic Review, 76(4),* 529–542.

Toedter, L. J., Lasker, J. M., & Alhadeff, M. A. (1988). The Perinatal Grief Scale: Development and initial validation. *American Journal of Orthopsychiatry, 58,* 435–449.

Tomassini, C., Rosina, A., Billari, F., Skytthe, A., & Christensen, K. (2002). The effect of losing a twin and losing a partner on mortality. *Twin Research, 5(3)*, 210–217.

Turnbull, A. (1993). *Cognitive coping: Families and disabilities.* Baltimore: Brooks.

Valentine, L. (1996). Professional interventions to assist adolescents who are coping with death and bereavement. In C. Corr & D. Balk (Eds.), *Handbook of adolescent death and bereavement* (pp. 312–328). New York: Springer.

van der Wal, J. (1989–1990). The aftermath of suicide: A review of empirical evidence. *Omega, 20,* 149–171.

Videka-Sherman, L. (1987). Research on the effect of parental bereavement: Implications for social work intervention. *Social Service Review, 61,* 103–116.

Webb, N. B. (2002). Deaths of grandparents and parents. In N. B. Webb (Ed.), *Helping bereaved children* (pp. 45–69). New York: Guilford.

Weinbach, R. (1989). Sudden death and secret survivors: Helping those who grieve alone. *Social Work, 34(1),* 57–60.

Weisman, A. (1991). Bereavement and animal companions. *Omega, 22(4),* 241–248.

Weiss, R. (2001). Grief, bonds, and relationships. In M. Stroebe, R. Hansson, W. Stroebe, & H. Schut (Eds.), *Handbook of bereavement research* (47062). Washington, D.C.: American Psychological Association.

Werth, J. J. (1999). The role of the mental health professional in helping significant others of persons who are assisted in death. *Death Studies, 23(3),* 239–255.

Wilson, L. (1995). Differences between identical twin and singleton adjustment to sibling death in adolescence. *Journal of Psychological Practice, 1(2),* 100–104.

Wolowelsky, J. (1996). Communal and individual mourning dynamics within traditional Jewish law. *Death Studies, 20,* 469–480.

Wood, J., & Milo, E. M. (2001). Fathers' grief when a disabled child dies. *Death Studies, 25(8),* 635–661.

Woodward, J. (1988). The bereaved twin. Acta Geneticae Medicae et Gemellologiae: *Twin Research, 37,* 173–180.

Worden, W. (1982). *Grief counseling and grief therapy.* New York: Springer.

Worden, W. (1996). *Children and grief: When a parent dies.* New York: Guilford.

Worden, W. (2002). *Grief counseling and grief therapy.* New York: Springer.

Wright, L. (1997). *Twins and what they tell us about who we are.* New York: John Wiley.

Yager, J. (1997). *The power of friendship and how it shapes our lives.* Stamford, CT: Hannacroix Creek Books.

Yoffe, E. (2002, August 4). Afterward. *New York Times,* pp. 36–41.

Index